The Media in Wales

The Media in Wales
Voices of a Small Nation

David M. Barlow, Philip Mitchell
and Tom O'Malley

UNIVERSITY OF WALES PRESS
CARDIFF
2005

British Library Cataloguing-in-Publication Data
A catalogue record for this book is available from the British Library.

ISBN 0-7083-1839-8 (pb)
     0-7083-1840-1 (hb)

The rights of David M. Barlow, Philip Mitchell and Tom O'Malley to be identified separately as authors of this work have been asserted by them in accordance with sections 77 and 79 of the Copyright, Designs and Patents Act 1988.

The publishers wish to acknowledge the financial support of the Higher Education Funding Council for Wales in the publication of this book.

Jacket designed by Darren Watts
Printed in Great Britain by Cromwell Press, Trowbridge

Contents

PART III: WALES AND THE ASSEMBLY: COMMUNICATIONS AND CULTURAL POLICY

Acknowledgements

In addition to the scholarly debts we owe to others, especially those authors we have mentioned at the end of our introductory chapter, we would like to acknowledge the support of staff at the University of Glamorgan's Learning Resource Centre, and at the Hugh Owen Library at the University of Wales Aberystwyth.

We would also like to thank colleagues and students at Aberystwyth, Glamorgan and elsewhere, who wittingly and unwittingly have stimulated our interest in this topic and provided insights and information on which we have built. Any errors of fact or interpretation, however, must be attributed to the authors.

Part of the material in this book stems from our research project on commercial radio in Wales, which was funded by the Economic and Social Research Council. Our work on this project was greatly enhanced by the efficiency and enthusiasm of Kelly Lock, our Research Assistant, to whom we also extend our thanks.

We are keen to record our gratitude to University of Wales Press for their highly supportive collaboration.

Finally, we would like to thank our families and friends for their patience and support while this book was being written.

David M. Barlow, Philip Mitchell and Tom O'Malley
Wales
September 2004

I

Approaching the Media in Wales

1

Introduction

Three factors in particular prompted this book. First, in Wales as elsewhere, media, culture and communications are central to everyday life in the twenty-first century. Second, the establishment of a National Assembly for Wales (NAfW or the Assembly) is a significant development and indicative of a major rearrangement of the UK political landscape.[1] Third, an additional factor was the need for a volume providing a unified historical and contemporary overview of the media in Wales.[2]

Whether reliant on private or public funds, organizations involved in the production, distribution and transmission of cultural goods are increasingly referred to as the 'cultural industries' (see, for example, Hesmondhalgh, 2002; McGuigan, 1996). The cultural industries are both similar and different to other industries. Similar in the sense that they produce and distribute goods and are part of the wider industrial context. Different because the goods produced, such as newspapers, films, television and radio programmes, generate many of the images and discourses that people use to interpret, understand and, ultimately, act upon their own social, cultural and economic environment (Golding and Murdock, 2000: 70).

The cultural industries are of interest to Wales for a number of reasons. Economic interest focuses on the employment opportunities they provide and the financial benefits that accrue from the production and distribution of cultural goods – symbolic or otherwise – throughout Wales, the wider UK and Europe and, increasingly, globally. While organizations such as BBC Wales, S4C, ITV1 Wales and the *Western*

Mail are generally considered to be the major employers, there are numerous other small and medium-size enterprises engaged in activities associated with broadcasting, film and new media in Wales.[3] For instance, in 2004 the trade association for Welsh independent film and television producers, Teledwyr Annibynnol Cymru (TAC), included in its membership over ninety businesses, most located around Cardiff and Caernarfon.[4]

The economic and global dimensions of the cultural industries are illustrated by S4C's sales of animation products overseas and the decision by BBC Wales to dramatize the books of Welsh-born author Catrin Collier, a project that was expected to generate £20m over a four-year period (Jury, 2002: 5). More generally, the film industry is a major contributor to the UK's balance of payments. This is before taking account of indirect or 'trickledown' impacts such as tourism. In this regard, findings by the UK Film Council are apposite. The UK film industry is considered more influential than the BBC World Service in promoting 'British culture' abroad, with evidence suggesting that around 20 per cent of tourists who visited the UK in 2001 were attracted as a result of its portrayal on film or television (Film Council, 2003: 12–13).

In Wales, the Assembly prefers the term 'creative industries' to 'cultural industries', including broadcasting, film and new media under this banner (Post-16 Education and Training Committee, 2000a: 25; Welsh Assembly Government, 2002: 48). In addition to their obvious capacity to create employment and generate wealth, the creative industries are also envisaged as a means of reinvigorating cultural and social life in Wales by helping to facilitate a more active and engaged citizenry (National Assembly for Wales, 2000: 8–9; see also Smith, 1998). More specifically, 'arts and cultural heritage' was one of the areas of responsibility devolved to the Assembly (Welsh Office, 1997: 33). As a result, one of the first tasks of the Assembly was to initiate a review of arts and cultural policy in Wales. The resulting publication, *A Culture in Common*, articulated a vision for Wales and set out principles for future policy development (Post-16 Education and Training Committee, 2000a). The later appointment of a minister for culture, sport and the Welsh language led to the production of *Creative Future/Cymru Greadigol*, a cultural strategy for Wales (Welsh Assembly Government, 2002). Broadcasting, film and new media have been harnessed to aid the achievement of this strategy. There is, though, some irony in this situation. This becomes evident when we turn to the powers of the Assembly.

Since the 1536 Act of Union that formally united Wales with England, much has been written about the relationship between these two countries. Within Wales, this relationship has often been characterized, at best, as generally less than positive and, at worst, even destructive, impacting negatively on the economy, the environment and the social and cultural life of Wales.[5] During the latter period of the twentieth century, government from London, through a Welsh Office in Cardiff, produced what one commentator described as 'quangoland' – a bureaucratic rather than democratic Wales (Osmond, 1992: 16). A 'yes' vote at the 1997 referendum – even though by a narrow margin – and the subsequent establishment of an Assembly were seen as the first steps in bringing about greater democracy in Wales.[6] The first Assembly Members (AMs) were elected in May 1999 and Queen Elizabeth II formally opened the NAfW later that same month (Jones and Balsom, 2000: 275, 282).

An Assembly, or similar type of institution, had long been recognized as an essential first step in the process of ensuring that the nation's media would eventually become accountable to the people of Wales through their democratically elected representatives. However, while 'culture' was devolved to the Assembly, powers relating to broadcasting, communications and film were not. Responsibility for these areas remains with the secretary of state for the Department of Culture, Media and Sport in London, who is obliged to consult the Assembly on all matters relevant to Wales (Department of Culture, Media and Sport, 2000: 5–6). While such decisions might prompt questions about what actually constitutes 'devolution' and whether reference to 'post-devolution' is somewhat premature, the practical implications soon became evident when the UK government signalled its intention to launch new communications legislation, which eventually materialized in the form of the Communications Act 2003. While the Assembly made submissions to the appropriate UK bodies to highlight the particular needs and nature of the Welsh context in terms of media, culture and communications, its recommendations carried no legislative weight.

Despite the Assembly's lack of powers in this area, the relatively recent history of civil disobedience in Wales over the allocation of broadcasting and communications services – the most recent example being the campaign to establish S4C – virtually guaranteed that such matters would soon be on the political agenda.[7] The Welsh Affairs Select Committee (1999) report, *Broadcasting in Wales and the National*

Assembly, paved the way. Since then, the Assembly has held plenary debates on broadcasting, communications, film and new media, and work relating to these areas has been undertaken by the (now dissolved) Post-16 Education and Training Committee and its successor, the Culture Committee.[8] Broadcasting and communications more generally were also the subject of submissions to the Commission on the Powers and Electoral Arrangements of the National Assembly for Wales, established in 2002 under the stewardship of the Rt Hon. Lord Richard QC (see, for example, Randerson, 2002a; Talfan Davies, 2003).

Two points can be made on material already published on the media in Wales. The first is to recognize that significant and substantial texts have been produced on the history of the BBC in Wales (J. Davies, 1994a; Lucas, 1981); on the press (A. Jones, 1993); and on cinema and film (Berry, 1994). Policy and related issues have also been addressed (see, for example, Mungham and Williams, 1998; K. Williams, 1997a) and a variety of other publications have dealt with media institutions and media-related issues (see, for example, Allan and O'Malley, 1999; Blandford, 2000a; Hume, 1986; Mackay and Powell, 1997; O'Malley, Allan and Thompson, 1997; Talfan Davies, 1999). However, there is no single published source that brings together a historical and contemporary overview of the media in Wales. The second aspect relates to the extent to which Wales and its media feature in publications that take as their focus the history and development of mass communications in the UK. It is not unreasonable to suggest that in some such accounts, England and the UK appear to be interchangeable, one and the same, with developments in Wales (as in Scotland and Northern Ireland) very much peripheral to metro-centric accounts which commence in London. This book takes the media in Wales as its focus and the nation of Wales as its starting point.

Organization

Beyond this introduction the book comprises eight chapters. While the first seeks to contextualize the book's title, essentially it is chronology that determines the order of the next few chapters. So, for example, the press is addressed before cinema and film and the latter chapter is followed by radio, television and the Internet. The penultimate and final chapters deal with policy and related matters.

Chapter 2 locates Wales and its media by way of a general and wide-ranging orientation before outlining the theoretical ideas that inform this and subsequent chapters. In taking the idea of 'voice' and using it as a metaphor for presence, it explores Wales's voice at home and abroad before moving on to examine the notion of a media, cultural or communication deficit. The final section of the chapter considers the idea of Wales as a 'small' nation, bringing into focus its status within the UK, its relationship with England and illustrating why the mass media are necessarily implicated in any such discussion.

Chapter 3 explores the historical development of the newspaper press in Wales, concentrating on the period after the industrialization of the press. It provides a synopsis of the key historical developments and the critical issues (industrialization, immigration, language) which influenced developments in the newspaper industry. This is followed by an overview of ownership and control in the contemporary Welsh press. In addition, it reviews the relationship between the press and key issues such as language, class and the national question, and examines some of the critical debates these relationships have stimulated.

Chapter 4 provides a historical and contemporary analysis of cinema and film in Wales. It tracks the introduction of film-making, the emergence of the travelling showmen, the growth of commercial cinemas and the development of an alternative cinema circuit in the valleys of south Wales. The chapter illustrates why cinema became such a popular pastime in Wales and explores the ways in which Wales and its people have been represented on screen. It examines the emergence of a film and video workshop sector and the role played by S4C in catalysing indigenous film-making in Wales. The chapter ends by considering the contemporary state of the industry in Wales and, in doing so, reflects on long-held ambitions to establish a 'Welsh cinema'.

Chapter 5 begins by tracing the key historical events in radio broadcasting in Wales, identifying the chief issues for critical debate arising from these developments. The subsequent review of the contemporary situation focuses on the evolving role of BBC Radio Wales and Radio Cymru since the advent of competition from the commercial radio sector. The rest of the chapter addresses the most salient contemporary issues, focusing in particular on the various regulatory frameworks that have controlled Welsh radio's development, and on an assessment of the extent to which present-day stations genuinely serve their target audiences.

Chapter 6 traces the history of television in Wales from its earliest days up to the advent of digital broadcasting. It covers issues such as the development of BBC Wales, Welsh commercial television, the debates leading up to the establishment of S4C and developments around digital TV. The chapter proceeds to survey the structures of control and ownership in Welsh television and examines aspects of programming, staffing, language and audiences. It explores some of the critical issues raised by the relationship between television, language and the national question in Wales.

Chapter 7 focuses on the Internet. It begins by outlining key areas of global debate and then proceeds to examine the problems which surround a full deployment of public and domestic Internet access throughout Wales, assessing the initiatives put in place to tackle these problems. The chapter then assesses the contemporary situation in more detail, paying particular attention to: Internet use by existing media; the role of Usenet newsgroups; the use of the Welsh language on the Internet; the technology's potential role in enhancing a sense of identity at regional and local level, as well as amongst the Welsh diaspora; and its role as a forum for mediated public debate. The final section evaluates the case for firmer state intervention in facilitating implementation of Internet-access policies.

Chapter 8 considers the context in which policy emerges and the economic, social, political and cultural forces to which policy responds, thus requiring attention to the wider context of the UK. The chapter moves on to examine the Communications Act 2003 and the preceding policy instruments that heralded a 'new' era of communications in the UK. It considers the implications of this legislation and, in particular, what a new and centralized regulatory body, OfCom, the Office of Communications, will mean for Wales. In a final section it explores and outlines the ways in which the Assembly has engaged with matters relating to broadcasting and communications in the course of developing cultural policy for Wales.

Chapter 9 begins with a review of the chief policy issues which relate specifically to the press, broadcasting, film and the Internet in Wales. This review includes an account of relevant historical developments and an evaluation of the role of the NAfW in each of these areas. The chapter then sets these considerations within an overall assessment of the media in Wales. This section draws together the core themes of the book by examining the key forces that have shaped and continue to shape the media in Wales, with particular emphasis on issues of economics, technology, geography, language, national identity and diversity.

Preliminary note

One of the overriding objectives of this book is to make a contribution towards filling the 'knowledge gap' identified by Talfan Davies (1999: 14–15) in his observations on the relative lack of academic research concerning policy-making and mass communications in Wales.[9] Given the range and complexity of the topics under review, this book does not claim to make a definitive statement on the media in Wales. We hope nonetheless that it will stimulate further research – from a variety of methodological and conceptual perspectives – and we have signalled this at various points in the text. In addition, we have tried to take into account the fact that different readers may wish to approach the book in different ways. With this in mind, each chapter has been written so as to be relatively self-contained. By the same token, we have sought to keep cross-referencing between chapters to a helpful minimum. A cumulative bibliography is provided in the references at the end of the book, which we hope will prove to be a useful resource for other researchers.

Certain parts of this book contain material arising from our own research project on commercial radio in Wales, which was funded by the Economic and Social Research Council[10] and from some original documentary research, data collection and analysis. Nonetheless, for the most part this book has drawn largely on published sources. While our debt to this material is clear from our textual references and bibliography, we are particularly keen to acknowledge the pioneering work on mass communications in Wales by David Berry, John Davies, Aled Jones, Geraint Talfan Davies and Kevin Williams.

We have made every effort to ensure that this book covers developments in the Welsh media in both languages, but we may have overlooked some material. In the case of the Welsh language none of the three authors reads Welsh at a sufficiently sophisticated level to guarantee the absence of such oversights. On this issue, as on the general content of the book, we welcome responses from readers.

Notes

[1] We have been unable to integrate the findings of the Commission on the Powers and Electoral Arrangements of the National Assembly for Wales (the Richard Commission) into our analysis. The *Report of the Richard*

Commission was published on 31 March 2004 and can be accessed via the Assembly website *www.wales.gov.uk*.

2   The lack of such a source became apparent when we were developing a course of study at the University of Glamorgan in 2000.

3   HTV was re-branded as ITV1 Wales in 2003.

4   See TAC website, *www.teledwyr.com*.

5   Debates of this nature, drawing on post-colonial theory, can be found in Williams and Aaron (2005).

6   The official turnout for the referendum was 50.15 per cent. The votes cast for an Assembly were 559,419 (50.3 per cent) and the votes against were 552,698 (49.7 per cent). See Wyn Jones, Trystan and Taylor (2000: 162).

7   See chapter 6 for a discussion of the history and development of S4C.

8   The influence of the Welsh Affairs Select Committee and the work of the Post-16 Committee and the Culture Committee are discussed in chapter 8.

9   Others have also expressed concerns about the limited amount of research on Wales carried out by its higher education institutions (see, for example, Wyn Jones, 2004: 29).

10   Grant number R000223668.

2

Voice(s) of a Small Nation: A Critical Context for the Study of the Media in Wales

The aim of this chapter is to contextualize the book's title. It is organized into four sections. The first provides an orientation to the media in Wales. The second outlines the main theoretical ideas that have informed much of the analysis. The third considers the ways in which 'voice' is linked to discussions about the media and how this idea can be utilized to inform a discussion about mass communications in Wales. The fourth explores the notion of Wales as a 'small nation' and, in doing so, considers its status within the UK, its relationship with England in particular, and why the mass media are necessarily implicated in any such discussion.[1]

Orientation

In anticipating a readership beyond the UK and Europe, what is the best way to begin a book on the media in Wales? Is there a need to 'locate' Wales, or is its global profile sufficient to render this unnecessary? While the latter question might appear frivolous, its relevance soon becomes apparent when people from Wales recall and reflect on their experience of travel overseas. These accounts – some related despairingly and others humorously – centre on issues of nationality and identity. Whether it be in Asia, North or South America, Africa, Oceania, or even in parts of Europe, the response to questions such as, 'Where are you from?', is just as likely to be 'Britain' as 'Wales'. Why? Because experience suggests that to answer 'Wales' necessitates further explanation which may not be possible due to time constraints or other social conventions in such an initial encounter. The following scenarios are not uncommon. When Wales is mentioned there is not even a flicker of recognition. On the other hand, the enquirer may have heard of Wales but is unsure of its geographic location. However, more commonly, mention of Wales prompts the response: 'Oh, you mean England.' Moreover, an attempt to correct this misapprehension is likely to underline Wales's 'invisibility' and further camouflage its distinctiveness. This is because the language needed to effect a successful communicative outcome is more than likely to be English. Perhaps, then, it comes as no surprise that one of the key objectives of the recently established National Assembly for Wales (NAfW or the Assembly) is to '[d]evelop the influence and profile of Wales in Europe and internationally' (National Assembly for Wales, 2000: 8; see also Post-16 Education and Training Committee, 2000a: 27–9).

On a more optimistic note, if the citing of Welsh cultural icons in such introductory encounters is likely to assist in situating Wales, modern-day globetrotters may be better placed than their elders in earlier years. For most of the twentieth century, the prevalent images of Wales in overseas climes included all or some of the following: picturesque scenery; rugby; coal and slate mines; iron and steel manufacturing; male choral singing; and a strong sense of family and community. The majority of these elements were combined in one of the most commercially successful 'Welsh' films, *How Green Was My Valley* (1941). That the industrial context was sanitized, family life romanticized, cultural practices misrepresented and the pit-head and Valley scenery fabricated on a film set constructed in the United States, mattered not to the American director and 'money-men', nor to the many who flocked to view this film. Interestingly, perhaps the most commercially successful Welsh film of the contemporary era, *Twin Town* (1997), also attracted barbs and bouquets. While its irreverent tilt at traditional Welsh icons was applauded by some, others were less convinced. Those in the tourism business were worried that the exposure of a Swansea 'underclass' would impact on the flow of visitors to Wales, while the clergy were more concerned about the potential for 'copycat poodle beheadings' (Blandford, 1999: 123; Morris, 1998: 27).

As the twenty-first century began, young Welsh travellers were more likely to find their initial conversations overseas marked with refer-ences to bands such as the 'Stereos' and the 'Manics' (respectively the

Stereophonics and the Manic Street Preachers), Catatonia, or second-wave outfits such as the Lost Prophets from Pontypridd. Tom Jones might even have been cited following his career relaunch with *Reload* in 2001, or Charlotte Church, known as much for her wealth, 'boyfriend troubles' and nomination as 'rear of the year' in 2002 – at barely sixteen years of age – as for the quality of her voice. But, however prolific the output of such artists, the listener was unlikely to become acquainted with the first language of Wales. In the popular music genre, this would require listening to the Gorky's (Gorky's Zygotic Mynci), the Super Furrys (Super Furry Animals) or the many less well-known artists who perform in Welsh but find difficulty getting airplay on commercial radio, even in Wales.[2] In the words of one such musician: 'We live our lives in Welsh. We don't just do it to be awkward. We order our drinks at the bar in Welsh. Why the hell should we sing in English?' (cited in Llewellyn, 1998: 62).

It is primarily S4C and BBC Radio Cymru that provide the performance space for these latter artists. S4C has also been a prime mover in illuminating the international profile of Wales through its investment in film and animation. Films such as *Hedd Wyn/The Armageddon Poet* (1992) and *Solomon a Gaenor/Solomon and Gaenor* (1998) have received Oscar nominations in the Best Foreign Language Film category. In the animation genre, S4C's current status was helped considerably by *SuperTed* becoming the first British animation series to be accepted by the Disney Channel in the USA (Robins and Webster, 2000: 112). But achievements such as these are more difficult to match in other areas. Although the soap opera *Pobol y Cwm* ('People of the Valley') remains a mainstay of S4C's programming schedule, achieving an audience beyond Wales will continue to be problematic. Nevertheless, while lacking the 'street cred' of BBC's *EastEnders* and the 'imagined nation' escapism offered by Australia's *Neighbours*, *Pobol y Cwm* does enable non-Welsh speakers to access soap 'Welsh-style' through the inclusion of subtitles. Moreover, audience research undertaken with a group of young Welsh speakers suggests that *Pobol y Cwm* should receive wider exposure. It was seen as a 'cultural ambassador' for Wales, a programme to be dubbed and broadcast on mainstream channels 'in order to challenge the perceived ignorance of the non-Welsh viewer' (Griffiths, 1993: 22).

While there is little doubt that Wales's profile within and beyond the UK and Europe is gradually expanding, questions have long been asked about aspects of self-familiarity and self-knowledge. Osmond

(1992: 5) laments how little people seem to know about their own country, suggesting, by way of example, that residents of the Valleys in south Wales are more likely to have visited Marbella than Machynlleth.[3] Furthermore, while earlier religious, political and regional tensions may have contributed to a limited national familiarity, poor communications infrastructure in the form of roads and railways, particularly between north and south, continues to inhibit in-country exploration. The mass media in Wales are also implicated, shaped as they have been by the all-powerful economic and political centre of the UK, London. As Raymond Williams (1989: 8) has reminded us, the visual and aural similarities of 'HQ' and 'UK' are powerfully suggestive. Moreover, the ramifications of British (or English) hegemony, exemplified by London-centric decision-making, continues to impact on the media in Wales.

For newly arrived visitors to Wales who turn to the mass media as a way of acquainting themselves with the local culture, the experience is likely to be one of bemusement. They are likely to be puzzled about the limited amount of locally produced material broadcast by ITV1 Wales, previously HTV, and BBC Wales, and how little the programming schedules of these two services differ from the UK-wide ITV and BBC networks. On the other hand, they may be impressed by the range and quality of local programming offered in Welsh on S4C, although mystified by the 'wrap-around' additional English-language material made available through Channel 4. If visitors are resident in hotel or bed-and-breakfast accommodation in south-east, mid or north-east Wales, they may find that the television news originates from Bristol, Birmingham or Manchester, respectively. Initial confusion may turn to frustration once it is realized that these news broadcasts seldom include any references to Wales. When this occurs in Cardiff – the nation's capital city – such an occurrence might, understandably, be experienced as bizarre.

Radio also has its peculiarities. Visitors who tune to radio when driving around Wales will quickly become accustomed to stations 'dropping out'. Furthermore, in some areas, the BBC's analogue services, Radios 1, 2, 3, 4 and 5 (originating from London), will be easier to access than Radio Wales and Radio Cymru, the two national services for Wales. There will also be disappointment for those hoping to sample the nation's cultural diversity by tuning to commercial Independent Local Radio (ILR). For instance, in north Wales the A55 passes through the reception areas of three such stations, Champion

FM at Caernarfon, Coast FM at Colwyn Bay and MFM 103.5 at Wrexham. However, as they are all owned by one company and networked as a result, at certain times of the day, evening and overnight, listeners will hear the same – predominantly music-based – programmes across all three stations. The origins of Champion FM may also be usefully recalled. From the outset, the station's commercial backers sought to target a working-class and largely Welsh-speaking audience, one allegedly ignored – or not adequately catered for – by Radio Cymru. By 2002, the ramifications of this development for the BBC had become apparent, with surveys indicating that Champion FM had achieved a greater audience share in this part of Wales than Radio Cymru.[4]

While visitors will hear a number of programmes in Welsh on Champion FM – unlike some other ILR stations in Wales – they are unlikely to be aware of the lively debates about the use and 'quality' of the Welsh language being broadcast. Essentially, arguments centre on whether the battle for radio ratings has contributed to a 'dumbing-down' of spoken Welsh on BBC and commercial radio.[5] Such idiosyncrasies, however, are not restricted to radio and television. The nation has no genuinely national newspaper and the biggest-selling daily papers in Wales are produced in England, the *Sun* being the market leader.[6] Visitors may also be somewhat perplexed to find the editor of a local newspaper in mid Wales describing it as an 'English paper' and the column detailing upcoming cultural events, albeit in Welsh, entitled – when translated literally – 'For the Welsh'![7]

Analytical framework

While it might be considered unusual in a book of this kind for authors to be explicit about the use of theory, there are three reasons for doing so. First, it illustrates and makes transparent how we, the authors, have approached our task. Second, it demonstrates how theory can shape and inform the practical tasks of enquiry and analysis. Third, it provides a model that the reader may wish to utilize, or, of course, reject![8]

Today, Wales represents itself to the world as a multicultural nation, even though this might be considered more a process in motion than an ambition achieved. In such nations, Jakubowicz (1995: 170) argues that studies of mass media must pay attention to the ownership and organization of production – plus the texts, or content, that emerge from this process – in order to judge the extent to which this output is representative of minorities and inter-group relations. Guided by these goals, this book aims to provide a critical analysis of the media in Wales. In this context, 'critical' means more than just posing difficult or unpopular questions. It has a number of strands, being theoretically informed, relying on empirically based historical and contemporary analysis, seeking to expose relations of domination and emancipation and suggesting ways of democratic reformulation (see, for example, Downing, Mohammadi and Sreberny-Mohammadi, 1995: xx–xxvi; Stevenson, 2002: 227).

The analytical framework adopted here draws on critical political economy and the Habermasian 'public sphere'. Why these two approaches? Three reasons are offered. First, they are both similarly theoretically informed – being broadly neo-Marxist. Second, while different in terms of history, scope and focus, they are complementary and offer significant explanatory potential when used in combination. Third, each encourages a holistic view, enabling consideration of the wider contexts of production and consumption. Like all approaches to the study of media, culture and communication, political economy and public sphere perspectives have limitations. Despite this, their currency and power as analytic 'tools' is widely recognized (see, for example, Boyd-Barrett, 1995; Curran and Gurevitch, 2000; McGuigan, 1996; Mosco, 1996; Stevenson, 2002).

Critical political economy

At the risk of over-simplification, one starting point is to suggest that political economy begins with the macro in order to understand micro-contexts. Attention is focused on the power relations that underpin and are integral to the production, distribution and consumption of resources, which in this case are 'communications' and 'cultural' (Mosco, cited in Boyd-Barrett, 1995: 186). It is a critical – rather than classical – approach to political economy for three reasons (Golding and Murdock, 2000: 70–2; see also Hesmondhalgh, 2002: 30–3). First, the central concern is with power and how it is constituted and exercised – unlike classical political economy where the focus is on exchange, consumer choice and freedom. Second, critical political economy is realist and materialist, in that it directs questions to both agency and structure in order to illuminate the constraints that shape the lives of 'ordinary' people and how unequal access to material resources impacts on the representational environment. Third, critical political economy recognizes the limitations of a 'free' market economy and argues for public intervention – through government – to 'correct' the resultant deficiencies.

Four key characteristics are core to a critical political economy perspective. First, it is holistic, in that it seeks to make connections between economic organization and political, cultural and social life; second, it is historical, requiring attention to core processes such as the expansion of media, the extension of corporate reach, commodification and changes in state intervention; third, it focuses attention on the 'balance between public intervention and capitalist enterprise'; fourth, it stresses a moral dimension, necessitating interest in – broadly speaking – issues of social justice (Golding and Murdock, 2000: 14; see also, Mosco, 1996: 27–38). By way of example, the next three paragraphs indicate how a critical political economy approach, focusing on the contexts of production, texts and consumption, can assist in a study of the media in Wales.

Beginning with 'production', the material realities of this process demand that analysis takes account of the patterns of ownership and their consequences, as well as the relationship between state regulation and communications institutions. In Wales, this requires a historical and contemporary analysis of press ownership and a similar exercise in respect of ILR. Such an analysis needs to take account of how changes in UK regulation have helped facilitate greater cross-media ownership and enabled ownership, in both these sectors, to become consolidated and – for the most part – located outside Wales.

In focusing on 'texts' – the content being produced – the aim is to illustrate how the material realities of production and consumption are related to representations. It is, therefore, important to recognize the relationship between the wider ownership and control of the television industry, the degree of local autonomy that exists, the legislative and regulatory frameworks and the level of locally produced television by BBC Wales, ITV1 Wales and S4C. If attention is directed to radio rather than television, the broadcast output of ILR stations might be scrutinized for 'localness' and 'quality', while considering the degree to which re-regulation and the economic dynamics of the industry impact on what is being broadcast.[9] Whether it is the output of television, radio or the press, there is a further dimension here. To what extent does the economic organization of the media in Wales impact on the process of citizenship? Here, questions centre on whether the mass media provide an adequate range and depth of information and a 'space' for debate in which a plurality of voices and viewpoints are accommodated.

In turning to 'consumption', the emphasis here is on exposing the relationship between material and cultural inequality. In other words, how are people's consumption choices structured by their position in society? In Wales, for example, concerns about the gap between the 'information rich' and 'information poor' direct attention to the costs involved in updating computer software, maintaining Internet access and retaining a mobile phone in order to participate in the so-called information, communication or knowledge society.[10] These costs impact disproportionately on the disposable incomes of low socio-economic groups (see, for example, Golding and Murdock, 2000: 86–9). Similar concerns arise in response to plans by the UK government to switch off the analogue television network in order to introduce digital transmission, with a similar transition expected for radio at a later stage. Aside from the immediate costs involved in ensuring a digital connection and the longer-term financial implications of replacing analogue television sets and video-cassette recorders, some households in Wales will face an additional access barrier due to topography. Overcoming this hurdle may involve additional expenditure. A further point might be made about broadband, touted as the latest 'big thing' in the early twenty-first century. In the United States the 'red-lining' of poor neighbourhoods acts as a reminder that certain urban and rural locations in Wales could remain 'unconnected' if the required investment is thought unlikely to ensure profitable outcomes in the desired timeframe (Communications Update, 1994: 15–16).[11]

The public sphere

The second element of our analytical framework uses Jürgen Habermas's concept of the 'public sphere' (Habermas, 1964; 1989; 1992). Habermas, a German philosopher, traced the evolution of what he called the 'bourgeois public sphere' in Britain, France and Germany from its origins in the seventeenth century, to its peak in the eighteenth century, through to its subsequent decline in the late nineteenth and early twentieth centuries. For Habermas, 'the bourgeois public sphere was the medium through which the middling classes wrested power from absolute rulers and the feudal aristocracy' (McGuigan, 1996: 25).

According to Habermas the public sphere was a set of physical and cultural institutions which were not controlled by the state, nor were they part of the private world of the home or business. He argued that the public sphere existed in the coffee houses, newspapers and literary journals of eighteenth-century London, the 'salons' in France and 'Table Societies' in Germany (Calhoun, 1992: 12). The public sphere was, he argued, unusual at the time because it was open to everyone. In a coffee house or a salon, a trader and an aristocrat could mingle without the normal inhibitions associated with their different social status. In the public sphere people could engage in rational, critical debate about literature, society and politics, and as such the public sphere was the first social and cultural institution in Europe to develop a form of public opinion (see, for example, Boyd-Barrett, 1995: 230; McGuigan, 1996: 23–5; Peters, 1993: 544; Poole, 1989: 14–15; Verstraeten, 1996: 347–9). In 'acting as a mouthpiece for the public', it provided an opportunity for private citizens to debate issues of public concern and engage in critical discussion of the state (Stevenson, 2002: 49).

The decline of the public sphere from the nineteenth century onwards is attributed to a combination of developments. For Habermas, the world of business invaded the sphere, in the sense that as the press became increasingly commercialized it no longer provided the same kind of free access to the public for rational debate. Equally, the growth of the modern state, with its accompanying institutions of pressure groups, political parties and a centralized electronic media, in a sense took over the sphere, ordering, regulating and controlling the flow of debate and public opinion. This process is described by Habermas (1964: 54) as the 'refeudalisation of the public sphere'. State and private control over the flow of public information became a matter of the manipulation of public opinion, rather than the promotion of rational public discourse designed to create public opinion. This was embodied, some have argued, in the increasing use of public relations and advertising (Dahlgren, 1991: 10; Poole, 1989: 16; McGuigan, 1996: 24). Curran (1996: 82) aptly captures the transformation that took place when he describes the public being squeezed out as economic interests and the state began to bargain with each other.

Habermas's historical account of the bourgeois public sphere and the characteristics attributed to it have been criticized for a number of reasons. However, detractors and advocates alike agree that the ideals of a public sphere retain relevance in any study of communications and culture in contemporary society (see, for example, McLaughlin, 1993: 599–601; Thompson, 1994: 41; Stevenson, 2002: 48). For Peters (1993: 559–61), one of the key insights emerging out of Habermas's work is the idea of mass media as 'ambiguous institutions' with 'ambivalent potential'. Ambiguous, because two often indistinguishable and intertwining roles – the 'civic' providing information for public debate, and the 'economic' providing entertainment to attract audiences for advertisers – cast mass-media institutions as agents of both political enlightenment and economic enticement. Their ambivalent potential is evident because the media can be employed for the purpose of ideological manipulation or emancipation. More generally, though, the most frequently cited insights associated with the public sphere relate to the principles it invokes and its potential as a model, or vision, for the role of the media in a democratic society (see, for instance, Curran, 1996: 82; Dahlgren, 1991: 5; Garnham, 1986: 31; Husband, 1994: 3–4). In other words, the public sphere can be envisaged as an 'ideal' public communications system – an open, independent, diverse and accessible communicative space.

It is at this point that both the theoretical strands adopted merge into a single framework, maximizing their explanatory potential. In its 'ideal' form, the public sphere is envisaged by critical political economists as a 'yardstick' against which judgements can be made about existing systems of public communications and corrective measures suggested (Golding and Murdock, 2000: 77; see also McGuigan, 1996: 28). Thus, the combination of a political economy perspective and insights from the public sphere help in illuminating a number of critical issues which require attention when focusing on the media in Wales. In no particular order, they are ownership and control, regulation, national identity, language, geography, governance, social class, gender, diversity, plurality, access and technology. To varying degrees and in a variety of ways, this chapter and those that follow engage with these critical issues.

Voice(s) – local and global

For the reader, reference to 'voice' or 'voices' may prompt recollection of past or present experiences at school, university, in one's family, the workplace, or in the neighbourhood or community that constitutes home. In all of these contexts certain voices will have been more prominent than others. Some will have been confident, others less so. Some will have been respected, influential and listened to, while others will have been ridiculed, banished, 'talked-over', or just simply ignored. Certain voices holding sway will have claimed to speak for absent others. In fact, presence or absence will have been influenced by factors such as gender, ethnicity, social class, role, attractiveness and power in its various guises.

Relatedly, the idea of 'voice' is often used as a figure of speech when referring to media, culture and communication. In this context, voice operates as a metaphor for presence, be that visually, aurally, or textually. Although something of a cliché, television and radio in particular are sometimes credited with providing a 'voice for the voiceless'. In other words, they provide those individuals and groups who have previously been denied communicative opportunities the chance to be heard, seen or read (see, for example, Scannell, 1989: 142). While this notion may be contentious, its employment here is useful because it draws attention to certain voices – be they individuals, groups or nations – being excluded, marginalized, or misrepresented in the mass media. For instance, Kevin Williams (1997b: 61) makes reference to the stereotyping of Wales and its people by London-based mass media.

'Voice' has been associated with Wales in two ways and the media have a role in both. The first relates to external concerns and draws attention to Wales's place and voice in the wider world. The second involves voices at 'home' – the people and institutions of Wales. The former becomes apparent in 'New' Labour's White Paper, *A Voice for Wales/Llais dros Gymru* (Welsh Office, 1997), which outlined proposals for a NAfW. Its emphasis was twofold: first, to increase Wales's voice in Britain, Europe and the wider world and, second, to enable a democratic voice – via the Assembly – to be brought to bear on the development of legislation and policy at the UK level (Welsh Office, 1997: 8–9). It suggested that the benefits for Wales would be economic, cultural and political.

The economic dimension is evident in the fact that the generation of wealth and employment and the maintenance of a skills-base in Wales are dependent on being able to sell cultural and other goods in a global market place. Likewise, the cultural dimension is apparent because it is via the media, in all its forms, that the cultural heritage of Wales becomes accessible to the wider world. Thinking particularly about the extent to which television drama can be envisaged as promoting or legitimizing minority cultures in an increasingly global media maze, Talfan Davies (1992: 23) argues 'no drama, no nation'. Moreover, while the hegemony of the English language dictates that English-language Welsh-produced texts are likely to be more marketable, the use of subtitling and dubbing has assisted in widening the potential reach of

Welsh-language material. Moreover, it might be argued that S4C's investment in animation products is particularly astute, as it provides a means of overcoming potential language barriers.

The political dimension relates to issues of citizenship. In other words, the extent to which the media in Wales provide its citizens with a sufficiently comprehensive and critical interpretation of world events and a sense of Wales's place in the world. In this regard, Hume's (1986) analysis of the English- and Welsh-language news media in Wales provides insights that remain helpful in any contemporary analysis. He argued that the English-language news media in Wales were hardly distinguishable in their use of language and presentational style from their counterparts in Birmingham, Bristol and Manchester. He also maintained that the Welsh-language news media, Radio Cymru and S4C, covered international news not only more thoroughly than Welsh-based English-language news services, but also from a more distinctly Welsh perspective (Hume, 1986: 334–5, 340).

While the situation has changed dramatically in the last decade or so, it remains the case that English-produced daily newspapers continue to garner a significant readership in Wales and that most of the nation's ILR stations continue to use the UK-wide networked Independent Radio News service. One further aspect is relevant here. While the longer-term future of the Assembly will be dependent on the will of the people, the media in Wales will play a major role in shaping perceptions of this institution in the wider UK, Europe and beyond (Mungham and Williams, 1998: 116).

In turning to discussions about 'voice' in the academic and political literature on Wales, the overriding sense is that most writers consider there is a media, cultural or communication *deficit* of one form or another. The idea of a media deficit is associated with the diversity and plurality of the mass media in Wales. Attention is drawn to the limited number of voices that provide the news, views and analysis of daily life in Wales and the resultant narrowness of political perspectives, viewpoints and opinions being expressed (see, for example, Hannan, 1998; Talfan Davies, 1999; K. Williams, 1997a).[12] This lack of diversity and plurality of voice has generated particular concerns on the grounds that information, public debate and knowledge are essential if a viable political public sphere is to emerge in Wales following the establishment of the Assembly (see, for example, Talfan Davies, 1999: 46–51).

The idea of a cultural deficit has arisen as a result of suggestions that the limited diversity and plurality of the media in Wales relates to issues of national identity. In particular, concerns have centred on the extent to which the media portray adequately and represent fully the diversity of Wales: its regions, languages, social classes, age groups, rural and urban communities, ethnic groups and general multicultural make-up. With the Assembly and other key bodies based in Cardiff and with events such as the Aberystwyth Film Festival gradually moving south and turning into the Cardiff Screen Festival, references to Cardiff as the 'octopus of the south' are unlikely to cease (see Hume and Pryce, 1986). In addition, there have been many concerns expressed about the ways in which the mass media in Wales rely on traditional stereotypes of what constitutes Welshness and have proved reluctant to embrace the changing nature of contemporary Wales (see, for example, Beddoe, 1986; Blandford, 2000a; M. Ryan, 1986; K. Williams 1997a).

Debates of this nature were reignited – if only briefly – by the much-hyped claims of 'Cool Cymru' shortly before and immediately after the turn of the twenty-first century. Most proclamations were based on the commercial success of a few (predominantly English-speaking) Welsh rock bands. However, this is to ignore the impact of some pioneering examples of Welsh theatre and of the artistic, rather than commercial, success of Welsh films in both languages (see, for example, Blandford, 1999; 2000a). Inevitably, the temptation to use Cool Cymru as an easy explanatory and promotional tool, plus its unavoidable association with Cool Britannia and 'New' Labour, has since encouraged a sense of vacuity, tempered earlier illusions and helped kick-start a more critical assessment of this period. Perrins (2000: 153), in particular, has questioned just how 'cool' Cymru actually was, arguing that the Welsh establishment 'hijacked the medium and in some cases the message of these so-called "indie" bands'. In particular, he rails against the detachment and co-option of Catatonia's catchy and allegedly ironic chorus in *International Velvet* – 'Every day, when I wake up, I thank the Lord I'm Welsh' – by the mass media and BBC Wales in particular:

> this partitioned chorus quickly gained favour, and reached a zenith when it was used almost as an alternative national anthem, or rather more fittingly in this land of 'New Labour' – national sound bite, at the climax of the *Voices of a Nation* concert in Cardiff Bay, to mark the official opening of the Assembly in May of 1999. (Perrins, 2000: 153)

The idea of a communicative deficit has its roots in the way public life was organized in Wales in the three decades prior to the arrival of the Assembly. The basis of complaint was that a multiplicity of public bodies – quangos – had been established in Wales and that their members were appointed rather than elected (see, for example, Osmond, 1992; 1994). It was the unsupportable nature of the assumption that members of such bodies were able to represent the interests and views of the wider population that led to calls for a more participatory democracy (Day et al., 1998: 291–2). The manner in which people have been appointed to broadcasting bodies such as the BBC Broadcasting Council for Wales, the S4C Authority and OfCom has mirrored the ways in which appointments have been made to quangos in Wales. This has led to calls for greater public participation in appointments to such bodies and, in turn, to demands for greater public participation at all levels of mass media. The current exclusion of the wider public from these processes means that individual citizens are unable to express their views directly through the media to the public in any meaningful way, and, because of the policy and practice of mass media institutions, cannot be assured that their views will be accurately reported. In addition, the wider public is deprived of the opportunity to hear or read in full the views and opinions of their peers, as they remain reliant on the 'filtered' news and information provided daily by the mass media.[13]

An enhanced public voice, however, does not emerge simply as a result of increasing the number of 'chat shows', 'talk-back' or 'phone-ins'. Here, in most instances, the agenda is pre-set. Entertainment takes priority over debate, the presenters – as 'stars' – are not to be upstaged by their guests, and a barely adequate amount of time is allocated to consider complex issues. Not surprisingly, there are suggestions that, in order to reinvigorate social, cultural and political life in Wales, there needs to be a more meaningful connection at local and national levels between the people and the media (see, for example, Day et al., 1998: 299; K. Williams, 1994: 257). It follows, then, that if there is to be greater participatory democracy in Wales, a more genuine form of media democracy is a necessary precursor.[14]

In essence, the concern, so frequently expressed in writing about the media in Wales, is that media, cultural and communicative deficits have ramifications for citizenship, national identity and democracy. A number of factors are seen to have contributed to this situation. They include: the consolidation of media organizations through mergers and take-overs; the centralization of control over public broadcasting bodies; mass-media organizations being generally unaccountable to the public; ownership of public and private media beyond the boundary of Wales;

a preference for market-led systems of delivery over those of 'public service'; and an increasingly re-regulatory environment. While these factors also operate in other countries, their impact is thought to be particularly significant during a period in which Wales is undergoing a major period of transition. At such times, it is argued, the nation needs to be able to 'dialogue with itself' (see, for example, Hannan, 1998: 12; Talfan Davies, 1999: 33–4). Inevitably, this invites attention to Wales's status within the UK and its relationship with England.

Small nation blues

It is not unusual to find Wales described as a small nation or a small country (see, for example, Griffiths, 1993: 10–11; Talfan Davies, 1992: 25; R. Williams, 1979: 1). According to Schlesinger (1991: 302–3), this generally self-imposed label is used to denote any, or all, of the following: a nation's territory, its landmass and population size, and its independent cultural viability. When Wales is referred to as a small nation it is more often than not the latter category that is being invoked.

Wales's cultural vulnerability may be understood in three ways. The first centres on Wales's ability to assert itself in an increasingly global media environment. One aspect of this is whether Wales has the capacity to produce and sell cultural and other goods in a global market place. Another relates to the perception that the globalization of the media poses threats to national identity and, in particular, the survival of the Welsh language.

The second area where commentators perceive Wales as vulnerable stems from the number of people relying on news sources from England. While the figures are disputed and the rationales various, 87 per cent of the population are judged to read daily newspapers produced in England and up to 14 per cent do not watch television channels broadcasting from Wales (see, for example, Talfan Davies, 1999: 7; Welsh Affairs Select Committee, 1999, para. 46; K. Williams, 2000: 96). While this 'leakage' of readers and viewers may rankle with the major media organizations, there are obvious implications for democracy. For instance, one analysis of voting patterns at the 1997 referendum noted a tendency to vote 'no' in those border areas of Wales and England where television leakage was most prevalent (K. Williams, 2000: 96).[15] Furthermore, if a sizeable segment of the population of Wales draws its news and current affairs from England, it does not bode well for an Assembly struggling to establish its credentials. As one Assembly Minister remarked, '[i]f people aren't getting their news about the Assembly from Welsh sources, they sure as hell won't get it from English ones'.[16]

A third way in which Wales may be perceived as culturally vulnerable relates to its stateless identity. While one school of thought may consider the nation-state as moribund and increasingly powerless, with borders no longer sacrosanct, there is evidence to the contrary. The obvious examples are to be found in the former Soviet Union where a number of nations have sought and gained statehood. Schlesinger (1991: 299) outlines a useful analogy that illustrates how media policy and mass media may play a role in the quest for sovereignty. He reminds us that the ultimate power of a nation-state is the right to defend its territory and to do so by military means if necessary. Territory can also be imagined as a 'communicative space' over which the nation-state still retains significant control, even in the face of satellites and the Internet. The nation-state 'defends' these spaces by means of legislation and regulation. With the advent of the Assembly, Wales might be conceived as a sub-state, but it still remains part of a unitary nation-state, the UK. It is, therefore, the British state that continues to exercise control over Wales's communicative space.

Wales's relative powerlessness in this area has been starkly illustrated by passage of the Communications Act 2003.[17] This legislation and the resultant regulatory framework will impact significantly on the communicative space of Wales (and Scotland and Northern Ireland). As the UK government is only obliged to *consult* the Assembly on matters related to communications, the latter's formal input to the legislative process has been to make submissions to the Department of Culture, Media and Sport outlining issues of particular importance to Wales (National Assembly for Wales, 2001a; 2002c). It is, therefore, not surprising that questions have arisen about whether Wales should have some form of local control over the media that operate within its boundaries. The underlying issue here is that if Wales can have some control over this space the media may be deployed for purposes of 'cultural defence' (Meech and Kilborn, 1992: 247). Such an idea invites attention to Wales's status within the UK.

There is a tendency for accounts dealing with the history and development of the mass media in Britain to commence in London before moving ever outwards to incorporate the peripheral regions and nations of the UK. Some of these accounts also ascribe to Wales (and

Scotland) the status of region – rather than nation – or assume or allude to such a position, and fail to address the significance of such matters and the underlying assumptions. Even in relatively recent accounts of the media in Britain, minimal attention is paid to the regions and nations. Not surprisingly, accounts of British media developments from a Welsh perspective are more likely to approach the task with the mindset of Wales as a nation. In doing so, the view from Wales portrays an omnipresent England with London looming large. By way of example, Jones refers to the 'media powerhouse of Fleet Street' being viewed with 'awe, anxiety and suspicion' (A. Jones, 2000a: 313), and John Davies has made mention of the 'struggle between Cardiff and Head Office' from the very beginning of BBC radio in Wales (cited in Morris, 1995: 6).

Clearly, the nature of these observations suggests, at the very least, an imbalance in power, even a colonial relationship. Whether it is appropriate or not to conceive of the relationship between Wales and England (or the British state) as colonial (or post-colonial), such views do exist. Either implicitly or explicitly, most authors writing about the media in Wales suggest a strong sense of powerlessness. There are numerous references to infiltration, exploitation, hegemony, stereotyping, imposition, conquest, dependence, centralism and domination. Where matters such as these are concerned, the BBC attracts particular criticism. One employee, a senior producer, described the BBC's promotion of 'Britishness' – or 'Englishness' – as 'undermin[ing] our consciousness as Welsh people' (Bevan, 1984: 109). Berry (2000: 138) cites a similarly placed source, who claimed that BBC Wales was treated by London as if it were a 'colonial outpost'. Geraint Talfan Davies, a former Controller of BBC Wales, has acknowledged that the 'obstacles of metropolitanism' have impacted negatively on local operations (1992: 25). In a similar vein, Osmond (1993), when writing about the accountability and transparency of the Broadcasting Council for Wales, called his article 'The last outpost of imperialism'.

Wales has been variously understood as a 'region', 'principality', 'western extension of England' and 'national region' – which until recently was the term used by the BBC (A. Jones, 2000a: 313; Talfan Davies, 1992: 20).[18] Whether past or present, Wales has never been a completely separate entity and neither has it ever been fully integrated. Confusion, or denial, about its status has had some obvious and far-reaching ramifications. Wales was initially 'attached' to the west of England in 1926 to form the BBC radio 'West Region' (J. Davies, 1994a:

39). The same ties were imposed when 'Television Wales and the West' (TWW) was established to provide the first commercial television service to Wales (Mackay and Powell, 1997: 9; Medhurst, 1998: 336). The linking of south-west England and Wales was not based on cultural grounds. In the case of radio, the regional arrangements took no account of cultural or geographical identity, thereby undermining local autonomy on creative and editorial matters and disregarding the needs of listeners (Crisell, 1997: 25; K. Williams, 1998: 25). 'Engineering-led' is the way Talfan Davies describes such decisions (1999: 7).

The rationale for the organization of television was similar to that of radio. Links with the west of England were encouraged because it was believed that Wales alone was not affluent enough to sustain a commercial service (Curran and Seaton, 1997: 184; Medhurst, 1998: 336). Furthermore, the reason for introducing a regional ITV structure throughout the UK was to counter the predominantly centralist structure of the BBC (Curran and Seaton, 1997: 84; Talfan Davies, 1992: 20). Yet, somewhat ironically, in 2003 the last two remaining ITV companies, Granada and Carlton, merged to form one UK-wide organization, thereby reversing the rationale of the structures put in place by the Independent Television Authority (ITA) set up by the Television Act 1954.

Essentially, then, the primary criterion to be satisfied in determining the regulatory arrangements for commercial television in Wales (and elsewhere) was 'the convenience of the market' (Curran and Seaton, 1997: 184). Even in recent years there are examples of decision-making that resonate with the past. For example, without consulting the Assembly, in 2000 the UK Radio Authority allocated a commercial radio licence for a regional station, Real Radio, to serve a swathe of south Wales. While it may seem so when looking at a map in London, very few people in Wales would consider an area incorporating Newport, Cardiff, Swansea and other population centres in south-west Wales as a discrete and 'natural' region. There is, therefore, ample evidence to suggest that ambivalence over Wales's status has influenced decisions which have, in turn, helped shape the nation's communications infrastructure.

Questions about infrastructure provide an opportunity to introduce Hechter's controversial thesis that 'Britain developed "internal colonies" in its Celtic fringe' (Hume and Pryce, 1986: xxiv). Hechter's (1986: 217–18) observation that infrastructural developments in colonial territories are determined primarily by the needs of the metropolitan

centre is insightful. Even a cursory examination of Wales'
network suggests that England's needs were prioritize
decline of the indigenous press in Wales has been explained, a.
part, by the availability of direct rail services into this country from
England (A. Jones, 2000a: 314). This ensured the timely and efficient
delivery of daily newspapers produced in London to all major
population centres in Wales. It is, therefore, difficult to see how any
account of the history and development of the media in Wales can be
told without recourse to the idea of 'struggle'.

While debates about the effective delivery of health, welfare and
education services can always be expected to provoke heated discussion,
in Wales broadcasting can be added to this list. The veracity of this
observation is evident in the widely supported, lengthy and sometimes
vitriolic campaigns to establish the BBC radio Welsh Region and S4C.
These and other matters prompted John Davies (1994: 38) to describe
broadcasting in Wales as 'one of the most contentious of all issues'. In
the case of the press, Aled Jones (1993, 1998, 2000a) provides a
comprehensive analysis of the struggle during the nineteenth and
twentieth centuries to maintain a vibrant Welsh press in both languages.
In recent years, television has also been a site of disquiet owing to the
apparent inability, or unwillingness, of BBC Wales and ITV1 Wales to
produce an adequate supply of quality local drama (see, for example,
Berry, 1996, 2000). In the case of film, the struggle has been concerned
with trying to maintain a Welsh presence on screen in both languages
and to balance the twin – and sometimes conflicting – goals of
economics and culture while maintaining the dream of an indigenous
film industry.[19] In the period preceding the passage of the Communications Act 2003, the Assembly strove to ensure that Wales was adequately
represented on the new regulator OfCom, even though it did not win a
place for a Welsh representative on its main board.

Using 'struggle' as a way of conceptualizing the role of the media is
both helpful and legitimate. Schlesinger (1991: 299) has suggested that
media can be understood as 'battlefields' or 'spaces in which contests
for various forms of dominance takes place'. Similarly, Ashcroft (2001:
4) has encouraged people to think of the media as 'sites of struggle',
because radio, television, film and to a lesser extent the press, can be
considered the key 'means of representation' in contemporary society.
In this context, 'representation' is envisaged both as 'the site of identity
formation and the site of struggle over identity formation' (Ashcroft,
2001: 4).

If both these ideas – media as battlefields and as sites of struggle – are accepted, it follows that change can only come about by gaining some form of control over the means of representation, the aim being to transform existing mass media into 'culturally appropriate vehicles' (Ashcroft, 2001: 5). This perspective forces a consideration of whether the existing patterns of control and accountability support or militate against the creation and sustenance of a culturally appropriate mass media in Wales. These issues underpin much of the debate in the following chapters.

Notes

1   Parts of this chapter were initially produced for a conference, 'Postcolonial Wales', held at the University of Glamorgan on 13 July 2002 and provided the basis for a contribution to a similarly titled edited volume (see Barlow, 2005).
2   This became evident in the course of interviews conducted for a research project, 'The role of Independent Local Radio in post-devolutionary Wales', funded by the UK Economic and Social Research Council (ESRC). Initial findings can be found on the Regard website (*www.regard.ac.uk*).
3   See also Talfan Davies (1999: 7–8), who reminds us that Wales has a lower percentage of its population born within its borders than either Scotland or Northern Ireland.
4   This ratings success was reported during interviews with staff at Champion FM in 2002. A further point might be made here. Unlike in England, the BBC has no local radio stations in Wales. BBC Radio Wales and Radio Cymru are considered national operations. ILR stations, therefore, provide Wales's only *local* radio services (see chapter 5). We are using the original terminology – Independent Local Radio – although the sector is now sometimes referred to as commercial radio.
5   This issue is discussed in chapter 5. Suffice to say at this point that there is significant pressure within the ILR sector to maximize audiences. This, in turn, means that local managers and presenters are constantly forced to justify decisions to include Welsh-language songs and spoken-word material.
6   Chapter 3 addresses and expands on this and related issues.
7   This emerged during an interview with a member of a community group in Newtown, mid Wales, undertaken in 2002 for the radio research project (see note 2 above). The paper referred to was the *County Times and Express*.
8   It should be noted that this section aims to provide an abbreviated overview of what are, essentially, complex theoretical perspectives. A fuller understanding of their derivation, development, limitations and potential will be enabled by consulting the sources identified.
9   Re-regulation – rather than deregulation, co-regulation or self-regulation – is preferred because it more accurately reflects the changes taking place;

namely, that regulation is being constructed in favour of private interests over those of the public (see McChesney, 2002: 2).

10 This issue is addressed in detail in chapter 7.

11 In this instance the term 'red-lining' is used as a metaphor to illustrate a decision to rule out – or draw red lines around – a location, or community, that will not be 'wired' to receive advanced communications services.

12 These matters are taken up again in chapter 3.

13 Reference to the use of 'filters' draws on Herman and Chomsky's 'Propaganda Model' (see Herman and Chomsky, 1988; see also Herman, 2002).

14 See Barber (1984: 178–9) who identifies nine functions of 'democratic talk' that are essential to participatory democratic communication. He argues that the ultimate aim of democratic talk is community building, which results from the 'creation of public interests, common goods and active citizens'. Such a goal requires media institutions to go beyond what neo-liberal theorists understand as the main aspects of democratic talk, that is 'the articulation of interests, bargaining and exchange . . . among competing individuals who seek to maximize their self-interests' and 'persuasion', its aim being 'to convince others of the legitimacy of one's own interests' (Barber, 1984: 179–80). See also Stein (2002) who examines Barber's taxonomy of democratic talk in relation to a number of radical access television projects in the USA.

15 Talfan Davies (1999: 7) concludes differently, arguing that 'the truth . . . is both more complex and less dramatic'.

16 This observation arises from an interview conducted in the course of the radio research outlined in note 2 above. All interviews were conducted on the basis that the respondent's views would be anonymous.

17 The Communications Act 2003 is the subject of extensive discussion in chapter 8.

18 This is not to suggest that such linkages have ended. Research undertaken by the UK Film Council on cinema admissions in 2003 showed 'Wales and the West' as one category (Wainwright, 2004: 5).

19 This issue is taken up in more detail in chapters 4 and 8.

II

Sectors and Industries

3

The Newspaper Press in Wales: Print, Culture and Society

The precursors of newspapers – almanacs, pamphlets and ballads – were printed in England and Wales throughout the sixteenth and seventeenth centuries. The first Welsh-language book was printed in Wales in 1546 (Williams, 1991: 152–3). If we include only those publications that are characterized by their regular (weekly, bi-weekly, daily) publication, the first newspaper in Wales dates from 1804 when the Swansea-based *Cambrian* was launched (A. Jones, 2000b: 1–3).

Nonetheless the boundaries between newspapers and other forms of printed materials were permeable. News journalism has always inhabited a much wider world of printed and other forms of communications, such as – to cite a modern-day example – the Internet. So, focusing on newspapers is, in part, a method of disentangling one important form of literary communication in Wales from the many others with which it is related. In addition, newspapers in the twenty-first no less than in the nineteenth century have to be viewed historically and in relation to the range of political, industrial, economic, technological and cultural forces which shaped them and with which they interacted. Pinning down the exact relationship between newspapers and society over time is impossible. It is, however, possible to grasp key elements of this relationship and to recognize the variety of ways in which they have related to society and culture in Wales.

Newspaper growth to 1900

In 1694 the Licensing Act which embodied the law relating to pre-publication censorship in England and Wales lapsed and was not renewed. This withdrawal of direct government pre-publication censorship contributed to the growth of English newspapers and periodicals in the eighteenth century. There were, however, laws in place from the early 1700s until the 1860s which used various types of taxation to limit the number, size and circulation of newspapers and thereby allow a measure of government control. These included newspaper stamp duties, taxes on advertising, and security, or 'good behaviour', bonds levied on publishers. In addition, successive governments in the eighteenth and early nineteenth centuries prosecuted authors and publishers for seditious libel, as well as seeking to control opinion in the press through bribery and subsidy.

During the Napoleonic Wars (1789–1815), a time of intense political agitation in the United Kingdom, the number of prosecutions increased. Yet, as the nineteenth century progressed, a combination of factors led to a gradual lifting of controls. These included pressures from the printing industry to remove unnecessary economic restraints on trade, the difficulties of policing the controls, and constant pressures from reformers inside and outside Parliament who argued for greater press freedom. As a result, advertisement duties were lifted in 1853, stamp duties in 1855, paper duties in 1861 and security controls in 1869 (O'Malley and Soley, 2000: 7–18). These changes led to a steady growth in the numbers of newspapers established in the UK up to the mid-nineteenth century, and then an explosion. Between 1800 and 1830, 136 newspapers were established in the UK; between 1830 and 1855 the number was 415, and from 1855 to 1861 it rose to 492 (A. Jones, 1996: 23).

In Wales, periodical publication in Welsh was established in the eighteenth century, with short-lived magazines like *Tlysau yr Hen Oesoedd* ('Gems of Past Ages', 1735), which may have only run to one issue, and *Trysorfa Gwybodaeth, neu Eurgrawn Cymraeg* ('A Treasury of Information, or Welsh Periodical', 1770). Aside from these generalist periodicals, politics and religion – later such driving forces in the Welsh press of the nineteenth century – inspired other periodicals. Thomas Evans's *Miscellaneous Repositry neu Y Drysorfa Gymysgedig* (1795) sought to promote the ideals of the French Revolution in Wales, while Thomas Charles's and Thomas Jones's *Trysorfa Ysprydol* ('A Spiritual Treasury', 1799), prefigured the explosion of Welsh denominational publishing in the next century (A. Jones, 2000b: 1–3).

It was not until the early nineteenth century that generalist news-papers modelled on earlier English versions began to appear: the *Cambrian* in Swansea (1804), the *North Wales Gazette* (1808) in Bangor and the *Carmarthen Journal* (1810). These heralded the arrival of almost five hundred titles in Wales in the nineteenth century. As Aled Jones has explained, there were

> two surges of activity, one in the 1830s, when the number of new titles jumped from seven to twenty-eight following the reduction . . . of the news-paper stamp from 4d to 1d, the other in the 1850s, following the complete abandonment of the stamp tax in 1855, when numbers rose steeply from twenty-six to sixty-nine. Numbers of new titles continued to increase steadily each decade for the following thirty years, culminating in the 1880s when one hundred new titles were launched. The majority of these newspapers were published in the English language, but . . . the rate of growth of the one hundred or so new Welsh language titles established during the nineteenth century also increased in the same critical decades. (2000b: 1–5)

This explosion in daily and weekly papers was precarious. Around 25 per cent of all titles failed every decade from the 1830s onwards. This was often due to lack of advertising and readers or because of difficulties in distributing papers across the difficult terrain of the country. But these failures did not dampen the faith of politicians, printers and journalists in the medium, and they continued to found new ones. Amongst these was the Tory, Cardiff-based daily, the *Western Mail* (1869) and its Liberal rival, the *South Wales Daily News* (1872), which between them reflected the two major political divisions of late nineteenth-century Wales. They emerged into a culture which, as in the UK in general, was saturated with print; but this was especially so in Wales with its news-print in both English and Welsh and with home-grown newspapers as well as those from England, including the *Liverpool Daily Post*[1] in north Wales (A. Jones, 1993: 129–30; 2000b: 8).

Decline, but not quite a fall – newspapers in Wales 1900–2003

The late nineteenth and early twentieth centuries witnessed a peak in the numbers of titles produced in Wales. The decline set in during the

1920s, mirroring developments in the provincial press in England
(Curran and Seaton, 2003: 351–2). Table 3.1 illustrates this process.

Table 3.1: Decline in newspaper titles in Wales 1914–60

Year	English-language titles	Welsh-language titles	Total
1914	119	20	139
1920	131	21	152
1930	116	18	134
1940	112	14	126
1950	105	9	114
1960	101	8	109

Source: Adapted from A. Jones, 1993: 209.

The number of English-language titles declined by 23 per cent between
1920 and 1960, in the context of an overall decline of 28 per cent. Yet
the figure of a 62 per cent decline in Welsh-language titles in total, and
from 16 per cent of all titles in 1920 to 7.9 per cent in 1960, indicates in
one sense the scale of a widely perceived crisis in the twentieth century
in Wales, that of the decline of Welsh as an organic language of home
and community. A combination of factors, not least the spread of
cheap English-language dailies such as the *Daily Mail* and the *Daily
Mirror* in Wales – and, as the century progressed, rivalry from film,
radio and TV – contributed to a long-term decline in the number of titles
published in Wales. The impact of intense competition from London was
facilitated by improvements in transport, allowing easier penetration for
these titles across Wales. The Second World War (1939–45) saw the
imposition of restrictions on newsprint and a squeeze on advertising,
both of which contributed to the economic problems of the press in
Wales (A. Jones, 1993: 219). The decline in the number of titles continued
thereafter, although it was offset, to some degree, by the spread after the
1970s of free, often weekly, papers as illustrated in Table 3.2.

Papurau bro and Y Byd

Set against the decline in the numbers of commercially produced English-
and Welsh-language titles has been the phenomena of the *papurau bro*
(local papers). These highly localized, Welsh-language publications,

usually monthly and based on voluntary labour, grew from the 1970s. Serving populations of varying size, they cover news about local people and organizations and contain columns aimed at segments of the readership: young readers, Welsh learners, and those interested in poetry or gardening. These papers have been criticized for being too focused on the past, rather than on the issues facing contemporary Welsh-speaking communities (Huws, 1996: 90–1). Nonetheless, one estimate put their number at fifty-one in the early 1990s, with average sales of around 1,292 each and an estimated total Welsh readership of 70,000 per month (Huws, 1996: 84–5).

Table 3.2: Numbers of newspapers produced in Wales 1966–2003

Year	Morning	Evening	Weekly/bi-weekly	Sunday	Free	Total
1966	1[a]	3	89			93
1970	1	3	87			91
1975	1	4	75			80
1980	1	4	67			72
1985	1	4	51		26	82
2003	1	5	33	1[b]	30[c]	70

[a] Excludes *Liverpool Daily Post*; [b] *Wales on Sunday* launched 1989; [c] this figure subsumes different titles for different districts in the same area and owned by the same company.

Sources: Figures for 1966–85 adapted from figures for Wales and Monmouthshire in the annual reports of the Press Council (various dates). Those for 2003 are calculated from data on the website of the Newspaper Society, 2003a.

The 1960s and 1970s were periods of heightened activism in Wales around the issue of the defence and promotion of the Welsh language. As Table 3.3 illustrates, the majority of *papurau bro* (83.8 per cent) were created between 1973 and 1983, with the peak years between 1975 and 1979 when 58.8 per cent were started. In this sense they were a reflection of that period of enhanced language activism.

The absence of a national Welsh-language daily paper prompted the Mercator Centre at the University of Wales, Aberystwyth to apply for grant funding to examine the feasibility for such a paper. The research prompted the formation of a project to establish a Welsh-language daily paper by 2005. Using information technology, employing up to forty people, sixteen of whom were to be journalists, the company established to run *Y Byd* was planning to gain 5,000 subscribers plus

2,000 casual sales in its first year. Thereafter its target circulation was to be between 15 and 17,000 copies per day (N. Thomas, 2003/4; *Y Byd*, 2004).

Table 3.3: Papurau bro

Year	Starts	Closures*	Year	Starts	Closures*	Year	Starts	Closures*
1973	1		1980	3		1990		1
1974	4	1	1981	2	1	1991	1	
1975	8		1982	4	1	1992		
1976	9	2	1983	3	1	1993		
1977	8	1	1984		1	1994		
1978	7		1985	1	1	1995		
1979	8		1986			1996	1	
			1987	4		1997	1	
			1988	2	1	1998		
			1989			1999		
						2000		
						2001	1	
Total	**45**	**4**		**19**	**6**		**4**	**1**
Total Starts 1973–2001 = 68				**Total Closures = 11**				

* Excludes papers closed and subsequently restarted.

Source: Calculated from National Library of Wales, 2001.

The Welsh press in context

The development of the press in Wales has been, and remains, linked directly to changes in the economy, population, occupations, politics and linguistic characteristics of the country.

The expansion of the newspaper industry in the UK in the nineteenth century was, as Brown has argued, the product of a complex of factors:

The period from the 1860s to the end of the century was one of rapid development, and much was not peculiar to Great Britain. In France and the United States we have a similar record: theories which explain the expansion in relation to British considerations such as the taxation of newspapers and the *Education Act* of 1870 fail to take account of this general development. If there is a common cause of the expansion, the most likely explanation lies in the urbanisation of these countries and in the speeding up of transport arrangements. Railways, which made the provisioning and employment of large concentrated populations possible, also made possible the larger markets for newspapers. (1985: 8–9)

In addition, the mechanization of printing presses and their increasing power and sophistication in the nineteenth century boosted circulations and increased the capital needed to start up a newspaper.

Wales benefited from a slow improvement in educational provision prior to the 1870 Education Act, but the development of the press was held back until after the 1850s by general economic conditions and the legal restraints on the industry. After the 1850s, population growth, urbanization and legal change combined with advances in print technology and the spread of the railways to create the conditions for the rapid expansion in the numbers of titles up to the 1920s (A. Jones, 1993: 107; 2000b: 6–7). This combination of transport, technology and concentrated markets remained key factors in the continuance of the newspaper press in Wales, in all its forms, during the twentieth century.

In Wales population growth was rapid and essential for the creation and sustenance of newspapers. The population of Wales rose from 587,000 in 1811 to 1,163,139 in 1851. It reached 1,572,000 in 1881 and then leaped to 2,523,500 in 1914, under the pressure of the expansion of the south Wales coalfields. Between 1851 and 1911 the coalfields received a net immigration of 320,000 people, while rural Wales suffered a net migration of 388,000. Thus the balance of the population shifted towards the industrial south and the Bristol estuary, with an accompanying growth in urban markets for newspapers and a depletion in the rural population that was to prompt grave concerns amongst nationalists concerned about the survival of Welsh-speaking culture (J. Davies, 1994b: 398–9; D. Evans, 1989: 232). The population growth was reflected in the rapid expansion of Merthyr Tydfil, which grew from 11,000 in 1811 to 80,000 in 1911, and Cardiff, which mushroomed from 1,800 in 1801 to 164,000 in 1901 (A. Jones, 1993: 91).

This expansion underpinned the markets for Welsh publications in both languages and for publications produced in England. The population was made up of a workforce that went through a series of major changes over the two hundred years from 1800. In 1851, 35 per cent of the male labour force were in agriculture, with 10 per cent in coal. By 1914 the relative positions were reversed, with 10 per cent in agriculture and about 35 per cent in coal. The twentieth century saw another shift – the retreat from extractive industries like coal, the decline in manual work and the rise of service-related industries such as transport, communications, financial and professional occupations. By 1982, 60.8 per cent of the population worked in service-related industries, 32.4 per cent were in manual occupations and only 6.7 per cent in the extractive industries. This last figure has since collapsed with the closure of the coalfields in south Wales after the 1984–5 coal dispute. Running parallel with these changes were the growing numbers of women entering the paid workforce in Wales during the twentieth century (J. Davies, 1994b: 398; G. A. Williams, 1991: 256–7).

The changes in population and occupations shifted the culture of Wales through a number of registers, raising issues at different times about the survival of Welsh-speaking culture, the impacts of urbanization, and, in the last quarter of the twentieth century, the consequences of the decline of heavy industry. The newspaper press, like the other media operating in Wales, was embedded in these shifts, and in particular was implicated in the political life of the country and the question of linguistic change.

In the nineteenth century, for instance, journalists, printers, politicians and the reading public believed in the power of the press to shape society, politics and culture (A. Jones, 1996). In the 1840s, Chartists used the press to propagate their ideas about social equality, through publications either from England or produced in Wales, like the *Northern Star*, the *Advocate* and the *Merthyr Free Press* (J. Davies, 1994b: 378; D. Evans, 1989: 171). Political parties and religious groups throughout the nineteenth century used the newspaper and periodical press produced in Wales and England to focus campaigns, to rally the faithful, to dispute with rivals and to promote their ideas. As in England, especially after the end of the restrictive economic duties and the expansion of the electorate in 1867 and 1884 (Koss, 1990), the major political parties, the Liberals and the Conservatives, founded and subsidized newspapers in pursuit of electoral success. In Wales the end of the nineteenth century saw the emergence of the Liberals as the dominant beneficiaries of these changes. The *Western Mail* (1869) was founded in Cardiff by the Conservative Bute family to promote that party's interest and counter the influence of Liberal publications. The Liberal interest responded with the foundation of the *South Wales Daily News* (1872).

In the twentieth century politics remained central to the content of the press, but, as in the UK in general, not to its financing. The *Western Mail* changed ownership over the next 100 years at various times. Like the English press, the Welsh papers of the twentieth century became reliant on advertising and circulation, rather than subsidy, for their survival. While remaining politically involved (see below), the Welsh papers became largely commercial concerns, with strong political dimensions. As the historian of the *Western Mail* has put it, the 'key to the *Western Mail*'s success in Wales was commercial, not political. The paper capitalised on its status as a title which had the advantage of being local, in its production and national in its appeal' (Cayford, 1992: 8).

Politics and religion were two of the bedrocks on which newspapers in Wales rested for many years. The other major social issue to which they, like broadcasting, have been related is the issue of linguistic change in Wales. During the nineteenth century, the impact of industrialization led to rural depopulation and the emergence of large urban centres, where the bulk of the population was concentrated. Because of the integration of these urban centres with the economic, transport, educational and administrative structures of the British state, English gradually became the dominant language of commerce, politics and culture. The changes were dramatic. In 1850 two-thirds of the population, or about 750,000 people, spoke Welsh. By 1914 this was about 40 per cent of the population, or 1,000,000 Welsh speakers. Thereafter the absolute and relative numbers of Welsh speakers went into dramatic decline. From 909,261 or 36.8 per cent of the population in 1931, through 714,686 or 28.9 per cent in 1951, the numbers of Welsh speakers reached a low point in 1981, with 508,207 or 18.9 per cent of the population claiming to speak Welsh. By 2001 there had been a slight upturn in the numbers of those claiming to speak Welsh, to 575,640, or 20.5 per cent of the population. The causes of these changes are complex, but they have resulted in considerable controversy and acted as a spur to political action (Aitchison and Carter, 2003/4: 55; J. Davies, 1994b: 399, 644).

This decline in those able to speak Welsh was reflected in the precipitous decrease (in both relative and absolute terms) in the number of Welsh-language papers, described above, from the late nineteenth century onwards. The significance of this for our purposes is that the relatively healthy, long-term presence of English-language newspapers in Wales, published in Wales and England, combined with linguistic change to fuel intense concerns about the impact of English-language media on that decline. These concerns were reflected in debates not only about the press, but also about cinema and broadcasting, and illustrate the fact that popular and political concerns about the impact of the media on society and culture remained as deep in the first decade of the twenty-first century as they did in the nineteenth (A. Jones, 1996).

Ownership

The issue of ownership has been – and remains – a source of controversy in media studies. In the UK generally there is no doubt that ownership of newspapers moved from small, individually owned papers, through ownership by joint stock companies, and then, by the first decades of the twentieth century, increasingly into the hands of large press groups with interests in more than one form of media; however, the exact implications of these changes have remained controversial (Curran and Seaton, 2003; A. Jones, 1993; A. Lee, 1976; Tunstall, 1983). The ownership of the newspaper press in Wales has followed a pattern similar to that of the United Kingdom.

Early nineteenth-century newspapers in Wales were often produced by local printers, journalists or businessmen. As the century progressed, two of the driving forces behind ownership were religion and politics. The Baptists were responsible for a highly regarded weekly Welsh-language newspaper title in the nineteenth century, *Seren Gomer* ('Star of Gomer', 1814), and from 1869 the Calvinistic Methodists produced *Y Goleuad* ('The Illuminator'). Although political parties were wary of committing themselves to long-term ownership of newspapers, political motives lay behind the foundation and sustenance of titles. The Liberals were keen supporters of papers, especially following the expansion of the electorate after the 1867 and 1884 Reform Acts. David Lloyd George helped establish *Udgorn Rhyddid* ('The Clarion of Freedom', 1888) and was involved in the 1880s and 1890s with the Welsh Nation Newspaper Company, which published *Y Genedl Gymreig* ('The Welsh Nation') and the *North Wales Observer*. Tory interest, too, helped set up newspapers, such as the *Western Mail*, which between its establishment in 1869 and 1873 received around £30,000 in donations from the Conservative Marquess of Bute (A. Jones, 1993: 2, 119, 128–9, 134–5; 2000b: 10–11). Regardless of contemporary claims to the contrary, ownership in the nineteenth century meant that 'the sovereign powers of decision were exercised by the proprietors, and not by the editors' (Brown, 1985: 89).

From the 1890s onwards, the relative diversity of ownership in the Welsh press, as in the English, was reduced, at the same time as the number of titles decreased (A. Jones, 1993: 202). The effects of increased production costs and an increasing dependence on advertising revenue as the main source of income encouraged concentration of ownership. By 1918, D. A. Thomas, Viscount Rhondda, had purchased – from different companies – the *Western Mail*, the *South Wales Journal of Commerce*, *Y Faner* ('The Flag'), the *North Wales Times*, *Y Tyst* ('The Witness'), the *Cambrian News* and the *Merthyr Express*.

These papers were subsequently bought by the Berry brothers, William Ewart Berry, who became Lord Camrose in 1929, and his brother, Gomer Berry, or Viscount Kemsley from 1936. Their empire, by 1928, was UK-wide, including the *Sunday Times* and the *Empire News*; this was the year they bought the *South Wales Daily News* and incorporated it into the *Western Mail*. They went on to buy the *Financial Times*. They were challenged in Wales by Lord Rothemere's Northcliffe Newspapers, with which they eventually reached an arrangement in the early 1930s. They exemplified a pattern which was to dominate ownership of the Welsh press thereafter, in which Welsh titles were owned by UK-wide publishing chains. By 1949 Kemsley controlled over 50 per cent of daily papers published in Wales (A. Jones, 1993: 210–13, 222).

In the 1960s five major newspaper groups controlled most Welsh titles. In south-east Wales it was the South Wales Argus (later a subsidiary of United Newspapers); in Cardiff it was Thomson Regional Newspapers; in the south-west it was Swansea Press Ltd, a subsidiary of Associate Newspapers. The other two were Woodhall's Newspaper Ltd (mid Wales) and the North Wales Chronicle Co. Ltd (A. Jones, 1993: 222–3) By 1979, of the Welsh-language publications, *Y Cymro* ('The Welshman') was owned by North Wales Newspapers Ltd, *Herald Môn*, by Herald Newspapers, with four of the remaining eight in church ownership (H. Jones, 1983: 171). By 2002, five companies dominated publishing in Wales (see Table 3.4).

The titles owned by the dominant company, Trinity Mirror plc, are listed in Table 3.5. In 2003 it was the largest UK regional paper publisher, owning 238 titles. The pattern of concentration in Wales mirrored that of the UK where the top twenty publishers controlled 85 per cent of regional titles and 96 per cent of total weekly circulation (Newspaper Society, 2003a; 2003b). Trinity owned the *Mirror*, a UK-wide tabloid, the *Western Mail* and the *Daily Post*, plus the *South Wales Echo*. From 1999, a *Welsh Mirror* was produced by Trinity, but because its circulation was in decline, at around 130,000 copies a day in Wales, the group closed it down in August 2003 (BBC, 2003; J. Thomas, 2003/4). By 2003 the Welsh press had largely become an extension of groups whose major commercial interests existed outside of Wales.

Table 3.4: Top five newspaper groups in Wales, 2002

Company	Weeklies*	Dailies**	Free
Trinity Mirror plc	12	3	12
Newsquest	8	1	5
North Wales Newspapers Ltd	4	1	6
Northcliffe Newspapers	2	1	4
Tindle Newspapers	6	–	4
Totals	**32**	**6**	**31**

* Includes *Wales on Sunday*; ** includes morning and evening papers.

Source: Adapted from Newspaper Society, 2003a.

Table 3.5: Titles owned by Trinity Mirror plc in 2002

Weeklies	Dailies
Caernarfon Herald (series)	*Liverpool Daily Post*
Chester Chronicle	*South Wales Echo*
Cynon Valley Leader	*Western Mail*
Glamorgan Gazette	**Free**
Gwent Gazette	*Bangor Mail*
Holyhead Mail (series)	*Barry Post*
Merthyr Express	*Bridgend Post*
Neath & Port Talbot Guardian	*Buy and Sell Flintshire*
North Wales Weekly News	*Buy and Sell S. Cheshire and N. Shropshire*
Pontypridd Observer (series)	*Buy and Sell Wrexham Edition*
Wales on Sunday	*Chester Mail*
Whitchurch Herald	*The Post – Cardiff*
	Vale Advertiser (series)
	Visitor (series)
	Wrexham Mail
	Yr Herald

Source: Newspaper Society, 2003a.

Circulation

Very little is known about the circulation of newspapers in nineteenth-century Wales (A. Jones, 2000b: 4). Estimates of newspaper sales in south Wales from the 1830s to the mid-1850s are in the hundreds (Rees, 1961–3: 319). In the 1850s one bookseller in Merthyr was selling 189 copies of the *News of the World*, a sign that the London-based sensationalist Sunday press had a firm foothold (G. A. Williams, 1991: 202). One report put the number of Welsh-language papers printed at about 120,000 per week in 1886. The *Western Mail*, which established itself as the first mass-circulation daily produced in Wales, moved from 6,000 in 1869 to 12,000 per day in 1873 (Brown, 1985: 53; A. Jones, 1993: 96–7).

By the early 1890s, newspapers like the *Manchester Guardian*, selling about 600 copies a day, and the Liverpool papers that circulated in north and mid Wales, with around 4,500 copies, were examples of how Welsh readers were consuming English titles in significant numbers (A. Jones, 2000b: 8–9). In 1946, in Tregaron, its population of 5,540 bought 139 copies of the *Western Mail* per day, 58 of the *Daily Mirror*, 46 of the *News Chronicle*, 40 of the *Daily Express* and 19 of the *Daily Mail*. The most popular weeklies were the *Welsh Gazette* (347) and the *Radio Times* (108), with 30 copies of *Y Cymro* and 9 of *Y Faner*. By 1947 one estimate was that 100,000 copies of British national dailies were being sent to Cardiff for sale in south Wales (A. Jones: 1993, 219–20).

Regional papers remained strong in the UK as a whole. The numbers of people in the UK reading a 'regional' (for which, in Wales, read a 'Welsh') paper was 80.6 per cent of the population in 2003 (Newspaper Society, 2003b). In Wales, however, papers produced outside the country achieved a powerful position in the twentieth century. In 1995 the *Sun* reached 22.5 per cent of Welsh households, compared to the *Mirror*'s 12.5 per cent and the *Daily Mail*'s 9.8 per cent (Mackay and Powell, 1997: 15). In 2002, 85 per cent of daily morning newspapers purchased in Wales came from the UK, outside of Wales. The *Western Mail* and the *Daily Post* made up just 13 per cent of the daily morning sales. The *Sun* reached 19.6 per cent of all Welsh homes, with an estimated circulation of 473,000 for its Monday–Friday editions. This was followed by the *Mirror* at 16.8 per cent and the *Daily Mail* at 11.7 per cent. The *News of the World* reached almost 20 per cent of all Welsh households (Thomas et al., 2003: 9, 35, 37).

In 1957 the daily national newspaper market in the UK stood at 17,320,000. In 1997 it had fallen to 13,835,841, a decline of 20.12 per cent. The paid-for local newspaper press in the UK has been in even sharper decline (Sparks, 1999: 54–5). Table 3.6 illustrates this process in relation to Wales and Monmouthshire from 1966 to 1990. Thus total morning sales declined by 28.2 per cent and paid-for weeklies by 34.8 per cent between 1966 and 1990. The overall decline was 30.8 per cent. This was offset by the rise in the circulation of free papers, which had reached 1,119,000 by 1986 (Press Council, 1987).

Table 3.6: Circulations of paid-for local papers in Wales, 1966–90

Year	Morning	Evening	Weekly/bi-weekly	Total
1966	103,000	285,000	679,000	1,067,000
1976	97,000	269,000	602,000	968,000
1986	76,000	229,000	526,000	831,000
1990	74,000	222,000	443,000	739,000

Source: Press Council, various dates.

Table 3.7 shows the relative circulations of different types of newspapers in Wales in 2002. Tables 3.7 and 3.8 show the relative stabilization of the situation by 2002. The categories used by the Press Council and the Newspaper Society reflect small differences in the classification of what constitutes a Welsh newspaper, which has contributed to the increased estimate for the weekly, morning and evening paid category. This came to a total of 834,910 in 2002.

Table 3.7: Relative circulations of local papers in Wales, 2002

Type	Circulation	% of total circulation
Paid weekly	494,714	26.00
Paid morning	160,146	8.41
Paid evening	180,050	9.46
Free weekly	1,068,231	56.13
Total	**1,903,141**	**100.00**

Source: Newspaper Society, 2003a.

Table 3.8: Relative circulations of press groups in Wales, 2002

Company	Weekly	Daily	Free	Total	% of total
Trinity Mirror plc	231,370	170,887	390,776	793,033	41.67
Northcliffe Newspapers	38,285	110,456	190,269	339,010	17.81
North Wales Newspapers Ltd	40,615	28,227	249,684	318,526	16.74
Newsquest	122,658	30,626	134,128	287,412	15.10
Tindle Newspapers	61,786	103,374		165,160	8.68
Total	**494,714**	**340,196**	**1,068,231**	**1,903,141**	**100.00**

Source: Newspaper Society, 2003a.

The stabilization in the number of papers circulating has resulted from the rise of free papers, and reflects Sparks's argument that, although paid-for dailies and weeklies have been in decline, the total amount of printed material in circulation in the UK has grown since 1900 (Sparks, 1999). Table 3.8 complements Table 3.5 in that they both illustrate the nature of Trinity Mirror's presence and dominance in Wales. The most precipitous and long-term decline in circulations occurred in the Welsh-language press. In 1866, one estimate put the circulation of the five quarterlies, the twenty-five monthlies and the eight weeklies at 120,000 (J. Davies, 1994b: 416). By 2002 *Y Cymro*'s circulation stood at 4,126, with *Yr Herald*'s at 1,832 (Newspaper Society, 2003a).

The press in Wales is essentially local, rather than national. Between January and June 2002 the *Western Mail*'s circulation was 49,904. It sold 6,122 copies in Cardiff, amounting to a household penetration of 4.4 per cent. In Swansea, where it sold 1,854 copies, its penetration was 2.89 per cent. Its reach was skewed to the south and south-west of Wales. As it is described as the 'national' newspaper of Wales this may seem surprising, but it was in keeping with the essentially local circulation of the rest of the daily and weekly press produced in Wales in 2002 (Newspaper Society, 2003a). Thus the newspaper press in Wales has declined in circulation, suffered a sustained assault by the non-Welsh papers for over a century and, yet, has survived in the hands of a few companies, which own papers spread over a wide geographical area, usually across the United Kingdom.

Advertising

From the 1800s it was the commercial trading classes that supported
the press in Wales, as advertisers and readers. Heavy industry (coal,
iron) did not need to advertise their goods in papers. Thus early
newspapers were centred on market towns, like Swansea, Carmarthen,
Bangor and Brecon. Later they grew up in industrial areas where
easy distribution fused with a commercial bedrock of small traders.
Denominational support for publications was an important source of
income, and Welsh-language papers keenly sought English-language
advertisements to boost their income.

Advertising has remained the basis of newspaper finance ever since.
In the UK, by 2000, local advertising provided the economic backbone
for the regional press. In so doing it provided information on a range
of subjects from home services, to shopping, to buying cars and job
hunting. Advertising underpinned the growth of the free-newspaper
sector in Wales (Future Foundation, 2000; A. Jones, 1993: 69–70;
2000b: 3–4).

Language

In twentieth-century Wales the absolute and relative numbers of people
claiming an ability in the decennial censuses to speak Welsh declined
(see above). The former leader of Plaid Cymru, Gwynfor Evans, has
articulated the widely held view that this was because of 'the English
education system provided in schools, English television, the English
press, and many another anglicising factors' (G. Evans, 2001: 164). In
this he was expressing a strongly held view about the importance of the
link between print and the maintenance of the Welsh language.

The translation of the Prayer Book and the New Testament into
Welsh in 1567, and the whole Bible by 1588, has been seen by scholars
as underlining the importance of print to the survival of Welsh. As
Glanmor Williams has argued, these translations meant that 'Welsh
had become the language of religion. This had profound consequences
for the future. It may well have done more than anything else to
safeguard the continued existence of the language . . . Quite definitely
it ensured its continuance as a literary language' (G. Williams, 1979:
133–4). The sheer volume of Welsh-language publications in the
nineteenth century was evidence of the continuity of both a literary and

a spoken Welsh culture. Indeed, as Aled Jones has pointed out, the English- and Welsh-language press did not exist in separate compartments:

> Welsh-language journalism, however, operated within the context of its English-language counterpart. The two journalisms, though distinct in style and vocabulary, and often in purpose, interrelated at a number of points: the same writers could be found writing for both Welsh- and English-language titles, they drew on similar sources of information, they depended on the same advertisers and distributors, were in some instances owned by the same proprietors, and sometimes even competed for readers. Furthermore, virtually all English-language titles carried some articles or poems in Welsh, or printed in English reviews and summaries of the contents of Welsh-language newspapers and journals. (A. Jones, 2000b: 10–11)

Thus the reality of the Welsh-language press in the nineteenth century was of a vibrant sector, in a close relationship with its English-language counterpart and reflecting the increasing bilingualism of much of Welsh life at that time.

The sense that regular, periodical publication in Welsh is essential to sustaining Welsh national identity found expression in the twentieth century in state funding for bodies like the Welsh Books Council, which subsidized books and magazines. It also underpinned the project to establish a Welsh-language daily, *Y Byd*, by 2005 (D. Thomas, 1996; N. Thomas, 2003/4; *Y Byd*, 2004). As Gwynfor Evans was aware, it is not possible to attribute the 'Anglicization' of twentieth-century Wales simply to the decline of a Welsh-language printed culture or newspaper press within that culture. Nonetheless, the decline in this kind of publication continued to exercise the minds of language activists throughout the twentieth century, echoing similar concerns focused on the influence of TV, radio and the cinema.

National identity

The question of the language used in Wales and by its newspapers has historically been associated with the issue of Welsh national identity. The question of what national identity is has been a source of ongoing debate. Is it invented by politically motivated elites seeking to create a nation, who use the institutions of politics, the media and administration to forge state unity out of linguistic, cultural and ethnic diversity – a kind of social engineering? In this model, largely as a result of the influence of Anderson, the printed word has been seen as an essential weapon in the armoury of those elites bent on forging national consciousness and nation states (Anderson, 1983; Hobsbawm, 1990). This emphasis on print has been attacked as an exaggeration by Anthony Smith. He has argued that the origins of nations are more an articulation of long-standing, historically rooted, distinct ethnic, linguistic and even territorial factors, 'that have in the past and continue today to select, shape and inspire modern nations' (A. Smith, 1991: 366–8).

In Wales, debate over the characteristics of Welsh national identity has pointed in different directions. For some, Wales has been typified by a rural, language-based, bardic tradition, for others by the diverse cultural identities of the industrial belts (G. A. Williams, 1991). In spite of this ongoing controversy, it has been claimed that

> to this day a consciousness of Welshness, whether it is given expression through the Welsh language, or the English, is a living reality to a host of people throughout Wales. During the twentieth century, national characteristics have found expression through an increasing variety of movements and institutions, and the concept of the territorial integrity of Wales is stronger today than it has ever been before. (J. Davies, 1994b: 500)

Newspapers in nineteenth-century Wales were 'started . . . often with the explicit intention of saying something in the public arena about Wales, about what was going on in Wales, and about what it meant to be Welsh' (A. Jones, 2000b: 22). The Welsh- and English-language press from Wales was part of a process, especially after the 1850s, when a strong middle class, often Nonconformist in religion, sought to reshape Welsh identities in its own image, using the press to push key 'Welsh' issues, such as land reform, the disestablishment of the Church of England in Wales and support for the *Cymru Fydd*, a nationalist current in the 1880s and 1890s (Day and Suggett, 1985: 100; A. Jones, 1993). While controversy existed over what constituted the national aspirations of Wales, the *Western Mail* and other papers asserted that Welsh interests were best served by being firmly part of the Westminster political system, based on Parliament and empire (O'Malley, Allan and Thompson, 1997). It was the expansion of English popular dailies into Wales, the decline of the issues of land reform and disestablishment (and their replacement by UK-wide issues of industrial conflict and social welfare in the twentieth century), plus the failure of the *Western Mail* to establish itself as a truly national paper, that made the press after 1900 appear far less of a national force than it had been in the nineteenth century. No contemporary commentator would say of the press in Wales in the twenty-first century what Aled Jones has said of nineteenth-century periodicals:

> during the second half of the nineteenth century . . . the expansion of print helped to generate, and, in turn, to be further stimulated by, a cultural mobilization which enabled new forms of national identity to gain currency . . . [it] articulated and shaped the desires of an important minority who, eager for self-expression, bequeathed to Wales its modern, but fractured array of self-images. (A. Jones, 2000a: 310–11)

Yet the idea that the newspaper press does help to forge popular identities, and that the press in Wales should actively foster a Welsh national identity, was a recurring theme in commentary on the Welsh media during the late twentieth century (Talfan Davies, 1999). Whether the press does foster national identity is a question that awaits detailed work which looks systematically at the relationship between reading, understanding and perceptions of national identity. This difficult work has yet to be done in such a way as to be able to draw firm conclusions, and so the jury must still be out on the validity of claims made about the link between newspapers and national identity. For the indeterminacy of the newspaper as a form of communications is what 'makes the discussion of its social influence . . . so problematic, and ultimately, perhaps, so sterile' (A. Jones, 1998: 218). The point is not that the perception of a link between national identity and the press is wrong, nor that this has not been central to the production and arguably the consumption of newspapers; it is that we should be cautious about making too strong a causal link between the presence or absence of nationalist sentiments in newspapers and the appearance of those sentiments in popular culture or voting behaviour, either now or in the nineteenth and twentieth centuries.

Class

Class, or social division, has always been an important dimension in the history of the press in Wales. Wales's first working-class paper,

Y Gweithiwr ('The Worker'), was produced in 1834, helping to organize the intervention of workers into local elections and the anti-Poor Law campaign of the period. In the turbulent 1840s, Welsh Chartists launched the *Udgorn Cymru* ('Trumpet of Wales') and the *Advocate* at Merthyr, as part of the workers' struggle for democratic rights. *Udgorn Cymru* 'produced high-quality political argument in good-quality Welsh' and was run by a workers collective, Argraff-Wasg y Gweithiwr (The Worker's Printing Press) (G. A. Williams, 1991: 190–7). Later, in 1898, *Llais Llafur* ('Voice of Labour') was established.

As the organization of the industrial working class in south Wales improved from the early twentieth century onwards, and as industrial conflict sharpened, the workers' organizations continued to rely on producing their own papers to counter what they saw as the bias of the commercial press. The left-wing Labour Research group singled out the *Western Mail* in the 1920s for its attempts to 'create a public opinion which is hostile to organised labour' and for seeking 'to divide the workers against themselves'. During the 1926 General Strike, the *Western Mail* 'was vicious in its condemnation of the strikers' (Labour Research, n.d.: 28–9; J. Davies, 1994b: 554). In general,

> Relations between the labour movement and the Welsh daily press were strained. Reporters told of being threatened by Maerdy miners, where they were regarded with hostility as outsiders. The *South Wales Daily News* famously referred to Maerdy as 'Little Moscow', and both it and the *Western Mail* were banned from the Maerdy Institute during the General Strike of 1926 on the grounds that they were printed by scab labour. (A. Jones, 1993: 215)

In 1927 A. J. Cook, the miners' leader, denounced the newspapers of south Wales as the 'dirtiest and the most vile press in the country'. From the 1930s the Communist *Daily Worker* circulated in Wales, while the *Western Mail* 'continued to blame industrial unrest on "red plots", secret societies and paid agitators' (A. Jones, 1993: 214–15).

The miners' union produced two official journals, the *Colliery Workers' Magazine* (1923–7) and the *Miners' Monthly* (1934–9), a revived South Wales Miners' Federation newsletter. Pit papers like the *Bedwas Rebel*, of the early 1920s, and the *Cwmtillery Searchlight*, of the mid-1930s, appeared for a time, and in the 1930s the Rank and File Movement produced the *South Wales Miner* (1933–5) (A. Jones, 1993: 214–15).

The gap between the south Wales commercial press and organized Labour was still acute in the late 1940s. In a speech of October 1946, which was part of the pressure that led to the establishment of the first Royal Commission on the Press (1947–9), Michael Foot MP attacked the private ownership of the press thus:

No one can really imagine it is by the democratic choice of the people of South Wales that they read the *Western Mail* if they want local news . . . These decisions as to which newspapers are to be sustained in different areas, are not made by the people or the public; they are made by the process of financial manipulation. (House of Commons, 1946)

In the 1950s, with the easing of industrial conflict and the establishment of the welfare state, much of the bitterness of the earlier period was dissipated. Thereafter, a small-scale workers' and radical press had an intermittent – but continuous – presence in Wales, with papers like the *Welsh Republican* in the 1950s and *Y Faner Goch* ('The Red Flag') in the 1990s, alongside the UK-wide publications of the Communist Party, the *Morning Star*, and the International Socialists, *Socialist Worker*. All of these circulated in very small numbers, largely amongst politically active people. The commercial press, a press not owned by or run for the political or industrial organizations of the Welsh working class, continued to dominate circulation. Although not overtly anti-working class, this press did not propagate the ideas associated with the tradition of working-class papers we have sketched here, yet it retained the majority of working-class newspaper readers in Wales amongst its readership (J. Davies, 1994b: 623).

Aspects of content

The press produced and circulating in Wales from 1800 cannot be classified easily in terms of content. As Aled Jones has pointed out, 'so elusive is the paradigmatic Welsh newspaper that it is easier to search for a definition by contrasting it to other print forms than it is to describe its characteristics as a discrete medium' (A. Jones, 1998: 217). In the nineteenth century the key division was that, unlike other forms, such as the novel or the monthly or quarterly reviews, 'newspapers were regarded as being more accessible' by authors aspiring to print (A. Jones, 1998: 217). They could gain access to the pages of the press through contributing items of local news, or reporting a meeting, or even contributing some poetry. During the nineteenth century much of the content of newspapers produced in Wales, in both languages, relied on contributions from networks of amateurs and cutting and pasting from London newspapers; these practices diminished with the emergence of journalism as an organized occupation at the end of the nineteenth century. This marked the newspaper as a miscellaneous form, one which has survived into the twenty-first century (A. Jones, 1993: 19–20).

A central element of the nineteenth-century press was religion. The idea that the periodical press could help mould and sustain religious groups was a powerful stimulant to publication. Journals like *Seren Gomer* (1814), founded by the Baptists, sustained not only religious argument, but also debates about the nature of the church and its relations with the state. Nonconformist ministers controlled significant parts of the press, in particular the Welsh-language press, as either editors or major shareholders. The all-pervasive religious dimension in much of the press found expression, for example, in *Y Genedl Gymreig* ('The Welsh Nation'), whose editor declared in 1895 that he had to 'defend the interests of Nonconformity, and to teach the principles of Liberalism and Nationalism' (D. Evans, 1989: 167; A. Jones, 1993: 157; 2000b: 2). In the twentieth century, the emergence of other leisure pursuits, increases in disposable income and increased mobility all contributed to a precipitous decline in church-going in Wales. By the last quarter of the twentieth century only 13 per cent of Welsh people regularly attended a place of worship. Under these circumstances the decline of religious titles is unsurprising (J. Davies, 1994b: 642–3).

Political content, in one form or another, has always played a major role in Welsh newspapers, and preoccupied the minds, especially in the nineteenth and early twentieth centuries, of those involved in funding, producing and reading the press. The Nonconformist press was 'unanimous' in its condemnation of the 1834 Poor Law Amendment Act, for its cruelty. The Welsh press sprung to the defence of the Welsh nation in the 1840s, in response to accusations of criminality from England. It was the failure of the Conservative Bute Estate to regain the Cardiff Parliamentary seat in the 1868 general election, which it blamed on the lack of a Conservative paper, that led to the launch of the *Western Mail* on 1 May 1869. We have seen how fiercely the south Wales press engaged with organized Labour in the early twentieth century. All of this testifies to the centrality of politics in the history of the press in these years (D. Evans, 1989: 68, 141; J. Davies, 1994b: 431–2).

When the First World War broke out in 1914, the *Western Mail* was openly supportive of the conflict from the outset, with support also from Welsh-language papers such as *Cymru* and denominational ones like *Y Tyst*. While explicitly anti-war publications had little support during the war, there were some of these in Wales, such as *Seren Gomer*. Other papers, such as those of the north Wales Herald group, started off as anti-war, but switched sides in the early months (A. Jones, 1993: 204–5).

Welsh nationalists also found grounds to be critical of some Welsh papers. In the 1970s Gwynfor Evans found the *South Wales Echo* 'tiresomely anti-Welsh in its editorial attitudes' (G. Evans, 2001: 203). By the time of the 1979 referendum, 'the editorial position of most of the English language press in Wales was hostile to the Labour government's proposals for devolution of power to Wales'. In this case the *Western Mail* supported the proposals, as did the Welsh-language press, with the exception of the Herald group (A. Jones, 1983: 175; Osmond, 1983: 161). After eighteen years of Conservative government (1979–97) and the growth in political circles – including the leadership of the Labour and Liberal Democrat parties – of support for a measure of devolution, the position of the newspapers shifted. As Kevin Williams has reported of the second referendum, 'The situation in 1997 was almost the opposite [to 1979]: the large proportion of local and national newspapers in Wales editorially was in favour of the establishment of a National Assembly; the rest were by and large neutral' (K. Williams, 2000: 100). The *Western Mail, Wales on Sunday*, and the *Daily Post*, all part of Trinity plc, were generally in favour of an Assembly. The editorials of two large-circulation evening papers, the *South Wales Argus* and the *South Wales Echo* remained neutral, with the *Echo* retreating from its fierce hostility to the 1979 proposals (K. Williams, 2000: 99–103).

In the late twentieth and early twenty-first centuries other concerns have been highlighted in relation to the press in Wales. Some writers have observed the perpetuation of a vein of anti-Welsh prejudice in papers produced in England. James Thomas (1997) has argued that in the 1980s and early 1990s a stereotype of the Welsh working class (macho, verbose, keen on drink) was played on to imply that the Labour Party leader, Neil Kinnock, who came from south Wales, was a risky choice for the electorate: 'It was not so much Kinnock being

Welsh that was the problem, but the way the press portrayal of his "certain brand of Welshness" linked up with and related to more fundamental explanations for his and Labour's defeat in 1992' (J. Thomas, 1997: 108). Thus, as others have pointed out, Welsh people buy papers produced in England which can and do repeat prejudices about the Welsh (Nurse, 2001). The one relatively serious attempt by the Trinity Mirror group to address Wales in the language of a UK-wide tabloid daily, was the creation of the *Welsh Mirror* in the late 1990s. After a lacklustre career, characterized by 'hammering its readers with a propagandist anti-Nationalist stick' and a 'constant diet of bad news about the devolution process', it failed to engage sufficiently with the Welsh tabloid readership to make it worth Trinity's while. It was closed in August 2003 (J. Thomas, 2003/4: 23–7).

Within the Welsh press, coverage of sensitive issues such as asylum seekers highlighted both the more open-minded attitude of some of the Welsh papers and their tendency in some key areas to rely heavily, like their UK-wide counterparts, on official sources for information and to avoid systematic explanation of the causes of complex social issues. In a study of thirty-two English-language papers circulating in Wales (thirty of which were Welsh regional papers and two of which were produced in the English borders, between April and December 2001), Speers noted that, while the 'Welsh press covers the issue of asylum seekers without the hostility or hyperbole that can be seen in the UK-wide national media', there were problems. Little attention was given to the question of why asylum seekers left their countries, and more to how the authorities 'managed them'. Quotes from, and photographs of, officials rather than asylum seekers dominated representations. Also an analysis of the language used to describe asylum seekers showed that they were discussed as a group to be 'feared', and as a 'financial burden' to local communities (Speers, 2001: 4, 35).

Yet this kind of evidence needs to be viewed in the light of polling evidence which suggests that among the most popular reasons for buying a newspaper in Wales is the desire to be entertained, the perusal of TV listings or reading about sport (J. Thomas, 2003/4: 26). Indeed, the centrality of entertainment to the UK national press has been a feature since at least the middle of the twentieth century. Overt, detailed political coverage did not occupy the same position in the press in 2000 as it did in 1900 (Curran and Seaton, 2003). This emphasis on entertainment was accompanied by the growing importance of advertising as a source of revenue. Advertising column space in the *Western Mail* tripled between 1869 and 1914, from around fifty to over 150 columns per issue. Paralleling this, the column space devoted to sport also rose. In 1879 both the *South Wales Daily News* and the *Western Mail* carried fewer than ten columns each of sport. By 1914 the *Western Mail* had nearly fifty and the *South Wales Daily News* approximately fifty-five columns each of sporting coverage per issue (Cayford, 1992: Appendices 2 and 5). The focus on lifestyle and entertainment in the Welsh press, which has been noted by recent commentators, illustrates the way in which it is integrated with practices in the UK-wide industry (K. Williams, 1994: 250–1) and expresses longer-term trends that go back to the end of the nineteenth century. From this point, small-scale publications, which depended on a mix of subsidy, advertising and circulation, were increasingly replaced by a press which depended on advertising and circulation for income and which became increasingly integrated into large-scale organizations, such as the Kemsley, Thomson and Trinity empires, where building and maintaining readerships that attracted advertising revenue was usually the dominant impetus (Curran and Seaton, 2003; A. Jones, 1993).

Yet an outstanding feature of the press produced in Wales has been and remains its localism. In the nineteenth century it 'was targeted primarily at small audiences', with the result that journalists produced a 'huge variety of periodicals' (A. Jones, 1993: 239). The development of the press in Wales in the next century only partly offset this. The *Western Mail*, as has been illustrated above, and the *Daily Post*, did not establish themselves as national papers in terms of geographical spread of their readership. In 2002, for instance, the *Western Mail* had a circulation of 46,732, but was closely rivalled by sub-national papers like the *South Wales Echo* (61,757) and outpaced in specific localities by weekly papers like the *Carmarthen Journal* (21,846) (Newspaper Society, 2003a). Again, while the London-based titles have a UK-wide readership, local publications continued to thrive at the start of the twenty-first century. One survey found that 'television and local newspapers run neck and neck' as sources for local news in the UK, with '45 per cent naming television as their main source and 39 per cent newspapers' (Hargreaves and Thomas, 2002: 64). Thus, while the lack of a strong national newspaper in Wales is evident, the localism of much of the Welsh press illustrates the popularity of this form of newspaper across the UK.

Influence?

It is very difficult to track the precise influence of newspapers in Welsh social and political history. It is, however, instructive to survey the variety of ways twentieth-century commentators, echoing a much longer tradition, have thought that the press has an influence on society (A. Jones, 1996). As Kevin Williams has put it, 'there is still a tendency amongst Welsh intellectuals and political activists to attribute great influence to the press. The 19th century myth of the newspaper as a "great engine of thought" is still firmly entrenched amongst the political and intellectual elite in Wales' (K. Williams, 1994: 252). Studies have shown the importance of the press in playing a part in the formation of opinion, under specific circumstances and on particular topics (see Miller, 1994); yet it is often the assumed general influence of the press which is the subject of commentary.

The nineteenth-century press was obviously an important part of Welsh political and social life (A. Jones, 1993), a fact testified to, for instance, by the way in which local government bodies after the mid-century, 'overcame their distaste for reporters, admitted, then welcomed them, and even began to order copies of the papers as reliable records of their proceedings' (Rees, 1961/3: 323). In 1891 the Liberal MP and nationalist, T. E. Ellis, 'informed the editor of the *South Wales Star* at an interview in the Reform Club that, "it is our new writers which are bringing to the minds of the Welsh people that they have a past and are a nation" '. Journalists saw themselves as actors in a process of social change, and their self-image has found endorsement in histories of Wales published in the twentieth century (A. Jones, 1993: 153, 156). D. G. Evans has asserted that the press – English and Welsh – of the nineteenth century 'stretched the mental capacities and broadened the experience of the working communities' in Wales. John Davies, likewise, has argued that it was through the Welsh-language periodical press 'that the Welsh people received their political education'. Davies has also argued that the great Welsh Nonconformist revival of 1904–5 was linked to the coverage it received 'from Cardiff journalists' which 'was a major factor in its spread' (J. Davies, 1994b: 350, 505; D. Evans, 1989: 221–2).

Welsh nationalists such as Gwynfor Evans held strongly to the view that the press was an important influence on opinion. During his campaign for a Welsh-language TV channel in 1980, when he threatened to go on hunger strike unless the Conservative government of Mrs Thatcher agreed to introduce the channel, the press was full of news, letters and articles about the campaign, including surprisingly sympathetic leading articles. *The Times* gave its support and the *Sunday Times* made history by publishing a helpful leading article in Welsh . . . Perhaps the most influential were the many supportive interviews and articles published in European and American papers. (G. Evans, 1997: 179)

The defeat of the Labour government's proposals for Welsh devolution in 1979 has been attributed to the way in which, through the influence of the 'penetration of Wales by London based daily newspapers', the press affected the negative result: 'Although one must not over-emphasise the persuasive and pervasive influence of the London dailies, the cumulative effect of their hostility or indifference to Welsh devolution . . . should not be ignored' (Jones and Wilford, 1983: 227–8). The press has therefore been viewed as part of a problem in contemporary Wales. This is the problem of an 'information deficit' which we raised in chapter 2, in which Welsh people and Welsh institutions suffer from the lack of a national publication, and so do not get sufficient information about Welsh political and cultural life (Wyn Jones et al., 2000: 172–3). One key figure in the media establishment in Wales has summed this up, deploring, in 1999, the lack of a 'plural, broadsheet press, able to act as a platform for the trading of information and contending ideas – facts, exposition, informed opinion. The result is that, to a greater degree than is desirable, the policy community is left talking to itself' (Talfan Davies, 1999: 18). The demise of the *Welsh Mirror* in 2003 elicited a similar response, as 'the absence of any newspaper coverage . . . which manages to reach and inform a disengaged mass electorate about Welsh affairs is now once again the most pressing area of concern' (J. Thomas, 2003/4: 27). It is clear that political and social activists and elites considered the press important, and, in so far as they allowed and continue to allow this to influence their behaviour, the press can be said to have played and to play a significant role in Welsh society (A. Jones, 1993: 176; 1996).

A complex beast

This brief survey of the press in Wales suggests a number of things. Welsh society since the late eighteenth century has gone through a series of dramatic and traumatic shifts. The newspaper press has emerged from that society and in different ways has participated in those shifts. It has been embedded in the cultural and political life of Wales, and, through the spread of London-based publications in Wales, the country has increasingly become part of UK-wide social, cultural and political developments. Its structural characteristics, with the exception of the lack of a national newspaper and the important qualification of the bilingual environment in which it operated, has reflected structural change in the wider UK industry. While assessing its influence is difficult, there is no doubt that people of all classes and political persuasions have been convinced of its importance as an engine of thought. In the long term, it is perhaps best viewed as part of the revolution in communications that began to overtake the world from the birth of modern printing in the fifteenth century, and which by the nineteenth century achieved its biggest boost from mechanization and the spread of railways and telegraphy. By the mid-twentieth century its importance in the life of Wales had diminished relative to that of radio and television, but it remained central to the fabric of communications that was woven across Wales at the start of the twenty-first century.

Note

[1] The *Liverpool Daily Post* had become the *Daily Post* by 2004.

4

Cinema and Film:
Casting Stereotypes?

Much of the contemporary literature on cinema and film in Wales ranges between pessimistic and optimistic forecasts about future prospects. At the heart of such debates is the perennial issue of whether one can actually speak of a 'Welsh cinema' or, in fact, a Welsh film industry.[1] In earlier years, one commentator even canvassed the idea of ' "Wales in the movies" as a non-subject' (Stead, 1986: 162). In part, at least, this scepticism is due to the domination of British screens by American films since the early years of the twentieth century. As a result, Wales finds itself doubly disadvantaged due to its own limited domestic market and its subsidiary position within a UK market that is constrained by Hollywood.[2] Not surprisingly, then, Britain has been described as a 'film colony' of America, with Wales 'a periphery of that colony' (Stead, 1986: 162). This situation continues to prompt concerns about work prospects for Welsh film-makers. It also ignites discussions about issues of identity and representation in Wales. In this regard, the UK Film Council offers a useful reminder about the importance of film:

Cinema is an immensely powerful medium which shapes the way the world sees us and the way we see the world. Films that tell British stories which reflect, explore and sometimes oppose the consensus of current cultural and political thought should always have a place on the creative map of any civilised nation. If the UK does not have the capacity to make such films and to ensure that they find their audience, our sense of cultural identity will be eroded and the way in which the UK is portrayed through an extraordinary powerful medium will be determined by external sources. (Film Council, 2003: 14)

The implication of this quotation, which focuses on British – or English? – identity, is unlikely to be lost on readers in Wales, where frustrations still exist about being framed by 'outsiders', particularly via the London-based electronic and print media. Indeed, this is one of the key concerns to emerge from a review of the first hundred years of cinema and film in Wales. Berry (1994: 10–11) asks whether audiences have received valid and accurate images of Wales from the cinema screen, whether conceptions of Wales from outside the country are based on sentimentalized or sanitized images and whether the work of incoming film-makers – particularly from the US and England – has resulted in superficial portrayals of everyday life. In summary, he concludes that 'national identity . . . has been surrendered too often to outsiders in the past' (Berry, 1994: 436). One consequence of this is that images and discourses about Wales and Welshness in the public domain are limited and restricted.

This has prompted calls for more filmic representations of Wales in order to move on from 'older sterile debates about Welsh identity' (Blandford, 2000c: 15). It has also catalysed demands for a national cinema – 'defined in opposition to Hollywood' – where questions about Wales and notions of what it means to be Welsh can be explored, debated and disseminated at home and abroad (Morris, 1998: 25).[3] Such aspirations may remain just that, as the hegemony of the Holly-wood product continues to undermine the viability of 'alternative "national" cinemas' (Petrie, 1996: 93). However, a cautionary note about 'external threats' is suggested – whether it be Hollywood or more general concerns about cultural imperialism – as this may distract from, or simply overlook, internal practices by a mainstream which itself marginalizes or excludes certain voices (Moran, 1996: 9–10).

This chapter is premised on the view that film must first be recognized as an industry before it can be considered as a cultural object. It is organized into three sections. The first focuses on the industrial context of film and cinema in Wales, providing a historical overview of developments from inception to present day, taking account of production, exhibition and distribution. The second section considers why cinema became such a popular pastime in Wales and explores how Wales came to be represented on film. The third and final section provides an overview of more contemporary developments, illustrating the role played by S4C and a fledgling film and video sector in catalysing a surge of indigenous film-making in Wales in both languages.

Always Hollywood, never Barrywood!

Although the early history of film-making in Wales features only marginally in British historical accounts, the country was awash with such activity shortly after the beginning of the twentieth century. Describing this era as a period of 'feverish film-making', Stead (1986: 164) queries why Wales, and south Wales in particular, never became an established centre for film-making. While 'Barrywood' – rather than Barry Island – does have a certain ring to it, Hollywood quickly became the dominant centre.[4]

The first projected film show in Wales was staged in Cardiff in April 1896. It followed similar exhibitions held in London earlier that year (Berry, 1994: 22; Corrigan, 1983: 27; K. Williams, 1998: 68). The films shown on these occasions were early forms of documentary, or *actualités*, first introduced by the Lumière Brothers in France in 1895. They featured ordinary events such as people leaving a factory, a train arriving at a station, or the rolling waves at the seaside (Desjardins, 1995: 405). The early pioneers, predominantly scientists and photographers, were more interested in the technological developments and their potential for educational purposes rather than entertainment (Berry, 1994: 31; R. Williams, 1983: 12–13). Likewise, the fledgling industry moguls expected profits to result from the manufacture of cameras and projectors rather than the films themselves, the primary role of the latter being to market the technology (Chanan, 1983: 45). The emergence of moving-picture cameras and projection facilities followed earlier advances in the nineteenth century when the light bulb, electric telegraph, telephone and phonograph were developed (R. Williams, 1983: 12–13; K. Williams, 1998: 69).

Travelling showmen

From these early projected screenings, it took ten to fifteen years – depending on location – for cinemas to be established around Wales. This period was filled by a number of travelling showmen who soon recognized the potential attraction of film for a predominantly urban working-class population 'weaned on music-hall acts, penny-dreadful

crime novels, comics, or the touring stage melodramas of the day'
(Berry, 1994: 46). Before the arrival of purpose-built cinemas, films
were shown in a variety of buildings. However, the large majority of
Wales's population received their introduction to this new medium at
annual fairs or other special events by way of a kinetoscope or
bioscope, towed around the country by the showmen:

> It is barely possible now to imagine the impact these travelling shows, with
> their gaudy colours, flashing lights and shimmering edifices, must have
> made when showmen arrived in towns and villages with their traction
> engines on wet and mournful midweek days. The entertainment must have
> seemed awesome to remote West Wales outposts often bereft of any other
> comparable form of entertainment for months on end. (Berry, 1994: 58–9)

Three of the more prominent showmen and film-makers were Arthur
Cheetham, John Codman and William Haggar (Berry, 1994: 35–63).
A brief overview of their work illustrates how film was literally taken to
the masses and why 'going to the pictures' suddenly became such a
popular pastime in Wales. Arthur Cheetham was born in Derby and
worked as a printer's apprentice in Manchester before moving to Rhyl
in 1889. Between 1897 and 1903, he made approximately thirty films on
location around mid and north Wales, including a May Day procession
in Rhyl, slate being loaded onto a ship at Porthmadoc, a royal visit to
Conwy and ladies boating in the sea at Aberystwyth (Berry, 1994: 39).
Cheetham exhibited films in Llanidloes, Dolgellau and Bala and also
established permanent locations for exhibition in a converted chapel at
Colwyn Bay, the Central Hall in Rhyl – thought to be north Wales's
first permanent cinema – and the Electric Picture Palace and Theatre at
Aberystwyth (Berry, 1994: 41).

John Codman, whose father was a Punch and Judy operator, exhibited
films throughout Wales prior to the First World War (1914–18). As a
travelling showman he towed his 600-seat theatre with a tractor engine
which also powered the projector (Berry, 1994: 43). As a means of
promotion when arriving at a new location, he would film members of
the local population promising that they would see themselves on
screen if they attended the show. Codman also leased halls – known as
'picturedromes' – for exhibitions at Nantymoel, Ogmore Vale, Llanelli
and Newtown, and, conscious of the cachet of American films, operated
variously under the names 'New Empire American and Royal Welsh
Electronic Animated Pictures' and 'New Empire American Animated

Picture Company' (Berry, 1994: 44). As well as exhibiting films, Codman is also thought to have made some short fiction films, although none has survived (Berry, 1994: 43).

William Haggar is generally regarded as the most esteemed and creative of Wales's travelling showmen.[5] With a background in entertainment, having worked as a member of a band and a puppeteer before establishing a theatre company in 1880, Haggar first screened films at Aberavon in 1898 (Berry, 1994: 47). Like Codman, Haggar also hauled his projection and theatre equipment around south, mid and west Wales, first by horse and later by traction engine, visiting showgrounds and seasonal fairs over a number of years (Berry, 1994: 47). He went on to make around sixty films, of which thirty-four are documented, and began by filming trains and trams, such as *Phantom Ride Through Swansea*, made around 1902 (Berry, 1994: 53). With his large family always ensuring an available cast, Haggar is best known for his fiction films. He was highly regarded by Gaumont who distributed his films in Britain and Europe, and Haggar's 1905 film, *The Salmon Poacher*, sold more copies than any other British film (Berry, 1994: 46). After years of travelling, and always subject to the fluctuating economic circumstances of the coal industry in south Wales, Haggar and his family transferred their operations into permanent cinemas at Llanelli, Pembroke and Aberdare from 1910 onwards (Berry, 1994: 59).

Dream palaces and fleapits

It soon became evident that the commercial potential of film would only be realised by securing a mass audience. This meant addressing public unease about what was still an unregulated market and one that attracted some unscrupulous operators (see, for example, K. Williams, 1998: 69–70). Cinema would have to be 'sold' as superior to all other forms of entertainment. While the introduction of 'picture palaces', or 'dream palaces', helped this process, it hastened the demise of the showmen, most having ended their travelling film days by the beginning of the First World War. A combination of reasons brought this about.

First, the new plush cinemas ensured, as Haggar's wife acknowledged, that people did not have to brave the muddy showgrounds to watch a film (Berry, 1994: 63). Second, films were now being purchased rather than hired, thereby introducing distribution as the third strand of an industry previously comprising only production and exhibition (Chanan, 1983: 48–9). This increased the turnover and availability of films in cinemas with the result that the travelling showmen struggled to find audiences to watch their now outdated material. Third, as the industry developed, the travelling showmen were unable to make films at a competitive price, nor could they match the increasing sophistication of the product now being manufactured. Fourth, business costs increased substantially with the introduction of the Cinematograph Act 1909, which imposed stringent safety requirements on operators in order to avert the risk of fire (Hogenkamp, 1985: 65). By 1914 it was evident that cinema would supersede the music halls as the preferred form of mass entertainment in Wales (Berry, 1994: 22).

From 1908 onwards the number of cinemas throughout Britain expanded rapidly (K. Williams, 1998: 70). Between 1910 and 1934 the number of cinemas in Wales increased from 162 to 321 and the seating capacity in nine venues exceeded 2,000 (Berry, 1994: 117, 126). Most of Britain's cinemas were located in urban, industrial, working-class areas, but south Wales had the highest number of cinemas per head of population in the UK (Ridgwell, 1997: 69).

In Wales, the buildings used for cinema exhibition during the period up to the Second World War (1939–45) were of three different types (Miskell, 1997: 60). One grouping comprised the purpose-built, relatively small, modestly designed cinema halls constructed before 1914. These 'fleapits' or 'bug-houses' catered for the 'poorer sections of society', reflecting not only the differing nature of the audiences to be served but the varied socio-economic conditions that prevailed in Wales during this period (Miskell, 1997: 65). A second group included buildings that had been converted specifically for cinema use, such as theatres, skating rinks and chapels. The third were the picture palaces built during the 1920s and 1930s, such as the 3,000-seat Capitol in Cardiff with its wide staircases, suspended balcony, orchestra, café, terrace and soda fountain (Berry, 1994: 120; Miskell, 1997: 65).

Cinema construction during the inter-war period took place in north Wales, south Wales and in some rural areas, but the 'depression-ravaged valleys' saw minimal development except for the Castle cinema built at Merthyr (Miskell, 1997: 61, 65).

'Cinemaization' and the miners

Alongside this burgeoning commercial cinema, a separate cinema network emerged in the south Wales valleys. By 1910 most of the mining towns and villages in south Wales had, or were building, a hall or institute, most financed by voluntary contributions from the miners themselves (Ridgwell, 1997: 71). Furnished with libraries and providing evening classes through the National Council of Labour Colleges, these halls and institutes established a 'tradition of providing an unparalleled working-class education' (Ridgwell, 1997: 70). Although there were some exhibition facilities in the halls and institutes prior to the First World War, the vast majority acquired their cinemas after 1920 with the aid of the Miners' Welfare Fund (MWF) (Hogenkamp, 1985: 65; Ridgwell, 1997: 70).

The MWF was established following the Mining Industry Act 1920, after recommendations by the Sankey Committee for a levy on the coal owners of 1d per tonne of coal produced. This was known as the miners' 'magic penny', its purpose being to create social and recreational facilities in mining communities and provide for research and education related to mining (Berry, 1994: 129; Hogenkamp, 1985: 66; Ridgwell, 1997: 72). As technology advanced, the MWF also helped many of the halls and institutes with loans and grants to convert from 'silents' to 'talkies' from the late 1920s, an era in which the term 'cinemaization' was coined to reflect the proliferation of new cinema developments (Hogenkamp, 1985: 66; Ridgwell, 1997: 70). With the addition of cinema to the recreational facilities offered by the halls and institutes, women and children were given the opportunity to enter what had previously been a male-dominated environment (Hogenkamp, 1985: 66; Ridgwell, 1997: 80).

Although cinemas were introduced to expand leisure and, to a lesser extent, educational opportunities, they were also seen as a means of supplementing the income of halls and institutes. This proved to be controversial, due to both the costs involved in the maintenance and upgrading of the equipment and also the types of films to be shown. While the majority of films exhibited were similar to the Hollywood product being shown by commercial cinemas throughout Wales, the halls and institutes attracted an 'alternative' label because documentary films, newsreels and selected European films of a politically 'left' persuasion were also screened (Berry, 1994: 142; Hogenkamp, 1985: 66–75).

The size of this alternative cinema network was substantial. At one point, seventy cinemas in halls and institutes operated in south Wales, an area in the 1930s which boasted more miners' cinemas than all the other mining areas in Britain combined (Berry, 1994: 128; Ridgwell, 1997: 70). In 1939, the halls and institutes in Wales and the west of England helped establish the Miners Welfare Workmen's Hall Cinema

Association, the aim being to assist with the material needs of its members and strengthen their negotiating position when hiring films (Berry, 1994: 128; Hogenkamp, 1985: 73).

The advent of 'sound' in 1929 impacted on both the commercial cinemas and the halls and institutes, not only because of the financial investment involved in introducing the new technology, but also because it coincided with a period of political turmoil and economic downturn in Wales (Berry, 1994: 116). An inter-war depression led to the closure of numerous pits in south and south-west Wales. There was a General Strike in 1926. The slate industry in north Wales was in terminal decline. High rates of unemployment throughout the country – up to 40 per cent in Wrexham in 1931 and 73.4 per cent in Dowlais in 1939 – led to one-fifth of the population leaving Wales and a proposal to move the entire community of Merthyr to Monmouthshire (Berry, 1994: 116; Miskell, 1997: 55). Some commercial cinemas went out of business and the halls and institutes faced the risk of investing heavily to make the transition to sound or losing their audiences (Berry, 1994: 116; Hogenkamp, 1985: 66).

Other complications also arose for the halls and institutes. In Ystradgynlais, where the workforce of one colliery was reduced from 550 to 12, and Cwmllynfell, where the pit ceased operations altogether, the loss of miners' contributions meant that the revenue from cinemas became essential to ensure the survival of halls and institutes (Ridgwell, 1997: 72–3). Another consequence, following the introduction of 'talkies', was the demise of cinema orchestras – some with up to thirty musicians – whose members had accompanied the earlier 'silent' exhibitions, putting many out of work (Berry, 1994: 117, 125). However, with 'talkies' now attracting audiences from the repertory theatres and owners adjusting admission prices to take account of the troubled times, some cinema operators continued to enjoy a profitable period during this economic downturn (Berry, 1994: 87, 126). A further consequence of this transition to 'sound' was that it reinforced the dominance of Hollywood (Mottram, 1990: 326).

Circuits and customers

Cinema 'chains' or 'circuits' developed in Wales as they did throughout Britain (Corrigan, 1983: 27–8). However, major companies such as Gaumont, ABC and Odeon invested minimally in Wales. Most cinemas in Wales were independently owned and the circuits that did exist were more likely to operate as family businesses (Miskell, 1997: 54). Berry

(1994: 84) refers to a number of small circuits that emerged between 1910 and 1920, with one operator, Leon Vint, running cinemas in Llanelli and Neath and advertising his film programme in seven languages at Barry Dock to attract visiting seamen. Some regional circuits also existed but these were influenced by geographic factors, with most operating on an east–west, rather than north–south, axis (Miskell, 1997: 58).

Welsh-based circuits increased only marginally in the inter-war period, but a decline in audiences during the 1950s led to consolidation in the industry with fewer, but larger, companies remaining (Miskell, 1997: 59). High unemployment and industrial decline deterred the major companies from investing in Wales, but other factors were also influential. While the large companies wanted to build 3,000-seat cinemas, most of Wales's population centres would not support a cinema of that size, and strong attachments to localities, particularly in rural areas, deterred people from travelling to other locations to watch a film (Miskell, 1997: 56). Although cinema attendance rose during the Second World War, peaking in 1946, a gradual decline thereafter resulted in patronage reaching an all-time low in the mid-1980s (Corrigan, 1983: 30; Dickinson, 1983: 74; Hill, 1999: 48). This led to closures of cinemas in Wales and throughout the rest of Britain (Berry, 1994: 280, 300; Corrigan, 1983: 28).

Three factors are suggested for this decline in cinema attendance. First, the changing social and economic climate of the 1950s and the so-called 'consumer boom' which resulted in changing lifestyles, work patterns and consumption, all of which helped to marginalize cinema amongst an increasing range of leisure options (K. Williams, 1998: 194). Second, the failure by governments to establish a consistent and realistic policy towards film in Britain added to the uncertainties of the British film industry and undermined the possibility of developing a national cinema in Britain (McIntyre, 1996: 215; Miskell, 1997: 53; K. Williams, 1998: 194). Third, television played a key role in the decline of cinema. Sales of television sets increased as cinema audiences dwindled, television companies began to acquire the rights to show film, and film companies began to invest in television, leading to a decline in their film-making activities (Hill, 1999: 51–2; K. Williams, 1998: 196). It is, therefore, somewhat ironic that by the mid-1980s, Britain's film industry was heavily reliant for its finance on television (Hill, 1996: 105).

Small screen developments

The television industry's involvement with film was affected by the introduction of Channel 4 in 1982. As a 'publisher broadcaster', required to purchase and commission programmes rather than produce them and with a brief to provide a distinctive and 'public service', Channel 4 prompted the expansion of an independent film production sector in Britain (Hill, 1999: 54–9). Other television companies such as Thames, Granada and Central also became involved in film production around the same time and the BBC extended its involvement by making films for cinema release as well as the small screen (Hill, 1999: 59–60).

In Wales, it was the emergence of S4C that heralded a new era for film-makers, many of whom had experienced little encouragement from BBC Wales and HTV, now ITV1 Wales, prior to the 1980s (Berry, 1994: 282, 310). Also operating as a 'publisher broadcaster' and with initial plans to commission around five films or documentaries on an annual basis, S4C catalysed the emergence of independent production companies in Wales. Both S4C and the independent sector were assisted by the availability of a number of able film-makers in Wales, some of whom had developed their skills through a film and video workshop sector which emerged throughout Britain during the late 1960s:

> In contradistinction to the mainstream industry, with its commitment to profitable entertainment, the search for a mass audience and a primarily 'box-office', or market, orientation towards the audience, this other ['independent'] sector developed in partial, contradictory and hesitating ways the 'conditions of possibility' for a more socially responsible recasting of the institutions of cinema. (Blanchard and Harvey, 1983: 232)

In Cardiff, the Chapter Arts Centre initiated film and video workshops, relying on a collective and cooperative approach to film production that involved sharing equipment, knowledge and skills (Berry, 1994: 344; McIntyre, 1996: 225–6). Other similar groups existed in Brecon and elsewhere in Powys, while Red Flannel, an all-women film and video workshop, was established in Pontypridd in 1984 (Berry, 1994: 344, 348). Red Flannel, along with a limited number of other workshops around Britain, was a beneficiary of financial support from Channel 4 under a Workshop Declaration. This arrangement, established in conjunction with the Association of Cinematograph and Television Technicians (ACTT), the British Film Institute, Regional Arts

Associations and the Independent Film-makers Association, enabled Channel 4 to provide funding for non-profit-making workshops in exchange for a supply of programmes (Berry, 1994: 348–9; Hill, 1999: 57–8).

More screens, less choice

By the mid-1980s, with increasing numbers of people watching film on television and video, it was the advent of the multiplex, pioneered in the USA, which began to reverse the decline in cinema attendance. Purpose-built, with multi-screen facilities and aiming to provide a total leisure package with cinema at the core, multiplexes rekindled interest in going to the cinema.[6] Growing in number each year since their introduction in 1984, multiplexes have expanded the number of cinema sites only marginally while increasing the number of screens substantially. This has resulted in the closure of numerous independent cinemas (Hanson, 2000: 49). Not only has cinema attendance risen numerically since the introduction of multiplexes, patrons now include more over-35s and more ABC1s (Corrigan, 1983: 32–5; Hanson, 2000: 54–5).

Multiplexes in Britain are predominantly American owned and the industry is dominated by a small number of large conglomerates (Hanson, 2000: 50; Murphy, 2000: 19). Despite the increase in numbers of screens, most of the films shown in multiplexes are American produced, making it increasingly difficult to secure the exhibition of British productions (Hanson, 2000: 55; Hill, 1999: 50–1). The first multiplex in Wales opened in Swansea in 1991 (British Film Institute, 1991). There are now eleven multiplexes in Wales operating a total of 112 screens. All are located in, or close to, Wales's major urban centres. Multiplex screens now easily surpass the number provided by the traditional cinemas in Wales (see Table 4.1).

Over the period 1985 to 2004, it is also interesting to note how the introduction of multiplexes has impacted on the number of cinemas and distribution of screens in Cardiff (see Table 4.2). Without the power to influence decisions over exhibition and distribution, the future visibility and viability of Welsh films will be dependent to a large degree on companies that are owned externally and have no particular affinity with Wales.

Table 4.1: Screens in Wales

Year	Cinemas		Multiplexes		Total
	Numbers	Screens	Numbers	Screens	screens
1985	61	86			86
1986	58	83			83
1987	52	75			75
1988	51	74			74
1989	51	74			74
1990	54	75			75
1991	51	70	1	10	80
1992	51	72	2	15	87
1993	57	77	2	15	92
1994	58	77	2	15	92
1995	54	73	2	15	88
1996	55	76	2	15	91
1997	54	73	3	20	93
1998	58	77	3	20	97
1999	57	75	7	61	136
2000	54	66	8	67	133
2001	52	63	9	79	142
2002	54	65	9	98	163
2003	54	67	10	98	165
2004	52	65	11	112	177

Source: British Film Institute, 1985–2004.

Table 4.2: Screens in Cardiff

Year	Cinemas		Multiplexes		Total
	Numbers	Screens	Numbers	Screens	screens
1985	7	12			12
1990	7	12			12
1995	6	11	1	5	16
2000	5	8	2	17	25
2004	2	3	3	41	44

Source: British Film Institute, 1985, 1990, 2000, 2004.

Framing Wales

A combination of economic and social factors was influential in ensuring that cinema became the most popular form of entertainment in Wales during the first half of the twentieth century. A booming economy enabled substantial economic growth between 1870 and 1914 and helped establish in south Wales a 'vibrant, cosmopolitan and highly politicised society . . . quite literally built on coal' (Miskell, 1997: 56; Ridgwell, 1997: 71).[7] The latter part of the nineteenth century also saw the introduction of better conditions for workers, including a reduction in the working week – but without a decrease in real incomes, which provided the scope for more leisure opportunities (Chanan, 1983: 40; K. Williams, 1998: 68). Cinema soon became the preferred leisure choice. Although early cinema-goers were predominantly working class, the quest to gain a mass audience involved targeting middle-class patrons by providing car-parking spaces, better seating, heating and improved ventilation (Miskell, 1997: 62–3).

Selling a habit

Initially, cinema's attempts to win the approval of the establishment and attract middle-class patrons proved to be problematic. Not only was repertory theatre the preferred option, but cinema was tainted for a number of reasons, such as the risk of fire due to the presence of celluloid film, the poor quality and unhygienic conditions in many early cinemas and the likelihood of sexual liaisons in darkened venues (K. Williams, 1998: 72). Moreover, the limited quality of early films and the association between cinemas and the somewhat risqué music-hall also deterred the middle classes, particularly those steeped in 'the dogma of the chapel and Nonconformist puritanism' (Berry, 1994: 21). Moral guardians were also in evidence, with a local councillor and 'temperance man' in Merthyr calling for cinemas to close by 9 p.m. because they were considered a greater moral danger to young men than the public house (Berry, 1994: 118).

There were also fears about the immorality of Hollywood films and the risk of American idioms being incorporated into everyday speech (Berry, 1994: 85–6, 125). Resistance to the new medium varied from place to place. For instance, the acceptance of cinema in west Wales was far slower than in other parts of the country due to the 'bloodcurdling anti-entertainment rhetoric of Revivalist preachers' (Berry, 1994:

44). Even the travelling showmen felt obliged to improve the reputation of the early industry, doing so by holding 'Sacred Services' on Sundays and raising money for charities and disaster victims (Berry, 1994: 32).

While the emergence of more palatial cinemas helped the industry gain middle-class patrons and respectability, two other measures were central to this achievement. One was the introduction of the Cinematograph Act 1909, which empowered local authorities to license venues where films were being screened. The other was the establishment in 1913 of the British Board of Film Censors (BBFC). Financed by the industry and with its head and board members approved by the Home Secretary, but without legal status and therefore acting only as a guide to local authorities, the BBFC classified and certificated films for exhibition (Corrigan, 1983: 29; K. Williams, 1998: 76).

Starting with only two rules of guidance for film-makers – 'no nudity and no portrayal of Jesus Christ' – the BBFC gradually extended the range of unacceptable practices and images, although not always to the satisfaction of local authorities, some of which imposed additional cuts before local screenings (K. Williams, 1998: 73). Initially, the rules imposed by the BBFC reflected the moral values of the era, but they were further extended during the 1920s to include powers over pre- and post-production censorship in order to address a changing economic and political climate (Corrigan, 1983: 29). Films focusing on social unrest and industrial conflict were rejected in favour of others showing more positive images of British society (Corrigan, 1983: 29; K. Williams, 1998: 121–2). This informal censorship was to influence how Wales appeared in the movies during the 1930s.

Cinema in Wales quickly became part of a weekly routine. It 'sold a habit' to the extent that a visit to the 'local' was just as likely to mean the cinema as the pub (Corrigan, 1983: 31). In Wales, for the many who attended twice weekly or more, cinema was their 'second home' (Berry, 1994: 116). Initially attracted by the novelty of the new medium as much as its entertainment value, cinema-goers were provided with opportunities for escapism, distraction and even a refuge during the economic downturn that followed the First World War and the Depression during the 1930s. However, despite the closure of collieries and the sharp rise in unemployment, cinema audiences in Wales continued to outstrip attendance at football and rugby matches, partly helped by cinemas 'pegging' their prices to accommodate the downturn (Miskell, 1997: 53). But what did people see in the dream palaces and fleapits around Wales?

Popular fare and partial visions

Westerns, romances, melodramas, travelogues and comedies emerged as the most popular genres during the silent era and fictional narratives had become the dominant film product in most industrial nations by 1910 (Desjardins, 1995: 407; K. Williams, 1998: 71). In order to transform a fledgling industry into a mass-entertainment medium, good business practices were essential, one being the steady flow of films required to attract and retain a mass audience. An almost formulaic approach to fictional narratives and a factory-like production process ensured their preference over the less predictable process of making documentaries (Desjardins, 1995: 406).[8]

Between 1912 and 1927, twenty-six films were set, or partly set, in Wales, of which fourteen were features (Berry, 1994: 66). However, the film-makers and their backers were attracted to Wales not for its culture or the vibrancy of its economic and social life, but because of the scenery and the lower costs of filming when compared with London (Berry, 1994: 60). In fact, the people of Wales featured only minimally in such films. When contemporary Wales did appear in the cinema it was more likely to be in a documentary, or 'topical', which acted as the filler before, or between, the major film(s).[9]

Overwhelmingly, the films exhibited in Wales before and after the First World War were American. This is not surprising given that almost 95 per cent of films shown in Britain during 1925 were Hollywood products (Corrigan, 1983: 26). Audiences loved the 'racy' American dramas and, with the arrival of sound, the first Hollywood musicals (Berry, 1994: 116). Wales's virtual non-appearance in film was matched by its sparse presence in the newsreels. The initial popularity of the newsreel, or 'animated newspaper', was helped by the poor picture reproduction in the press at that time and by the absence of pictorial magazines and of television (K. Williams, 1998: 71–2). Even when Wales did emerge in the newsreels, the coverage was restricted to 'soft' news, festive events and human interest stories; images of industrial disputes and any other contentious news were avoided (Hogenkamp, 1985: 71; Stead, 1986: 164). While the newsreels were not subject to control by the BBFC, the owners of such companies chose not to show this material, resulting in superficial reporting of hunger marches and demonstrations during the 1930s (K. Williams, 1998: 121–2). Most owners of newsreel companies had close connections with the Conservative Party, as did the Newsreel Association of Great Britain, their representative body (K. Williams, 1998: 127). Essentially, newsreel operators judged that it was in their commercial interest to toe the government line on how economic and social issues were to be handled. Reporting 'bad' news was not considered good for business.

Nevertheless, despite – or because of – a pervasive, hegemonic, commercially driven, capitalist cinema that focused almost exclusively on producing mass-entertainment products, alternative voices did emerge as the socio-political climate began changing in the late 1930s. As Stead (1986) notes, with the possibility of another world war on the horizon that would require the services of an acquiescent proletariat, perceptions of working-class lives were re-evaluated:

> the Welsh miners who had previously been thought of as undisciplined hotheads now became to many the classical expression of a long-suffering and democratic working class community. The largely unofficial but nevertheless very effective code of film censorship prevented both the newsreel and feature-film companies from depicting the politics of working-class communities but the new political dispensation and cultural debate made it inevitable that Welsh miners would make it into the movies, albeit in a highly controlled way. (Stead, 1986: 165)

Three related developments helped to create a context in which critical voices would be raised in Wales: the documentary film movement; 'left' film organizations; and the miners' halls and institutes, an institutional context more amenable than the commercial cinema to showing alternative or oppositional films.

Alternative voices

John Grierson, later associated with the development of the Newport Film School, is credited with devising the term 'documentary' and founding the documentary movement in Britain (Aitken, 1997: 58; Hood, 1983: 99; Stead, 1987: 39). Grierson joined the Empire Marketing Board in 1927 in order to make publicity films to promote trade links between Britain and its empire (Aitken, 1997: 58; Hood, 1983: 101). He moved to the General Post Office (GPO) in 1933 to establish the GPO Film Unit. As the GPO came to assume a key role in promoting government activities, its publicity budget was larger than all other government departments (K. Williams, 1998: 117).

With roots in realism and naturalism, the documentary movement was renowned for its use of collaborative approaches to film-making and its use of ordinary people rather than professional actors (Aitken, 1997: 62; K. Williams, 1998: 117). Essentially, the aim of the documentary movement was to bring to the attention of the wider public the impact of the Depression on working-class communities, in the hope that growing public awareness would result in political intervention (Aitken, 1997: 60–1; K. Williams, 1998: 116). Documentary films were seen by some as 'tools for change' – 'a new film genre which would halt the insidious influence of Hollywood's make-believe' (Berry, 1994: 131; Stead, 1986: 165).

While the documentary movement produced over 400 films between 1929 and 1939, the viewing audience was limited, mainly due to problems with distribution as the commercial cinema was reluctant to show such films (Stead, 1986: 167; K. Williams, 1998: 119). The movement was also constrained by its dependence on sponsorship – derived primarily from the British state – and its reliance on middle-class film-makers who tended either to romanticize the plight of working people or to 'other' them (Hood, 1983: 101–2; K. Williams, 1998: 118).[10] Furthermore, there were concerns that some of the films simply avoided, or glossed over, key issues such as low wages, poor working conditions and the risk of death or injury at work (Hood, 1983: 107–8). While the documentary-makers were sympathetic to the problems of working people, this did not result in beneficial concrete changes: 'Grierson and his colleagues were shocked by the waste of human lives, caused by the depression, but never offered anything but piecemeal improvements to the audience' (Hogenkamp, 1985: 67).

The documentary movement made two films in Wales, *Today We Live* (1937) and *Eastern Valley* (1937). A promotional film sponsored by the National Council for Social Service, *Today We Live* includes two segments, one filmed in Pentre, Treherbert and Treorchy during the winter months, and the other in England's Cotswolds. The Welsh segment focuses on unemployed miners building a community centre in Pentre where the pit had closed (Berry, 1996: 130–7; Hogenkamp, 1987). This film became notorious for its scenes of unemployed people scrambling over slagheaps searching desperately for coal to burn at home. *Eastern Valley*, filmed in Gwent and sponsored mainly by the Order of Friends, features unemployed miners as members of a Subsistence Society engaged in a 'social experiment'. This was a cooperative land scheme producing and distributing food and other goods for local impoverished families (Berry, 1994: 137–40). While both films use local people instead of actors and highlight the problems associated with unemployment, there are no references to the politics of the area, nor to the South Wales Miners' Federation (Stead, 1986: 166). While there were a few other documentaries made in Wales prior to the Second World War, they too tended to avoid references to the social, political and industrial tensions of the era (Berry, 1994: 143–4).

The documentary movement has been contrasted with other more radical organizations involved in the production, distribution and exhibition of film. These groups, sometimes referred to as the Workers' Film Movement (WFM), were closer to working-class people and more politically committed than the documentary makers (Hood, 1983: 105). They included the Workers' Film and Photo League, Kino, Progressive Film Institute (PFI), Workers' Film Association and the Federation of Workers' Film Societies (FWFS). The FWFS began operations in October 1929 with the intention of bringing Russian and other 'left'-oriented European films to the attention of working-class people, and a local branch was established in Cardiff in the same year (Berry, 1994: 132; T. Ryan, 1983: 114). To enable the importation, distribution and production of films, the FWFS founded Atlas Films, but due to financial problems, censorship restrictions and police harassment both collapsed in 1931 (T. Ryan, 1983: 114).[11]

Kino, established in 1933, continued to work with the FWFS and achieved a national reach by 1937, touring the south Wales valleys in 1935 with two films. One was a Soviet film, *Storm over Asia*, showing British imperialism in Asia, and the other, *Holiday from Unemployment*, featured a holiday camp for unemployed miners in Oxford (Berry, 1994: 141; T. Ryan, 1983: 116; Hogenkamp, 1985: 70). In 1935, both Kino and the PFI were registered as companies to distribute films that would otherwise not have been distributed in Britain and in 1936 and 1938 the latter also produced twelve films in Spain to be shown in support of the republican cause (Ryan, 1983: 118–20). In all, the WFM produced over 112 films between 1927 and 1939 which were used for entertainment, fund-raising and agitation, each offering an alternative to the fare produced by the commercial film industry (T. Ryan, 1983: 124, 128).

Not surprisingly, the miners' halls and institutes were seen as receptive venues for films produced and distributed by the WFM, although as most were set up with 35mm facilities this reduced the opportunity to show films produced in a 16mm format (Berry, 1994: 133; Stead, 1986: 167–8). Nevertheless, Russian, German and Spanish films were shown in some halls and institutes, but a 'labour cinema network' showing non-commercial films did not emerge. This was because mining communities – like the rest of Britain – enjoyed Hollywood blockbusters and the halls and institutes became increasingly reliant for their survival on achieving regular and sizeable audiences (Hogenkamp, 1985: 65–6; Ridgwell, 1997: 77–8).

There was, however, exceptional support in south Wales for the republican movement in the Spanish Civil War. This was in terms of both the number of volunteers who went to Spain to fight for the cause and those who remained behind to raise funds. It has been suggested that the contribution from south Wales far exceeded that of other parts of Britain (Ridgwell, 1997: 78). With public information about the Civil War rather muted, some halls and institutes set out to raise public awareness and elicit support for the republican cause by exhibiting films – generally provided by the WFM – and raising money via collections at these screenings (Hogenkamp, 1985: 71).

'Outsider' representations

The documentary films failed to attract large audiences. They did, however, pave the way for later ventures by the commercial film companies which recognized that social problems could provide an ideal subject for melodrama once the political climate was more amenable to the production and exhibition of such material (Berry, 1994: 131; Stead, 1987: 40). With its industrial landscape and photogenic scenery, Wales proved to be an attractive destination for visiting commercial film-makers.

Berry (1994: 160) lists a number of films made between 1938 and 1949 that drew on Wales's industrial context: *The Citadel* (1938), *The Stars Look Down* (1939), *Proud Valley* (1940), *How Green Was My Valley* (1941), *The Corn is Green* (1945), *Fame is the Spur* (1947), *Last Days of Dolwyn* (1949) and *Blue Scar* (1949). These films are considered significant because it is through their images and narratives that Wales has become 'known' both here and overseas. Three films, *The Citadel* (1938), *Proud Valley* (1940) and *How Green Was My Valley* (1941), are seen as particularly influential as they have 'borne the weight of Welsh folk-memory and created a mythic Wales unlikely to be dislodged from the mind of cinema goers' (Berry, 1994: 160). The apparent impact of these particular films is seen to be problematic. This is because not all were set or filmed in Wales, only a minority of the major roles were allocated to Welsh actors, most were made by 'outsiders' – English or American – and, not dissimilar to criticisms directed at the documentary-makers, political realities were minimized or distorted:

> the film studios came to make stunningly dramatic films that would broadly sympathize with the plight of the miners in a way that had been sanctioned by the kind of consensus that the government of the day was encouraging. In the United States and Britain censorship quite simply ruled out any attempt to depict meaningful trade union activity and in any case the vast majority of feature film producers and directors had very little sympathy with militant union activity which they thought of as being totally alien to the norms of democratic politics. (Stead, 1987: 41)

The most successful of the mining films, both critically and commercially, was *How Green Was My Valley* (1941). Awarded five Oscars and a success at the box office, this film has been suggested as 'the defining Welsh film' because it 'contains most of the elements of Welsh myth – the pit and the heroic pitman, the choir, the chapel, the beauties of the countryside . . . interwoven with the timeless elements of romance – growing up, falling in love, the joys and sorrows of family life, death' (Richards, 1997: 216, 221). Nonetheless, the film has attracted vehement and voluminous criticism, primarily on the grounds of its lack of authenticity: it used only one Welsh actor; it failed to distinguish between Celtic nationalities, showing an Irish jig being performed at a Welsh wedding; all filming took place on a film set in the United States where a Welsh village was constructed for the purpose; and it engendered anti-union and anti-socialist values which contradicted the prevailing political climate (Berry, 1994: 161–6; Richards, 1997: 217–20). Despite such criticism, Stead (1986: 172) insists that many people still believe the film to be 'the ultimate tribute to all that was best in the old Welsh communities'.

If *How Green Was My Valley* is the quintessential Hollywood 'take' on Wales, *David* (1951) has been suggested as a fine riposte – providing an authentically indigenous representation of the country (Richards, 1997: 221). Aaron (1979: 302) also acknowledges that *David* 'catches an authentic Welsh quality', even though the scriptwriter came from outside Wales.[12] Made by Paul Dickson, previously schooled in the documentary movement, *David* was commissioned in 1950 as Wales's contribution to the Festival of Britain. It was filmed in Ammanford and centres on a school caretaker 'who distils his crowded memories of his dead son . . . into a poem which takes second place at the National

Eisteddfod' (Berry, 1994: 246). But, although different, *David* does have similarities with *How Green Was My Valley*. This is because *David* embodies values of home, family and community life, illuminating 'those elements that go to make up Welshness: education, chapel, poetry, music, communality, the pit' (Richards, 1997: 221). It is, though, the realism and documentary traditions of *David* – its reliance on non-actors, alongside professional actors – and its use of genuine locations that distinguish it from the romance of *How Green Was My Valley* (Richards, 1997: 222).

According to Stead (1986: 171), *David* was an attempt to counter the films produced by Ealing Studios which played a major role in determining how Wales and the Welsh would be represented on screen during the 1950s. Michael Balcon took up the role of head of production at Ealing Studios in 1938 with the intention of producing films that were rooted in contemporary British life. While most of the post-war films produced at Ealing were shaped by this premise, 'the realism of their portrayal is more problematic' (Porter, 1983: 188). This was particularly the case in respect of Wales. In the Ealing heyday, token Welshmen appeared alongside the representatives of other UK regions and nations and, although Welsh actors, writers and musicians contributed significantly to the success of Ealing films, portrayals of Wales and the Welsh were generally limited to parodies, myths and stereotypes (Berry, 1994: 214, 228).

The Ealing comedy, *A Run For Your Money* (1949), is singled out for particular criticism, with Stead (1986: 171, 174–5) suggesting that the film paved the way for later depictions of the Welsh as 'music-hall stereotypes'. In reflecting on *A Run For Your Money* and two later successful comedies of the era, *Valley of Song* (1953) and *Only Two Can Play* (1962), Berry (1996: 230) acknowledges that some of the images and performances demeaned and patronized the Welsh. It was an era in which 'the screen Taffy' was 'likeable but insular, naïve and gullible' and later, sycophantic and duplicitous (Berry, 1994: 200). Similarly, Richards (1997: 227), writing about *Only Two Can Play* (1962), a film based on Kingsley Amis's novel, *That Uncertain Feeling*, argues that culture and education in Wales is 'mercilessly caricatured as bogus, pretentious and chauvinistic'.

By the 1960s, films made by British and American studios had established images of Wales and Welshness that would linger for some time. These images conveyed the importance of education, music, communality, comradeship, pit-work, and Wales's role in the British

Empire – epitomized by the presence of Welsh soldiers in *Zulu* (1964) starring Stanley Baker and Michael Caine – while occasionally hinting at tensions between Wales and England, sometimes over the Welsh language. Overall, though, Wales was portrayed on screen as 'consensual rather than conflictual' – partly due to the censorial restrictions of the era (Richards, 1997: 229). The large majority of films were made in English even though the first Welsh-language film, *Y Chwarelwr/The Quarryman*, was made in 1935. Another noticeable feature of these films was the absence, or stereotyping, of Welsh women. Reflecting on this era, Beddoe (1986: 227) concludes, 'Wales, land of my fathers, is a land of coal miners, rugby players and male voice choirs'. Welsh women, she suggests, were confined to certain roles: the Welsh Mam, the Welsh lady in national costume, the pious Welshwoman, the sexy Welshwoman or the funny Welshwoman (Beddoe, 1986: 229).

Indigenous rising

Two developments were particularly responsible for reviving film in Wales and enabling the possibility of a Welsh cinema. One was the establishment of S4C in 1982 and the other was a film and video workshop sector that had its genesis in Cardiff at the Chapter Arts Centre (Chapter).

Film and video workshops

Spurred by the involvement of groups such as the South Wales Arts Society and Cardiff Cine Society, Chapter opened its first cinema in 1974 and a second in 1976 (R. Hutchison, 1977: 78, 84–8). Ironically, the materials used to equip them came from previously closed cinemas in the south Wales valleys (Kinsey, 2001: 2). While Chapter showed the usual commercial movies, it also screened European films on the basis that the finance generated by the former would sustain the latter (R. Hutchison, 1977: 80). Success with the cinema programme led to the introduction of a film-production workshop, attracting existing film-makers and helping to nurture new talents in the field (Berry, 1994: 344; Kinsey, 2001: 3). Despite these developments, Chapter was not sufficiently embedded within the local community during its formative years (R. Hutchison, 1977: 94; M. Ryan, 1986: 191). Furthermore, an influx of English-born film-makers militated against the production of films with a 'recognizable Welsh identity', although this was later corrected to some extent with the introduction of a video workshop (Berry, 1994: 347).

The Chapter Video Workshop attracted funding from Channel 4 and the Welsh Arts Council, enabling a fully staffed and equipped unit. It produced films addressing sexism, domestic violence, poor housing, the 1984–5 miners' strike and the impact of changing industrial conditions in the south Wales valleys, topics not previously addressed by TV film-makers (Berry, 1994: 343–54). The Video Workshop was able to respond promptly to emerging political and community concerns by exhibiting their films in community settings such as pubs, clubs and community centres. For example, during the 1984–5 miners' strike the workshop made films with the intention of increasing public awareness and generating funds to support miners and their families (M. Ryan, 1986: 190–1; 2000: 45).

The Video Workshop also acted as a catalyst for other initiatives. The South Wales Women's Film Group (SWWFG) was formed by a group of women from Chapter in 1981 to provide peer support and to encourage other women to become involved in the medium (M. Ryan, 2000: 41–2). This initiative led to the establishment in 1984 of Red Flannel, a women's film workshop in Pontypridd. Its mission was twofold. First, to document the history and experience of local women in both the domestic and public sphere. Second, to illuminate the changing nature of women's roles in the face of a decline in mining and other heavy industries in south Wales (M. Ryan, 2000: 44). Productions such as *Mam* (1988), *Special Delivery* (1991) and *Otherwise Engaged* (1991) reflected these aims (Berry, 1994: 348–9; M. Ryan, 2000: 45).

Other independent documentary film-makers also visited south Wales with the intention of illuminating the experiences of women (Berry, 1994: 352–3). The London Women's Film Group produced *Women of the Rhondda* (1973) and Cinema Action, also from London, produced *So That You Can Live* (1982). In addition to its Video Workshop, Chapter also spawned an Animation Workshop, helping to expand the number of skilled animators operating in south Wales, some of whom later had work commissioned by S4C (Berry, 1994: 354). The film and video workshops were instrumental in helping develop a wide range of film-makers in Wales. They also enabled previously unheard or marginalized voices to enter the public sphere and provide a counter to the omissions and distortions of mainstream media. In so doing, the film and video workshops provided 'alternative forms of

representation' which challenged the existing cultural hegemony
(M. Ryan, 1986: 190).

S4C as catalyst

Without doubt, the introduction of S4C was the key moment for film in
Wales. S4C spawned a healthy independent production sector in
Bangor, Caernarfon and Cardiff (Berry, 1996: 22; M. Ryan, 2000: 46).
Nonetheless, the first few years of S4C proved to be problematic,
attracting criticism from a variety of quarters. Essentially, there were
concerns about the generally conservative nature of its programming,
its lack of a film policy and its over-reliance on 'period "rural and
folkloric" dramas' (Berry, 2000: 128; M. Ryan, 1986: 187). One of
S4C's early successes was in animation. *SuperTed*, launched in 1983
after being rejected by HTV, was sold to forty-five countries and
dubbed into seventeen languages (Robins and Webster, 2000: 112). The
series won a BAFTA award and was purchased by The Disney Channel,
establishing the reputation of Siriol, a small production company in
Cardiff (Berry, 1994: 330).

   Animation in Wales gained further exposure and prestige through
the work of Joanna Quinn, whose award winning *Girls Night Out*
(1987) prompted S4C to sponsor the follow-up, *Body Beautiful* (1993).
It was, in fact, S4C's interest in the project that transformed Beryl – the
'roly-poly heroine' of both films (Berry, 1994: 340) – from 'a Mancunian
to a bilingual "valleys girl"' (Robins and Webster, 2000: 123). Quinn's
work, which also included *Tea At No. 10* (1987) and *Britannia* (1993),
was the first by an animator in Wales to critique the status quo
and challenge prevailing perspectives on contemporary society (Berry,
1994: 340).

   S4C also showcased the work of other animators and in so doing
established Cardiff as a major international centre for animation,
attracting the International Animation Festival to the city in 1992. The
channel enjoyed more local and international success with its series
Animation Classics, which drew its inspiration from opera, religious
works and plays, most famously the work of Shakespeare (Robins and
Webster, 2000: 110, 115). While S4C's interest in animation may have
seemed surprising to some, it was a logical development for at least
three reasons (Robins and Webster, 2000: 111). First, animation was an
established and popular entertainment genre, and S4C required an
audience and was keen to stimulate popular support for the channel.

Second, it could be dubbed into other languages fairly easily and at reasonable cost, thereby ensuring it was saleable beyond Wales. Third, S4C was obliged to draw its programming from the independent sector and Wales already had a fledgling industry as a result of the Animation Workshop at Chapter and initiatives undertaken at the Newport Film School.

Intent on quashing claims that it was failing to engage with contemporary issues in its formative years, S4C approached two film-makers, Karl Francis and Stephen Bayly, neither of whom had previously worked with the channel.[13] As well as helping to rejuvenate S4C's credentials, the two films that emerged from this initiative made history in 1987 as the first bilingual films, in English and Welsh, to feature in London's West End commercial cinema (Berry, 1994: 329). *Milwr Bychan/Boy Soldier* (1986), directed by Karl Francis, centres on a Welsh squaddie's experiences in the British army in Northern Ireland (see Berry, 1994: 390–3). Stephen Bayly's comedy, *Rhosyn a Rhith/ Coming Up Roses* (1986), illuminates the impact of Tory policies on the south Wales valleys in the 1980s (see Berry, 1994: 328–9). These two films were followed by other Welsh-language productions, most supported directly or indirectly by S4C. Endaf Emlyn's *Un Nos Ola Leuad/One Full Moon* (1991), garnered a number of festival awards and was screened at the London and Edinburgh Film Festivals before being distributed to regional film theatres in 1992, but it failed to achieve a commercial cinema release (Berry, 1994: 416).

S4C's local and global credentials were further enhanced with the release of Paul Turner's *Hedd Wyn/The Armageddon Poet* (1992) and Endaf Emlyn's *Gadael Lenin/Leaving Lenin* (1992), each made in Welsh with English subtitles and both winning festival awards. *Hedd Wyn* was the first Welsh-language film to be nominated for Hollywood's Foreign Language Oscar (Berry, 1994: 412). Support by S4C for Steve Gough's *Elenya* (1991), shot 'back to back' in English and Welsh versions, and Ceri Sherlock's *Dafydd* (1993), *Branwen* (1994) and *Cameleon/ Chameleon* (1997) – the latter winning festival awards in Germany and the United States, enlarged and extended the body of work in Welsh.

There were more accolades for S4C and Welsh film in general following the release of Paul Morrison's *Solomon a Gaenor/Solomon and Gaenor* (1998), further encouraging the idea that Cool Cymru was displacing the previously hegemonic Cool Britannia. The film, made in Welsh, English and Yiddish, was nominated for an Oscar in 2000 under the Best Foreign Language Film category, despite a lukewarm review in

Sight and Sound where it was described as 'a typical BBC-type period piece' (Louvish, 1999: 56). Although it failed to win the award, the film's nomination prompted the *Western Mail* to judge the event a major boost for the Welsh film industry (Waters, 2000: 12). However, despite the critical acclaim accorded to many of these films, their commercial success at the box office has been minimal.

Reflection and renewal

During this period English-language Welsh films also generated mixed responses. Although *Twin Town* (1997) attracted a good deal of criticism, Perrins (2000: 152) has suggested that it was the most successful Welsh film at the box office since *How Green Was My Valley* (1941). Its critics, including the Welsh Tourist Board and church groups, rounded on the film's less than idyllic depiction of Swansea, its 'disrespect towards . . . rugby and male voice choirs' and expressed fears that it would lead to 'copycat poodle beheadings' (Blandford, 1999: 123; Morris, 1998: 27). As Perrins (2000: 153) notes, this 'somewhat jarring popular vision of Wales' was distinctly at odds with the Cool Cymru so avidly promoted by the Welsh establishment.

House of America (1996) offered a rather different take on Wales and Welshness, but hopes that the film would build on the success of the earlier stage play and be commercially successful did not materialize. However, for critics and would-be film-makers, the problems encountered during the seven years it took to reach the screen are revealing (Blandford, 2000b: 26, 27). Ed Thomas, the screenwriter, also illuminates the barriers associated with distribution and exhibition. He points out that, for a multiplex such as the Capital Odeon in Cardiff, 'it's more lucrative to play *101 Dalmatians* for an extra week than to show *House [of America]*' (cited in Blandford, 2000c: 83).[14]

Acquiring adequate funding was also a factor with Julian Richard's *Darklands* (1996). The film, a prizewinner at a film festival in Portugal, contributed to debates about national identity in post-devolutionary Wales (Blandford, 1999: 124). However, the reviewer in *Sight and Sound* was less than complimentary, noting that the film 'was made on 16mm for £500,000 (half of it from the Arts Council of Wales lottery funds) and looks as cheap as it is' (Monk, 1997: 37). While there are doubts about whether Justin Kerrigan's *Human Traffic* (1999) is a Welsh film, or simply uses Cardiff's clubland as a backdrop, it did receive positive reviews and was a commercial success, although the original funding came from Ireland (Blandford, 2000b: 36; Brooks, 1999: 46–7).[15]

With a background in short films, Sarah Sugarman is one of a small number of women who intrude on what still appears to be a predominant-ly male domain in Wales (M. Ryan, 2000: 48). Her short, *Anthrakitis* (1998), preceded *Mad Cows* (1999), an adaptation of a Kathy Lette novel, which was followed by *Very Annie Mary* (2000). Set in Wales and filmed in the small south Wales town of Pontycymer, *Very Annie Mary* received a positive review in *Sight and Sound*, the reviewer noting a not unusual theme, '[t]he film is run through with a Welsh ambivalence about ambition' (Jays, 2000: 57).[16]

This surge of film-making in Wales, in both languages, has begun to make its presence felt throughout Britain and overseas, albeit to a limited extent. This is reflected in recent accounts on the changing nature of filmic representations of Britain. Hill (1999: 241) notes how film in the eighties began to offer a more 'fluid, hybrid and plural sense of "Britishness" . . . representing the complexities of "national" life more fully than before'. Likewise, Luckett (2000: 91) saw a continuation of this trend in the 1990s with films suggesting 'a national identity in flux, producing multiple visions of the nation for an increasingly regional home market'. However, despite these apparent shifts, some British – or English – critics appeared uncomfortable with Wales's newly found confidence which enabled film-makers either to ignore earlier stereotypes and myths or to deconstruct them (Blandford, 2000b: 20). Morris (1998: 26), for example, describes how one critic, Spencer (1997: 45–6), depicted *House of America* as 'just another entertainment' and a 'wannabe *Trainspotting*', failing to recognize the film as a 'brilliantly cerebral contribution to the struggle to define Welshness'. Similarly, the suggestion by another reviewer, Thompson (1997: 53–4), that *Twin Town*'s disrespect towards Welsh institutions could not – or should not? – have originated in Wales is seen as patronizing by Perrins (2000: 155), who reminds us that Kevin Allen, the director, actually hails from Swansea.

Such debates are the 'stuff' of national film culture. Morris (1998: 28) aspires to a situation where film would become a 'formative cultural practice in Wales and a confident world cinema – a place where debates concerning language and identity were worked through'. Likewise, Berry (1994: 435) argues that more films should be produced that are 'rooted in or relevant to the present . . . reflect[ing] the traumatic changes, and hopes, for Wales'. For Ryan (1986: 185), the aims of a

Welsh film culture are 'to reclaim our past moments of struggle and place them in contemporary debates about Wales and its future'. Likewise, Blandford (2000b: 15) believes a more diverse range of representations of Welsh life will relieve the burdens experienced by contemporary writers and film-makers.

Such aspirations for a Welsh film culture imply not necessarily a 'homogenising and enclosing tendency', which Higson (2000: 72) associates with national cinema, but more the idea of a national cinema being able to reflect the 'lived complexities of "national" life' (Hill, 1996: 111). This is not new. There has always been an acknowledgement that, ideally, a Welsh film industry would initiate productions addressing indigenous cultural issues while still attracting outside productions to the country (Berry, 2000: 149). However, while history suggests that it has been relatively successful at the latter – and the scenic backdrops prove to be a continuing attraction – achieving the former remains a serious challenge. Sgrîn Cymru Wales (Sgrîn), the Media Agency for Wales, was established in 1997 to address both tasks.[17]

Sgrîn's brief is to raise the profile of film, television and new media in Wales. As the lead body for film, Sgrîn is charged with developing it both economically and culturally (Rowlands, 2002–3: 3). Both Sgrîn and the film industry more generally have been assisted by the emergence of the National Assembly for Wales (NAfW) and its devolved powers in respect of 'culture', although it has no specific policy responsibilities relating to film. The potential financial benefits of this sector for Wales are significant. A report by the Cardiff Business School argues that 'judicious policy shifts could increase not only the prosperity of the [arts and cultural industries] sector, but also the contribution of arts and culture to economic development in Wales' (Bryan et al., 1998: iv). With the NAfW in place, the chairman of Sgrin is confident that the 'cultural will' exists to create 'an indigenous Welsh film industry' (G. S. Jones, 2001–2: 2).

However, bodies such as Sgrîn attract critical attention, particularly in terms of accountability.[18] Interest focuses on the make-up and 'balance' of board members and whether there is adequate representation of all aspects of the industry and the nation more generally. Interest in such matters stems from concerns about the need to strike an appropriate balance between commerce and culture. In this regard, with Scotland so often suggested as a model for development in Wales, a glance to the north may be insightful.

It is generally accepted that initiatives such as 'First Reels', 'Prime Cuts' and 'Tartan Shorts' – and its Gaelic counterpart 'Gear Ghearr' – have provided a career development path for film-makers in Scotland and helped establish a 'distinct Scottish cinema' (Petrie, 2000: 162).[19] However, McArthur (1985; 1993; 1994) has expressed concerns about aspects of the Scottish film industry. He argues that it is dominated by conventional film industry figures and senior television executives whose aim is to create an 'orthodox narrative cinema' which will be internationally competitive, but will reduce the possibility of alternative approaches and result in the exclusion of already marginalized voices (McArthur, 1994: 112–13). This 'market-driven' approach is thought to ratchet up costs while paying scant attention to cultural concerns. According to McArthur (1993: 32), the current predilection by policy-makers for 'economics' over 'culture' should be reversed, as the ultimate aim should be to 'create in the first instance a culturally relevant and in the longer term economically viable Scottish cinema'. Achieving a balance in this area becomes more difficult when the UK government and the NAfW identify film as a key component of the much heralded creative industries sector (Film Policy Review Group, 1998; C. Smith, 1998; Welsh Assembly Government, 2002).

Filmic futures

Some of the issues raised by McArthur will resonate in Wales. There have long been calls for a Welsh film industry which represents the ethnic and cultural diversity of Wales, accommodating alternative and oppositional voices and avoiding what has been described as the 'superficial multiculturalism' evident in British film during the nineties (Luckett, 2000: 96). However, the hurdles imposed by commercial imperatives are ever present. This is evident in the words of a BBC drama director who asserted that it was a waste of licence fee money making programmes that 'less [*sic*] than 10 million people are going to watch' (cited in Oppe, 2000: 178). Not surprisingly, such observations fuel calls by Welsh film-makers for additional 'spaces', the most obvious example being the provision of a fifth television channel for Wales – a scenario that perhaps becomes more probable in a digital environment.

Such a development would advantage film-makers in both languages. BBC Wales and ITV1 Wales have long been criticized for their indifference towards film, and Channel 4's reluctance to intrude on what it sees as S4C's territory has further disadvantaged independent film producers in Wales (Berry, 1994; 1996; 2000; Blandford, 2000b). Another perspective on this debate is offered by Marc Evans, who argues that as BBC Wales considers the Rhondda to be the '"true" Wales' and because S4C are committed to promoting Welsh, 'you cannot make a bilingual film in a country which is bilingual' (cited in Blandford, 2000c: 86). It is for these reasons, Evans suggests, that Wales needs a 'film culture separate from television', one which is underpinned by an infrastructure that will enable independent film-making (cited in Blandford, 2000c: 86).

Beyond production, there remain concerns about the distribution and exhibition of film in Wales. In terms of the former, as indicated earlier, a number of Welsh films have struggled to find distribution. This is also the case in Scotland where, as Petrie (2000: 167) points out, if it continues, questions will be asked about the ethics of using public funding – such as the Lottery – to make films that fail to secure distribution. Unfortunately, annual reports produced by Sgrîn in 2001–2 and 2002–3 did not include detailed information on the distribution of Welsh films.

In the area of exhibition, two matters that attract attention are the location and number of screens in Wales and the diversity of the films being shown. Berry (1994: 428–30) refers to a number of initiatives undertaken in south Wales during the 1990s to try to compensate for the earlier closure of cinemas, noting that many of the south Wales valleys communities had no screens operating during the 1980s. Neither has the advent of multiplexes necessarily advantaged those living beyond Wales's major urban centres. Moreover, there is apprehension about the longer-term consequences of an expanding multiplex regime which offers a diet of Hollywood fare without the sort of balance – or corrective – enabled through initiatives such as the Regional Film Theatres (RFTs) network.

The first RFTs were established outside London in 1967 by the British Film Institute (BFI) with the aim of making cinema and film more accessible, and particularly so for 'disadvantaged' groups. In some locations, RFTs were seen as the 'only waterhole' in a 'cultural desert' (Docherty, 1987: 162). With funds now channelled through Sgrîn, the Chapter Cinema in Cardiff is the only venue in Wales that receives financial support under this programme. This contrasts sharply with the situation in 1993/4 when eight cinemas around Wales were beneficiaries of the RFTs scheme (British Film Institute, 1993, 1994).

As a result, Morris (1998: 27) is concerned that much of Wales – and particularly rural communities – is disenfranchised, with little opportunity to 'experience cinema that is relevant, challenging and innovative', a situation made worse because the terrestrial television channels are reluctant to show subtitled films made in languages other than English.[20]

Despite the difficulties facing film-makers in Wales, there is still optimism about what is variously referred to as a Welsh film industry, film culture, or national cinema – the three are often used interchangeably. The importance of this goal is captured by Ryan: '[o]ur small country needs a good film industry to act as an ambassador, a trade promoter and a mirror' (2000: 48). But what will people see when they look in this mirror?

Here, again, it is prescient to recall the era of 'cool' – Britannia and Cymru. With New Labour in view, Luckett (2000: 89) reminds us how public relations strategies have been employed with the explicit aim of generating images to 'promote unity (in the service of the dominant powers) by eroding class-based conflicts and radicalism'. In Wales, many will hope that the 'mirror' – in the form of the films produced – will both reflect and represent the complexities and contradictions of life in Wales, while still accommodating the populist, 'market-driven' cinema that has remained ascendant since its emergence in the early years of the twentieth century.

Notes

[1] Chris Monger (2000: 7) acknowledges that he had not fully understood what 'film industry' meant until he scanned the Yellow Pages while in New York to find endless pages listing numerous bodies involved in the making and distribution of film.

[2] This idea is prompted by Petrie's (1996: 93) analysis of Scotland's situation in the UK.

[3] 'National cinema' can be defined in a number of ways (see, for example, Moran, 1996: 8). In this instance it is being used in relation to an oeuvre of films which address national issues, including questions about national identity. However, discussions about national cinema may also centre on the domestic industry, leading to questions about production, distribution and exhibition within a national territory and information on the government agencies that support and protect film.

[4] It is somewhat ironic that plans are now afoot to establish film and television studios on a former opencast mining site at Llanilid, near Llanharan, in south Wales. Work was expected to commence in 2004 with the project due

for completion by 2006. One of the backers of Dragon International
Studios, dubbed Valleywood, is Sir Richard Attenborough. If the project
does proceed it may generate between 6,000 and 8,000 new jobs (see
www.members.lycos.co.uk/valleywood).

5 Details about William Haggar and his films can be found at the National
Screen and Sound Archive of Wales (*www.screenandsound.llgc.org.uk*) and
the British Film Institute (*www.bfi.org.uk*).

6 Essentially, the aim is to entice a greater spend by the consumer. Hence, the
expanse of foyer space made available today for the sale of sweets, ice
cream, popcorn, burgers and hot dogs, all of which can now be consumed in
the auditorium, much to the chagrin of those customers who would prefer
an odour-free viewing experience!

7 The south Wales coalfield produced its record tonnage in 1913 and the ports
at Barry and Cardiff were the busiest in the world shortly before the First
World War (Berry, 1994: 18, 116).

8 Early film production was referred to as manufacturing and the first film
studios were known as factories (Chanan, 1983: 43).

9 Examples of 'topicals' include a 1902 rugby game between Wales and
Scotland, a boxing match between two of Wales's best fighters of the era and
general interest films set in north Wales (Berry, 1994: 81–2).

10 In this instance, 'other' acts as a negative stereotype, connoting the idea of
difference and outsider; a person, group or race set apart, or peripheral to
the mainstream, and associated with notions of mysteriousness or danger.
For example, Williams (1998: 118) cites Orwell's reference to 'the "smell" of
working people' and Grierson's ventures 'into the jungles of Middlesborough
and the Clyde'.

11 Montagu (1980: 124) reports on subtle forms of censorship by way of police
harassment at a film event organized by the Peace Pledge Union (PPU) in
Cardiff prior to the start of the Second World War (1939–45). The films
being shown were *Kameradschaft* and three short films by the PPU.

12 *Noson Lawen/The Fruitful Year*, a drama-documentary made by the National
Savings Movement in 1949, is suggested by Aaron (1979: 301) as a film that
people from Wales will more readily identify with than *The Last Days of
Dolwyn* (1949) and *How Green Was My Valley* (1941).

13 Karl Francis's drama-documentary, *Above Us the Earth* (1977), which
centred on the Ogilvie Colliery in the Rhymney Valley of south Wales, is highlighted as a significant film because it marked the arrival of a talented director
and demonstrated the possibilities of an indigenous Welsh cinema (Berry,
1994: 4).

14 Further work by Evans (*Resurrection Man*, 1997; *My Little Eye*, 2001), and
Thomas (*Rancid Aluminium*, 2000), looks beyond Wales and Welsh themes.
Evan's latest work, *Dal: Yma/Nawr/Still: Here/Now* (2003), a film about Welsh-
language poetry involving, amongst others, Rhys Evans, Cerys Mathews,
Ioan Gruffydd, Siân Philips, Mathew Rhys, Nia Roberts and John Cale,
rounded off the 2003 Cardiff Screen Festival.

15 Kerrigan, who graduated from the International Film School Wales –
   previously Newport Film School – went on to work with Ridley Scott on
   another feature, *I Know You Know* (Sgrîn, 2003: 3).
16 Although initially slow to attract institutional support in Wales, short-film
   activity during the 1990s was spearheaded by a series of four films known as
   PICS, produced by Oppe (2000: 175–6). Reflecting on Scotland's fledgling
   film industry, Petrie (2000: 162) underlines the importance of short film in
   providing continuity of employment for the sector's workforce and, in doing
   so, developing the skills and resources to build a viable industrial base.
17 The emergence, role and operation of Sgrîn is considered in more detail in
   chapter 8.
18 McIntyre (1996: 230–2) offers a critical perspective on such arrangements,
   arguing that the broadcasters appear to get more benefits than the cultural
   agency. He goes on to ask: 'how far should arts money be used to subsidize a
   television industry in doing something that it should be doing anyway?
   What is the added cultural value?'
19 Funding for 'First Reels' is provided by the Scottish Film Council, while
   'Tartan Shorts', 'Prime Cuts' and 'Gear Ghearr' are financed by the Scottish
   Film Production Fund.
20 Sgrîn (2002–3: 10) has established an objective which aims to ensure that
   'commercial and cultural cinema' programmes are available throughout
   Wales within a forty-minute journey by car or public transport of any home.

5

Radio in Wales:
'Your Nation, Your Station'?

Radio broadcasting is sometimes seen as the 'Cinderella medium',[1] and its centrality to an understanding of the media's contribution to society in the twentieth century – and beyond – is easily neglected. In the case of Wales, moreover, there are grounds for considering radio's place in the development of mass communications as having been especially pivotal, particularly when viewed from a historical perspective. John Davies's claim that, in the Welsh context, 'broadcasting has played a central role, both positive and negative, in the development of the concept of a national community' has a particular resonance for radio (1994a: ix).

With a presence in Wales since the 1920s, radio's position at the start of the twenty-first century is one which embodies a number of key controversies, dilemmas and contradictions in relation to the construction and dissemination of Welsh identity, at nationwide and local community levels. These relate to debates, for example, about the ultimate role and value of public service radio broadcasting within a post-devolutionary Welsh context in which policy-making powers in connection with broadcasting remain in Westminster and in which the new regulatory framework appears to provide negligible scope for any meaningful Welsh representation on its decision-making bodies. Similarly, much controversy surrounds the development of the commercially operated radio sector in Wales. This sector's chief component, the Independent Local Radio (ILR) stations, show an increasing tendency towards non-Welsh ownership, and their degree of commitment to any thoroughgoing representation of the localities in their target catchment areas warrants close scrutiny.

This chapter's starting point, therefore, is the view expressed by Aled Jones in relation to Welsh radio's initial potential vis-à-vis other media sectors: 'The press had self-consciously sought to generate a sense of nationhood in nineteenth- and early twentieth-century Wales, and the potential of radio, far more than the cinema, to do the same was abundantly clear' (1993: 234). What follows is an examination of the extent to which radio broadcasting in Wales – in its various guises: public service or commercial, 'national', 'regional' or 'local' – has proved to be successful in making such a contribution.

This chapter is structured so as to strike a balance between a broadly chronological narrative of the key events in the development of radio broadcasting in Wales and, on the other hand, an evaluation of how these events fit into our broader understanding of the relationship between Welsh society and its mass-communication systems. It begins by tracing the early development of radio in Wales from the birth of the BBC to the Second World War (1939–45). This historical overview continues by looking at post-war developments in BBC Radio Wales and Radio Cymru up to the birth in the 1970s of the BBC's first real radio competitors with the advent of commercial radio. The rest of the chapter is divided into several sections which address the most salient issues of the last quarter of a century, focusing in particular on the various regulatory frameworks that have controlled Welsh radio's development, as well as on an assessment of the extent to which present-day stations – both public and commercial – genuinely serve their target audiences, and of the changing position of radio in the post-devolutionary media landscape.

The development of radio broadcasting in Wales

The circumstances of the initial, tentative stages of radio transmission in Wales carry a distinct resonance down the years, in that they foreshadow a number of enduring problems and peculiarities, some of which still give cause for concern in one form or another in the present day.

The first radio broadcast from within Wales was transmitted in February 1923 from an aerial in Cardiff,[2] chosen somewhat controversially as the site of one of eight transmitters which the British Broadcasting Company had distributed around the UK.[3] In fact, by that stage listeners in Wales would already have been able to capture radio signals from over the border in England, from transmitters in Manchester and Birmingham (J. Davies, 1994a: 4–5, 25–6, 34–5; Lucas, 1981: 15–26; Scannell and Cardiff, 1991: 304–8).

One of the very first voices given access to the microphone was that of the Lord Mayor of Cardiff, who expressed the hope that radio in Wales would ensure that 'the highest form of culture will be taken into the homes of the poorest in the land' (Lucas, 1981: 16). While John Reith, the first director-general of the BBC, would presumably have approved of such a patrician sentiment, given his own propensity for similar pronouncements about the role of public service broadcasting (Curran and Seaton, 1997: 112–13), his own disdainful view of Wales and of the Welsh soon became apparent (J. Davies, 1994a: 6 and *passim*; Mackay, 1999: 3; K. Williams, 1998: 108). This prejudice was one factor in the gradual creation of a highly centralized (that is to say, London-centric) radio system. Such a development was disappointing for Wales, given that during the first few months, following on from that first broadcast, 'everything Cardiff transmitted was unique to Cardiff' (J. Davies, 1994a: 6; see also Lucas, 1981: 29). Furthermore, '[t]he work of the early stations was local radio in its fullest sense, a form of broadcasting which . . . did not re-emerge until the 1960s' (J. Davies, 1994a: 6–7). Similarly, Scannell and Cardiff argue that there is solid evidence at a UK-wide level that 'radio was more genuinely local for a few years in the early twenties than it was some sixty years later in the eighties' (1991: 304). A point of contention is whether such an authentic 'localness' has ever fully been recaptured by radio broadcasting in Wales, even in the current age of ILR stations.

What did this early Cardiff radio material consist of? The initial pattern was for three hours each evening consisting chiefly of children's material, talks, news and, above all, music. Almost all of this broadcast output was in English. The first words spoken in Welsh were broadcast on St David's Day 1923,[4] but over a decade would pass before the first Welsh-language news bulletin was transmitted, there being in general very little managerial backing for Welsh-language material. The efforts of early pressure groups such as Cylch Dewi could make little headway in this regard (J. Davies, 1994a: 392; Lucas, 1981: 22, 24–6).

Overall, then, these first, faltering steps taken by the radio in Wales were characterized by a string of issues which have remained problematic ever since: controversy about the justification for Cardiff's allegedly privileged position; a strong sense that Wales's media development was hampered by the Anglocentric perspective of the overall controllers and policy-makers; a very marked ambivalence about the media's projection of a regional or local identity; and, lastly, the Welsh audience's consistently anomalous position as regards its physical access to broadcasting signals. This latter point meant that, for example, in the 1920s a listener in Abergavenny would have picked up a clearer radio signal from London than from Cardiff (J. Davies, 1994a: 15).[5] This has its present-day counterpart in both radio and television reception, in what is now known, for example, as eastern Wales's 40 per cent 'transmission overlap', a feature which 'underlines how porous Wales is, compared with Scotland and Ireland, in media terms' (Talfan Davies, 1999: 17).[6]

The early BBC was, of course, aware of this reception problem. One measure taken with the aim of addressing it was the setting up in 1925 of a 'relay station' at Swansea to increase coverage around south and south-west Wales. Curiously, though, and in common with other such relay operations set up around the UK, the station was given a direct link to London rather than to its nearest 'main station', which in Swansea's case would have been Cardiff. Such an arrangement was not what the BBC's director-general had planned, but it seems that the cause of this logistical anomaly in Wales, as elsewhere, was political rivalry between the localities in question (Scannell and Cardiff, 1991: 305). A second measure, approved by Reith in 1925, allocated increased power to the Cardiff transmitter (Briggs, 1965: 306). In this there was also a clear ideological interest at work since the director-general was anxious that miners in the south Wales valleys should be able to tune in, so as to 'combat the doctrines of Communism and Bolshevism so sedulously preached there' (Reith, cited in J. Davies, 1994a: 15).

Such an attitude on the part of the BBC management was also facilitated by rapid technological advances, which meant that by the mid-1920s simultaneous broadcasts had become possible. These permitted a programme from any one UK station to be broadcast by the others at the same time, in effect allowing the BBC to disseminate as much London-originated material as it saw fit, thus entrenching a centralist approach. It was immediately established that twice a week the entire evening's programming around the BBC's regions would be networked from London (Scannell and Cardiff, 1991: 306–7).

These regions had been created, in their initial form, by 1930 (in decisions made in July 1928). The initial 'local' perspective had given way to what were originally five regions which provided a 'regional programme', alongside the 'national programme' from London, from centres designated as serving 'the Midland', 'the North', Scotland, 'the South-East' and 'the West'. Wales was subsumed under this latter heading (Briggs, 1965: 321; Scannell and Cardiff, 1991: 16).

Across the UK, one effect these decisions had was, in Crisell's words, to 'destroy the local basis of early broadcasting' (1997: 25). In the specific case of the 'West Region', which served both Wales and the English West Country, the consequence was that neither of these target audiences was entirely happy (Briggs, 1965: 323; Lucas, 1981: 53–4), and that feelings in some spheres of Welsh nationalist opinion ran particularly high; Saunders Lewis, for example, complained that the 'BBC administers Wales as a conquered province' (Lucas, 1981: 52; K. Williams, 1998: 108). The overall arbitrariness of this process can be summarized as follows: 'the design of the regional scheme and the siting of the transmitters and stations were determined by administrative, technical and economic considerations before any notion of what regionalisation might actually mean in terms of people, places and cultural characteristics' (Scannell and Cardiff, 1991: 321–2; see also Crisell, 1997: 25). What ensued in Wales can best be characterized as a ten-year period of disgruntlement,[7] culminating in the eventual al-location of separate 'regional' status to Wales in 1936, which became operational with its own discrete wavelength two years later (Briggs, 1965: 321).

In these early years of radio transmission collective listening was common, due to the relative expense of radio receivers as a household purchase, and 'radio guilds' were formed in a number of places around Wales to facilitate this (Lucas 1981: 27). As wirelesses gradually became more accessible in price, however, a steady increase was recorded in radio licences during the 1930s (see Figure 5.1). This trend saw the gradual disappearance of the earlier phenomenon of collective listening, an early illustration of the media's influence in constructing what has been described by Raymond Williams (as cited by J. Davies, 1994a: 85), as the mass media's contribution to the 'privatisation of life'.

A further feature of this early period was a gradual erosion of the stylistic distinctiveness of any Cardiff-originated material that remained. In common with other stations around the UK, Cardiff was asked to prioritize speakers from London when allocating space at the microphone to those invited to give talks (J. Davies, 1994a: 28). Reith also took steps to minimize the use of non-Received Pronunciation accents and other markers of regional distinctiveness. This policy also meant that the tone of accessibility and informality that had been deliberately cultivated by those in charge of radio broadcasting in Wales was stifled and standardized into a more formal BBC register. This led, it would seem, to a marked drop in listener engagement, at least in so far as the number of listeners' letters declined as the standardization policy took root. The 'attitudes and values' of these early days were, in the words of Scannell and Cardiff, 'deliberately eradicated by the policy of centralisation' (1991: 304; see also Briggs, 1965: 315). The fact that those in the BBC's London hierarchy who were overseeing such standardization were, it seems, largely unable to conceive of a radio listenership outside of their own social milieu (questioning, for example, the need for anything at all to be broadcast between 7 and 8 p.m. given that all listeners at that time were assumed to be 'dressing for dinner') clearly exacerbated the problem (J. Davies, 1994a: 13–14).[8] This

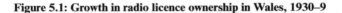

Figure 5.1: Growth in radio licence ownership in Wales, 1930–9

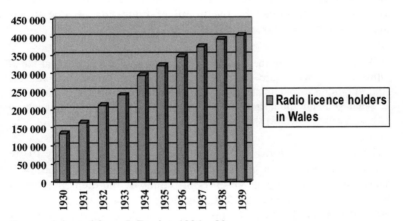

Source: Adapted from J. Davies, 1994a: 82.

blinkered approach also extended, crucially, to the BBC's centralized attitude towards the Welsh language. In John Davies's words: 'Equally incomprehensible to them was any notion that the 922,000 Welsh-speakers of Wales, 37.1% of the population enumerated in 1921, should be provided with programmes produced specifically for them in their own language' (1994a: 53).

There was a limited number of encouraging outcomes here. Briggs (1965: 322), for example, confirms that those programmes that the BBC did produce in the Welsh language were seen as 'genuinely innovatory'. However, as the dominance of music on the airwaves was gradually displaced by more speech-based programming, and as the transmission reach was steadily being extended around the Welsh geography, so the concern grew that a service broadcast almost totally in the English language constituted 'a dire threat to the survival of Welsh-speaking communities' (J. Davies, 1994a: 32). The campaigns and protests began to gather momentum and played a large part in the eventual attainment of 'regional' status for Welsh radio (see above). There was a certain ambivalence or confusion about these protests, however, in that what were in effect two separate – though related – demands, for 'a broadcast station wholly for Wales', on the one hand, and for more use of the Welsh language, on the other, became conflated into a single cause in much of the resultant public and political discussion (J. Davies, 1994a: 46–7; Lucas, 1981: 40). This was partly a consequence of the vehemence of the Welsh-language protests. In particular, a report on 'Welsh in Education and Life' commissioned by the Board of Education became widely discussed, notably its assertion that

> Wireless is achieving the complete Anglicisation of the intellectual life of the nation. We regard the present policy of the British Broadcasting Corporation as one of the most serious menaces to the life of the Welsh language . . . nothing short of the full utilisation of the Welsh language in broadcasting will meet the case. (J. Davies, 1994a: 48)

This was followed, over the course of the late 1920s and early 1930s, by further protests from the League of Nations Union, a delegation of Welsh MPs, a majority of Welsh county councils, and the University of Wales (J. Davies, 1994a: 51–5; Lucas, 1981: 41, 44–5; see also Briggs, 1979: 89). When the Welsh Region was eventually created, however, its commitments in terms of Welsh-language broadcasting were not as fully realized as some campaigners were demanding, and in any event the further development of this region would be affected firstly by wider historical events, and secondly by subsequent criticisms of the BBC from within the UK 'establishment'.

Post-war developments in BBC radio in Wales

The outbreak of war had to some degree delayed the full implementation of this devolution in radio broadcasting, just as it interrupted

developments in television.[9] This meant that in some senses Wales did
not become a fully fledged region until 1945, as part of the general
restructuring of the BBC's output, which saw the creation of the Light
programme and the regional Home Services. Even then, these moves
were accompanied by dissenting views from within the corporation.
The northern regional director of the BBC had tried to prevent this full
implementation on the grounds that those involved 'would be driven
into politics and twisted and warped away from their primary business
of broadcasting, as parts of the inclusive nation to which they belong'.
Needless to say, the 'nation' he was referring to was Britain, rather than
Wales. Such attitudes from within the BBC were now beginning to be
more rigorously questioned, initially by Undeb Cymru Fydd (the 'New
Wales Union') but subsequently by voices coming from outside Wales
(Briggs, 1979: 91, 97–8; A. Jones, 1993: 234).

The Beveridge Committee on Broadcasting, which was set up in 1949
and published its report in 1951,[10] criticized the BBC for being
insufficiently accountable to the public, as well as for being too London-
centric. It therefore recommended what it referred to as the 'democra-
tisation of broadcasting', and the creation of a 'public representation
service', a concept which involved endowing Northern Ireland, Scotland
and Wales with a stronger voice (Crisell, 1997: 76; Lucas, 1981: 164–5;
K. Williams, 1998: 115). In effect this led to the conversion of the
existing Welsh Regional Advisory Council (WRAC) into the Broadcasting Council for Wales (BCW) in 1953.

The WRAC had been set up in 1947, and had its origin in a 1946 UK
government White Paper on broadcasting, which had made the case for
a number of such regional councils, as well as arguing for a five-year
renewal of the BBC's Royal Charter. The WRAC's concerns, over the
five years of its existence, had focused in particular on linguistic issues,
such as the quantity and 'quality' of the Welsh spoken on the regional
programmes and the pronunciation of Welsh place names. The BCW's
existence became a formal requirement in the BBC's 1952 Royal
Charter, and its remit was significantly broader, not only in that it had
an advisory role in relation to television in Wales, as well as a fuller
responsibility for the radio, but also in the range of issues with which it
was forced to deal (J. Davies, 1994a: 160–171; Lucas, 1981: 199).

If the birth of the BCW coincided with the dawn of the television age
in Wales, it also marked 'the apogee of the sound radio era', as by 1952
a total of 82 per cent of Welsh households now held radio licences, a
rise of 17 percentage points from the end of the war (J. Davies, 1994a:

182). One of the first challenges presented to the BCW was the controversy surrounding the right of Welsh political parties to have access to the airwaves during election periods to make party political broadcasts.[11] This controversy was only resolved at the intervention of the post-master general, who at the time retained the right, technically at least – and however incongruously – to ban any BBC broadcast, on the grounds that it was the Post Office that administered the radio licence fee.[12] His eventual decision, in the summer of 1955, to forbid such broadcasts on account of their 'regional' status, aroused great controversy amongst the Welsh political parties, especially Plaid Cymru, who saw it as casting doubt on the degree of real influence wielded by the BCW (J. Davies, 1994a: 242–8). For its part, the BCW's protests against the decision were in turn seen by the wider UK political parties, and by other Welsh parties, as evidence of a pro-nationalist agenda on the part of the BCW and, in particular, on the part of the BBC in Wales, leading to a debate in the Commons the following year (Briggs, 1979: 677; J. Davies, 1994a: 248–50; Lucas, 1981: 172–6).

One positive outcome for Wales of the strength of such controversies is that they produced a climate in which there was an overall perception that Wales was an area with particular concerns relating to broadcasting (both television and radio). Partly because of this, the Pilkington Committee on Broadcasting, which was set up in 1960 and published its report two years later, heard ample representations from Wales (J. Davies, 1994a: 222–4).

One of the Pilkington report's many favourable references to the BBC's role was that the corporation was flagged up as the most appropriate site for the development of a local radio network (Crisell, 1997: 143). The report's generally withering view of the quality of commercial television had, it seems, extended to a conclusion that the nurturing of a local network needed to be entrusted to the public service broadcasters. An idea which then gained wide acceptance was that the existing regional network, of which the BBC's operation in Wales formed a part, would in due course be replaced by this local network initiative (K. Williams, 1998: 246). This regional network was indeed phased out by 1983. Arguably, however, in the context of these developments, the position of BBC Radio Wales – like that of its Scottish counterpart – was to become a somewhat anomalous one, in that its status has lain rather ambivalently between '(Welsh) national', 'regional' and 'local' (see below).

UK-wide, the BBC's first local radio station, Radio Leicester, began in 1967, the same year that BBC Radios 1, 2, 3 and 4 replaced the previous Light, Home and Third radio services. The first swathe of eight such stations were all in England, although Swansea lobbied – unsuccessfully – for its inclusion in the second batch. Swansea's hopes, and those of other Welsh localities which subsequently expressed a similar interest, were definitively dashed by the Sound Broadcasting Act 1972, which outlawed the setting up of any BBC local radio stations within any of the so-called 'national regions'. As confirmation of this, the BCW were informed by the managing director of BBC radio that – remarkably – 'local radio in Wales [would] be a station for the whole of Wales' (J. Davies, 1994a: 308).

As regards Welsh-language developments, partly due to the protests of Cymdeithas yr Iaith Gymraeg (Welsh Language Society) – which included a very detailed set of written proposals, presented to the BCW in 1971, relating to the future development of Welsh-language radio – and those of other groups, the BBC eventually agreed to the splitting of VHF and medium-wave services in Wales so as to allow English and Welsh programmes on different wavelengths, something which had been technically possible since the mid-1950s (J. Davies, 1994a: 311–15; Lucas, 1981: 230).

The Crawford Committee had been set up in 1973 to look at the development of broadcasting in the 'national regions' (as well as in rural areas of England). Its report, published in November 1974, raised a number of significant concerns about the need to protect and enhance Welsh-language provision, to the extent that it strongly endorsed a proposal which had come from the BCW for the setting up of a fully fledged Welsh-language public service radio channel.[13] As envisaged by the BCW, this channel would broadcast one hundred hours a week in Welsh, alongside the eighty hours to be broadcast by Radio Wales. The path had thus been cleared for the creation of BBC Radio Cymru. However, this channel was to begin transmission, a few years later, during a period when the plans for ending the BBC's radio monopoly – confirmed in the Sound Broadcasting Act 1972 – were beginning to be implemented.

The age of commercial competition

What can now be seen as the present-day age of competition between public service radio and a commercially funded radio sector – and of simultaneous competition within this latter sector – was ushered in by legislation passed by the Conservative UK government of the time, in the form of the Sound Broadcasting Act 1972. The Conservatives had been attracted by the idea of widening audience choice, and by the provision of an economic incentive to potential owners and advertisers (Crisell, 1997: 186).

One effect of this legislation was to create a regulatory body with responsibility for a radio sector which was about to expand. Before then, the UK-wide regulator with responsibility for broadcasting had been the Independent Television Authority (ITA), which had a remit restricted to (commercial) television only. The 1972 Act created the Independent Broadcasting Authority (IBA), one of whose specific briefs was to oversee the setting up of a number of commercially owned local radio stations, in effect sanctioning a certain amount of direct competition for BBC Radio, in particular its then burgeoning local network.

As regards the Wales-specific political debates which led up to the 1972 Act, there was a very distinct echo of the arguments put forward in the 1930s regarding the need to nurture and disseminate a genuine sense of Welsh identity, with the implicit view that the BBC had failed to take such a responsibility seriously. Witness, for example, the speech to Parliament of the MP William Gibson in March 1966:

> If local sound broadcasting was properly organised, and was not a monopoly of either the BBC or the independent companies . . . it could cater for local communities . . . It is important to foster the local communities and the differences which exist in language, accent, outlook and culture. We get far too much Londonisation throughout the country these days. (House of Commons, 1966)

Such sentiments carry a very clear resonance with those of, for example, Saunders Lewis in his representations to the BBC's director general (J. Davies, 1994a: 83). The idea took root, in other words, that Wales had particularly strong reasons for encouraging a wider diversity of voices – and, by logical necessity, of ownership – in radio broadcasting. This question of ownership became crucial, however, no less in Wales than in the rest of the UK. Under political pressure to ensure both independent ownership and public access in the new commercial radio sector, the IBA sought to foster local investment and public involvement. Such an approach was ratified by the Annan Committee's (1977) statement of priorities for local broadcasting. However, for a variety of practical, commercial and political reasons,[14] chief among them the deregulatory priorities of the Thatcher government which came to power in 1979, it would not be until the 1980s that a significant flowering of local, commercially owned radio stations was recorded, a process which has led to hundreds of ILRs being in existence around the UK by the early twenty-first century.

This process was mirrored within Wales, in that, while the first commercial radio station, Swansea Sound, began operating in 1974, the second, Cardiff Broadcasting Company (CBC), would not appear until the start of the next decade. There has subsequently been a steady increase in number, to the extent that by early 2004 there were a total of fourteen independent local radio services across Wales. UK-wide trends have also been reflected in the steadily increasing liberalization of the regulatory climate affecting the commercial radio sector. Both Swansea Sound and CBC reflected to some extent the IBA's priorities, in that the Swansea station was established under local ownership and the Cardiff station arose as a community-based initiative, being awarded the franchise at a time when the IBA was seen as proactively sympathetic to such initiatives and sceptical of more profit-oriented enterprises (Barnard, 1989; Crisell, 1997: 188). In line with the lobbying tradition which the city's early broadcasting campaigners had established in the 1920s (in reaction to the BBC preference for Cardiff as its operating centre within Wales), Swansea had campaigned hard during the late 1960s for the establishment of its own non-BBC station (Barlow et al., 2003).[15]

As a further echo of the initial decades of broadcasting in Wales, a distinct strand of this political and professional lobbying was a series of calls for Welsh-language broadcasting. Among other consequences, this led to these two pioneering commercial stations in Wales devoting a significant amount of airtime to Welsh-language programmes (Independent Broadcasting Authority, 1981: 41, 47–8; A. Jones, 1993: 235).

The technological background to this debate should also be kept in mind. The allocation of frequencies to Welsh broadcasting had been a source of concern in the 1960s (House of Commons, 1969) and 1970s. The growing profile of Scottish and Welsh nationalism in the 1970s and the delays in the spread of the BBC and ILR in Wales, alongside the growing demands for a Welsh-language TV channel, made technological issues highly political, hence the decision to set up the Crawford Committee. The relative cheapness of radio broadcasting compared to television, and latterly the proliferation of digital channels, underpinned the views of those who argued that radio could be made more local and accessible, and played a part in encouraging the idea that community radio was feasible (Lewis and Booth, 1989: 105–6).

Economic factors became especially important at this stage, however. From the 1970s onwards the economic fragility of ILR led to criticisms of the system administered by the IBA. Some argued that the IBA's public service requirements on ILRs undermined the financial health of the industry, others that the IBA eventually diluted these obligations in order to aid the licensees (Local Radio Workshop, 1978; Phillips, 1982, 1983). The structure of the industry, plus the precarious financial basis on which it rested for many years, contributed to the collapse of both CBC and Gwent Broadcasting by 1985 (M. Carter, 1998: 25; Independent Broadcasting Authority, 1986: 35; Lewis and Booth, 1989: 108–14), and provided a basis, until the 1990s, for a move in Wales away from such strongly community-based projects towards more commercially driven ones (Carter, 1998). By the late 1990s, the change in political climate and the growth of a more market-oriented system of radio regulation led to the growth of group ownership in Welsh commercial radio. The idea that Welsh radio should be locally owned and strongly related to the local community was thereafter no longer a main regulatory goal (*Airflash*, 1993: 8–9; Carter, 1998).

We might therefore sum up this early period of the post-monopoly radio age as being one in which, outside the BBC, two distinct, nascent models of radio could be identified in Wales, one 'commercial' or 'free market', the other 'community' (Lewis and Booth, 1989). The community model, where local people sought to provide a service for 'public good', inspired developments at CBC, Radio Ceredigion and Radio Maldwyn. By the end of the 1990s, however, it was clear that only the commercial model had survived, at least within the ILR sector itself.

Figure 5.2 shows the distribution of ILR services around Wales, as of 2004, revealing a certain concentration around the populous southern areas. Outside the ILR sector there remains a vestige of the 'community' model in the form of Access Radio.[16] Such organisations are non-profit-making, have emerged through 'grass-roots' community initiatives, and pursue goals concerned with 'public good' rather than private gain. Furthermore, they eschew the exclusivity of 'professional' media organizations by using volunteers alongside paid staff. Not only is this a demonstration of active citizenship, it also helps develop skills and may enhance employment opportunities.[17] Curran and Seaton argue that it is precisely this type of community-based radio station which provides the most perspicuous example of a controlled-market libertarian approach to the media (1997: 354), seen as a counterbalance to the gradual displacement of public service ideals by market ideology and the hegemony of professional codes of practice. Such potential benefits notwithstanding, as of 2003 Wales had only one Access Radio station, the GTFM 106.9 project, based near Pontypridd, although with the arrival of the Communications Act 2003 there have been calls for the new regulator OfCom to take proactive steps to foster the development of this form of radio around Wales (OfCom Advisory Group, 2003).

Figure 5.2: Location of ILR stations in Wales (with year of first award of licence)

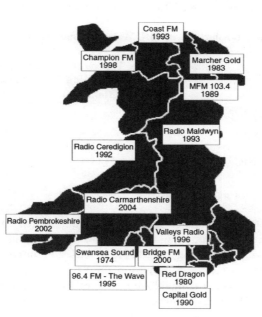

Developments in BBC radio

The launch in 1977 of the new dual service of the English-language Radio Wales and Welsh-language Radio Cymru was therefore carried out amidst the early years of commercial radio. This initial period was in reality rather limited in scope, since it consisted largely of 'opt-outs' from Radio 4. In recognition of this, the BBC in Wales actually 'relaunched' the channels just a year later, this time with a significant increase in the number of hours. By the mid-1980s, Radio Wales was broadcasting continuously for twelve hours a day, although Radio Cymru would not achieve this target until 1993, a discrepancy due partly to the BBC's use of Radio Cymru's wavelength for the broadcasting of schools' programmes (BBC Wales, 2003a; J. Davies, 1994a: 215; K. Williams, 1997a: 13). As part of a major refocusing of its broadcast output in 1995, Radio Cymru increased its time on air to eighteen hours a day (from 6 a.m. to midnight). By that stage, increased competition had arrived in the form of UK-wide radio networks created in the wake of the Broadcasting Act 1990: on medium wave, Virgin Radio and Talk Radio (subsequently renamed Talk Sport), and on FM, Classic FM.

Table 5.1: Allocation of BBC Wales's resources (2002/3)

	Hours per year	Expenditure allocation £ (millions)	Cost per hour £ (thousands)
BBC Radio Wales	6,992	9.6	1.4
BBC Radio Cymru	6,906	8.4	1.3
BBC Wales TV	788	23.8	33.0
BBC Wales on S4C	532	17.4	34.0
BBC 2W	400	5.9	36.0

Source: Adapted from BBC Wales, 2003a.

By 2002/3, the two channels' provision are summarized, in terms of both airtime and expenditure, in Table 5.1 (this table also incorporates, for comparative purposes, figures relating to television output produced by BBC Wales, including its provision for S4C). Table 5.2 gives an indication of the highly competitive nature of the provision of radio services around Wales, as it summarizes a 'snapshot' of audience figures for BBC Radio and the ILR sector (excluding Radio Ceredigion and Radio Maldwyn, as these stations were not participating in the Rajar system at the time of this survey). Also included, for comparative purposes, is the regional radio licensee, Real Radio, which is increasingly seen as a competitor to BBC Radio Wales (see Ellis, 2000: 196). The degree of competition and inter-outlet rivalry such figures engender, together with a growing UK-wide tendency since the 1980s for public service broadcasting to be judged in terms of its audience share, has the effect of placing particular importance on the regulatory regimes controlling the two sectors.

Table 5.2: Radio audiences in Wales (December 2003)

Service	Weekly reach[18] (000)	% Weekly reach[19]	% Share of listening[20]
BBC Radio Wales	459	19	9.2
BBC Radio Cymru	177	7	3.3
Total BBC	**580**	**24**	**12.5**
Bridge FM	49	31	12.4
Champion FM	35	30	13.8
Marcher Gold	22	6	2.7
MFM 103.4	72	20	10.8
Coast FM	64	29	11.8
96.4 FM The Wave	353	26	8.6
Swansea Sound	83	16	8.4
Valleys Radio	100	23	12.9
Red Dragon	312	35	14.0
Capital Gold South Wales	65	7	3.2
Real Radio	366	25	12.7

Source: Rajar, 2004.

Regulating the radio in Wales: who guards the guardians?

One of the original arguments in favour of regulating radio was that the airwaves constitute a scarce resource which can only accommodate a finite number of stations. In the words of Peter Eckersley, the BBC's first chief engineer (as cited in Curran and Seaton, 1997: 112), '[t]he BBC . . . owes its existence to the scarcity of airwaves'.[21] Such thinking is clearly still applicable, in that it is not only one of the enduring arguments in favour of public service broadcasting (Tracey, 1998), but also a key rationale for the existence of a regulatory body for the commercial sector. As a quid pro quo for access to the radio spectrum, for example, ILR stations are expected to provide services in the public interest. However, controversy has increasingly come to surround the extent to which such a body should be attentive not only to the need to protect the spectrum from overuse, in the interests of reception quality, but also to the range and quality of the material with which these airwaves are filled, and to the relationship the commercial sector has with its target communities.

Similarly, concerns have been raised about the representativeness and accountability of the mechanisms by which BBC radio in Wales is regulated. In addition, with regard to both 'public' and private sectors there are various issues surrounding the extent to which any Wales-specific components are incorporated in the regulatory set-up.

The expansion of the ILR sector in Wales has occurred under the aegis of first the IBA and subsequently – from 1991 to 2003 – the Radio Authority (RA), the regulatory body which emerged from the Broad-casting Act 1990. In addition to owning the radio transmitters, which it rented out to the ILR licensees, the IBA imposed obligations of 'range' and 'balance' (Crisell, 1997: 186). This in effect meant that, in Barnard's words: 'each of the ILR stations outside London had to provide the full range of BBC services within a smaller, localised framework, and entirely from commercial resources' (1989: 75). Towards the end of its existence, the IBA began the process of loosening these public service requirements, a process continued by the RA, which allowed the ILRs to use their own transmitters and brought in a further dilution of the 'range' and 'balance' obligations (Crisell, 1997: 216–17).

The RA in turn gave way to the 'super-regulator' OfCom, following the Communications Act 2003, and among this body's functions is the overseeing of the regulation and licensing of all ILR stations. However, at a UK-wide level criticisms were voiced from an early stage of this sector's fulfilment of its commitment to independence and 'localness' (ostensibly enshrined not just in the successive regulatory guidelines governing the allocation of their licences but also in the sector's very name).[22] The RA was, after all, a body which did not maintain any offices outside London and whose members, including the national member for Wales,[23] were appointed by the Secretary of State for Culture, Media and Sport, as opposed to the NAfW.[24]

In terms of accountability, the RA's guidelines on localness (dis-cussed further below) made no comment on ILR services being accountable to the localities they serve, a prime example of the RA's 'light touch' approach (Curran and Seaton, 1997: 337). Additionally, the NAfW has no role in relation to broadcasting, except that it is consulted on the appointment of the member for Wales on the RA Board (and other broadcasting bodies), a position supported by the Commercial Radio Companies Association (Commercial Radio Companies Association, 1998: 1).

The RA's approach and guidelines, in place during this period of main expansion of the sector and directly incorporated into the new regulator's practices (OfCom, 2004a) are worth examining in more detail, specifically from the point of view of re-licensing, 'take-over' targets and regulatory practice.

Prior to the point of licence renewal, if there were no other applicants and the licence holder is 'performing satisfactorily', the regulator was able to renew the licence automatically for a further eight years (Radio Authority, 1998: 3). Also, by obtaining a slot on a digital multiplex, an ILR operator is guaranteed an extension of the analogue licence for an additional eight years. The largest 'local' stations in Wales, Swansea Sound/The Wave 96.4 and Red Dragon/Capital Gold, are beneficiaries of this policy as their respective owners, The Wireless Group and Capital Radio, have key stakes in digital multiplexes in south and south-west Wales. In both the above scenarios there seems to be no role for members of the local community.

There appears to be a recurring pattern whereby the group or groups that pioneer radio initiatives in Wales are displaced. In considering a licence application, the regulator claims to be cautious about ensuring that 'external expertise is not merely taking over a local group, and marginalising its members to the extent that "localness" benefits might not be sustained' (Radio Authority, 1999: 5). One example is Bridge FM, where groups such as Chrysalis and Tindle Radio played the role of 'stalking horses' with minor shareholdings at the start. After approximately fifteen months, Tindle Radio gained a controlling influence, prompting the resignation of a number of local directors, a turnover in the station's personnel and, according to a number of respondents, a loss of local flavour in the programming.

There are issues about the consistency, transparency and policing of regulatory practice. As a senior person at one station indicated, being part of a large radio group enables an awareness of the decisions made in other parts of the UK by the regulator. For example, arguments which are accepted by the regulator in some contexts to support certain initiatives are rejected when put forward at other locations. Also, approaches to the regulator by one station to complain about a powerful competitor's breaching its stated music policy were met with, 'well, it's the spirit of the format rather than the words'. Perhaps not surprisingly, the same respondent concludes, 'it's a sort of "wet finger in the wind" form of regulation'.[25]

One consequence of this is that there appeared to be few expectations on the part of the stations – or of the RA itself – as to the rigour, detail or frequency of the publication of the programming schedules, nor of the need to monitor their appearance or accuracy. Moreover, even by the end of 2003 the opportunities provided by the World Wide Web for facilitating such dissemination appeared to be notably under-exploited. In fact, the ILR sector in Wales was at that stage generally making very limited use of the Internet's potential, with an almost total absence of on-line listening facilities via their webpages.

Within this context, the Communications Act 2003 has led to revival in debate over the degree of accountability of commercial broadcasting in Wales to Welsh people, in particular through the loss of a nominated Welsh member on the board of the new regulator OfCom (House of Commons, 2002; National Assembly for Wales, 2003).

Are we being served?

In view of the concerns summarized above regarding the relationship between both public and commercial radio broadcasters in Wales, on the one hand, and their respective regulatory systems, on the other, it becomes important to evaluate in more detail the service they actually provide. In particular, there is a need to bear in mind the optimism expressed by Scannell and Cardiff (1991: 304) that 'the rediscovery of local radio broadcasting by the BBC in the wake of the Pilkington Report' gave UK radio a chance to re-engage with the 'values and attitudes' of the very first period of radio broadcasting (see p. 98). The problem with such a hope was of course that the 'local' nature of BBC radio in Wales was compromised by the need to preserve the 'national region' status of Wales and Scotland. This in turn means that a particular onus is put on the ILR stations in terms of their 'localness'. In addition, it entails that the BBC's response to the challenge of incorporating a regionally and sub-regionally differentiated service becomes especially worthy of scrutiny.[26]

In the period since the arrival of BBC local radio and the ILR sector, there have been two main lines of criticism of the BBC's service, one UK-wide and one specific to Wales. A general criticism levelled at the

BBC's local/regional provision is that it has received insufficient financial resources and that there has been excessive control from London (see Lewis and Booth, 1989). Within Wales, a prominent criticism of Radio Wales is that it has shown a bias towards coverage of Cardiff and the south-west (Ellis, 2000: 194). Radio Wales's own promotional material indirectly alludes to both these criticisms, via slogans such as: 'Your Nation, Your Station. 19 hours a day of programmes made all over Wales.' In this same vein, by 2001 BBC Radio Wales had also developed a system of regional opt-outs involving Radio Gwent and Radio Clwyd (the latter had first been trialled twenty years earlier).

Figure 5.3 summarizes the overall content of the two BBC services, in terms of the number of hours of airtime devoted to 'general' programming and to news and current affairs. What is not readily apparent from such figures, however, is the extent to which the style and content of the 'general' programming, in particular, is shaped by the competitive climate summarized above. For example, while towards the end of the 1990s Radio Wales began recasting itself as a service for the whole of Wales rather than the south Wales valleys, its traditional heartland, Radio Cymru started to adopt a more populist approach to its programming than hitherto. Specifically, in changes initiated in 1995, the Welsh-language channel set out to increase the number of younger listeners by moving away from the 'sequence programming' associated with the previous period of Radio 4 'opt-outs' and towards 'strip programming'. This was a move, in other words, towards: 'fewer but longer programmes, which are personality-led, generally live and linked by the presenters rather than continuity announcers . . . an increase in personality-led music programmes . . . a more populist approach' (Ellis, 2000: 191). The effect of these changes was indeed to increase the audience in the 15–34 age group. However, this advance has arguably been achieved at the expense of the maintenance of a differentiated public service dimension, in that the changes described here have had the cumulative effect of making much of Radio Cymru's output increasingly resemble that of the ILR sector.

**Figure 5.3: Overall distribution of programme types on
BBC Radio in Wales (2002/3)**

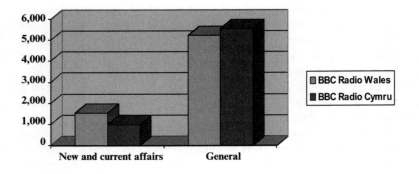

Source: Adapted from BBC Wales, 2003a.

Localness in the ILR sector

The Radio Authority's guidelines for would-be licensees, incorporated
into OfCom's framework, lay great emphasis on the concept of
'localness'. Applicants must demonstrate a 'feel for the local audience . . .
their understanding of the local community . . . and its needs', their
'involvement in local life', and so on (Radio Authority, 1999). However, it
is also the case that ever since the emergence of the ILR sector concerns
have been expressed about the accuracy of the descriptor 'local' in
commercial radio (Gorst, 1971: 6–7; Lewis and Booth, 1989: 199; Local
Radio Workshop, 1983: 15–17). The situation in Wales in 2003 indicated
that this term has an enduring flexibility. For example, while Radio
Ceredigion, Champion FM, Swansea Sound and Red Dragon were
all defined as local, they broadcast to populations of 60,000, 116,000,
500,000 and 900,000 respectively. Furthermore, evidence suggests that
Welsh-language communities located in the catchment area of Radio
Maldwyn were all but marginalized in the original licence application.
Interestingly, this is a station that continues to provide only a minimal
on-air Welsh-language presence.

Similarly, there is evidence that economic imperatives appear to take
preference over community, or broadly cultural, concerns when determining licence areas. For example, the area to which Valleys Radio
broadcasts is not seen as comprising a community, but the three

separate valleys that comprise this area are (G. Davies, 1991: 109).
Where else in the UK would a city the size of Newport be without its
own radio station? It is an integral element of the catchment area of the
Red Dragon/Capital Gold services broadcasting from Cardiff. These
decisions may have been influenced by the fact that most ILR licences
in Wales were determined and allocated over a period when the Board
of the RA operated without a member for Wales.

Networking

The trend towards consolidated and distant ownership together with
the introduction of technological developments has provoked an
increasing tendency for what Crisell has termed 'networking by stealth'
or 'a kind of syndication' (2002: 129). ILR formats for stations in Wales
indicate that local production varies considerably between stations, the
minimum being four hours, the maximum twenty hours. The overall
average is approximately fifteen hours out of a daily broadcasting
schedule of twenty-four hours. Some of these locally produced hours
may also be pre-recorded, so the broadcast is not 'live' with the presenter
in the local studio. The RA acknowledges that reductions in 'live'
presentation diminish the quality of the ILR service being offered
(Hooper, 2001: 4; Radio Authority, 2002). Such procedures have long
been a feature of US radio (see Crookes and Vittet-Philippe 1986;
Fairchild, 1999; Fornatale and Mills, 1980; Tunstall, 1986). In a sense,
they recall the first introduction, in the late 1920s, of 'simultaneous
broadcasting' technology, which essentially had a similar 'networking'
effect of allowing the same programme – usually originated in London –
to be transmitted by all other stations in the network. Though an
ideological desire for centralization may have given way to commercial
imperatives as the motivating force for such procedures, the outcome in
terms of a potential loss in local identity is comparable.

Once stations become part of a larger group there is an increased
likelihood that they will be subject to networked programmes. For
example, Coast FM (Caernarfon), Champion FM (Colwyn Bay) and
MFM 103.4 (Wrexham) are networked at certain times on a daily basis.
Along with the rest of the GWR group, these three stations are also
networked in the late evenings, allowing 'Late Night Love' to flow
across the whole of north Wales. While these developments increase
company revenue, they reduce opportunities for local employment,
local performers and other local 'voices'. This resonates with the notion

of commercial radio as 'omnisciently "local"' (Berland, 1993: 112). One respondent, proud that 'his' station did not revert to such practices, offered a view on networking: 'it doesn't matter where you are listening . . . you will hear the same jingles, the same music, the same presentation style, the same cue cards being read, and I think people, after a while, get to realise that it isn't coming from [the local station]'.[27]

ILR in Wales is far from unique in such sentiments. Crisell, for example, describes listening to a range of ILR stations around the UK as 'a reassuringly uniform experience . . . mediated by mostly "accentless" presenters whose pleasantries and platitudes seldom assume a knowledge of the locality or its culture' (2002: 128). In the Welsh context, the 'reassurance' in question might more appropriately be described as a reminder of the corporate influence on any sense of 'place' or of genuine diversity on the airwaves.

Ownership

Barnard's pithy observation (2000: 61) that 'independent' radio is now 'anything but' has a clear relevance for the Welsh situation. Many of the Welsh stations are subject to significant external and controlling interests located outside Wales. The situation as of 2003 is summarized in Table 5.3. Such ownership patterns raise issues about local accountability and public access. In our own study, a number of respondents reported that enquiries at a local station about changes in programming or style were explained as 'company policy', with the enquirer being directed to 'head office'. With major decision-makers located beyond the immediate locality, the opportunities for face-to-face communication are minimal. Furthermore, without roots in the immediate locality of a station, distant decision-makers were seen by some respondents as unlikely to have any personal commitment to the area, and thus relying on 'balance sheets' rather than a 'sense of place' to drive decisions. However, others, including some employees, stressed the benefits of being part of a large group. One in particular argued that this brings a 'national feel' and 'national resources', while still allowing the station 'to be local'.[28]

**Table 5.3: Ownership of commercial/ILR stations
in Wales (2003)**

Station	Ownership
Bridge FM	Tindle Radio
Champion FM	GWR
Marcher Gold	GWR
MFM 103.4	GWR
Coast FM	GWR
96.4 FM The Wave	The Wireless Group
Swansea Sound	The Wireless Group
Valleys Radio	The Wireless Group
Red Dragon	Capital Radio plc
Capital Gold	Capital Radio plc
Radio Ceredigion	North Wales Newspapers
Radio Maldwyn	Locally owned
Radio Pembrokeshire	Locally owned
Radio Carmarthenshire	Locally owned
Real Radio	GMG Radio Holdings

The ILR 'style' and format

The dominant commercial model has led to a format that pervades the airwaves across most of Wales. Hence, whether in Swansea, Ebbw Vale, or Bangor, 'breakfast' is likely to run from 6 a.m. to 10 a.m., followed by 'mid-day' (or similar nomenclature) between 10 a.m. and 2 p.m., with the 'prime-time' daytime period concluding with 'drive' through to 6 p.m. If 'breakfast' is 'served' by a single presenter, it will be a man, if it is a joint presentation then both sexes will be represented, but the man will retain the major role. The schedules also indicate how programmes have become increasingly homogenized. Even senior staff at Swansea Sound, where the medium wave (or AM) schedule still retains some distinctiveness, particularly in the evenings and at weekends, accept that the amount and range of specialist programming has declined significantly since the station commenced broadcasting in 1974. Hence, music is preferred over speech, popular music – itself restricted in range – is favoured over other musical genres, and most speech is non-controversial, thereby enabling an ambience that facilitates unquestioning consumption.

This process is known within the ILR industry as the construction of an ARP: an Authentic Radio Personality. In a sense, this has intriguing echoes of the Reithian policy of standardization of announcing style in the 1920s and 1930s. Reith, it will be recalled, had decreed in March 1924 that the style of announcing was to be the same in all stations in order to assert 'the collective personality of the service' (J. Davies, 1994a: 19). Reith's policy was, of course, driven more by ideological concerns, especially an antipathy towards regional identity per se. In the case of the ILRs' policy, it is born more of the desire to create and solidify a network brand and to ensure that local autonomy, including any stylistic latitude given to individual presenters, is ruthlessly constrained.

This curtailment of speech-based programming and concomitant dominance of music as the staple radio genre is another feature with curious echoes of an earlier age. The then recently established BBC service of the 1920s also prioritized music above other genres,[29] to the extent, in fact, that it gave rise 'to the belief that the transmission of music was virtually the sole function of the new medium' (J. Davies, 1994a: 7). Moreover, a 1936 article in the *North Wales Chronicle* (cited by A. Jones, 1993: 233) bemoaned the BBC's 'ten minutes of news in Welsh and an hour and a half of foxtrots!' and asked: 'Is Wales really alive?' While musical genres have clearly evolved since then, the question may well remain pertinent.

News provision

Another issue arises as a result of ILRs being described as 'music and information' stations. Given the preponderance of music, what is this information and to what extent is it representative of the local broadcast area? News comes in two forms. One is a pre-packaged format provided by the Independent Radio News service that targets the UK. This is coupled with a bulletin of two to three minutes' duration, which is described on the airwaves as consisting of 'local' news items. In fact, more than half of these latter items are, on average, either Wales-wide in focus or relating to a significantly larger regional area than the stations' stated catchment zones. Moreover, the total number of news items overtly signalled as 'local' – or otherwise identifiable as such – is almost always lower than the UK-wide items.

Some stations employ no journalists and receive their local news via a network arrangement from another station (see Radio Authority, 2002). Others generate the local news on site, while at one station it is outsourced to a company located some distance from the local area. One journalist operating in a Welsh 'heartland' confirmed that even the framing of local news was shaped by the station's 'ideal' target – the 29-year-old woman, adding, 'if you want current affairs, if you want political stories, you go to Radio Cymru'.[30] In terms of local news values, purely local items tend to relate to 'spot news' (reports of crime, accidents, fires, flooding etc.) and little attention is paid towards local authorities, institutions and other locally constituted groupings (see Hargreaves and Thomas, 2002).

Such patterns would appear to confirm the criticisms advanced by Talfan Davies, who bemoans the fact that, in the context of broadcast news, 'for too many people Wales has no locus in their personal matrix' (1999: 43) and that there is a lack of reporting of the local impact of NAfW decisions (1999: 18). However, BBC radio does not escape similar criticisms. For example, Kevin Williams argues that Radio Wales

> struggles to find a happy mean between local news, all-Wales news and British news. The main thrust of the programmes seems to be on Welsh presenters relaying British national news stories with the occasional Welsh or Welsh-based 'expert' commentating on the event. Such reporting locates the listener as being first and foremost part of a British audience. (1997a: 21)

Language issues

While Radio Ceredigion and Champion FM are seen as ILR stations with the strongest bilingual elements (Ellis, 2000: 190), most ILR services are reluctant to provide more than a minimal amount of programming in Welsh, and tend to consign it to the 'ghetto slots'. The words of a senior person at one station are insightful:

> I would suspect that our Welsh output has gone down by over 50% . . . But we had a very long conversation with [person at RA] and we said to him . . . very few people in our area speak Welsh [and] more to the point . . . I can't find anyone . . . to do the news in Welsh.[31]

Our research revealed that at a number of stations there was also pressure to justify to senior executives the extent and range of programmes being broadcast in Welsh, and to find ways of making them accessible to a wider audience. 'Presenter bilingualism' has been refined at Champion FM, and was introduced at Radio Ceredigion after North Wales Newspapers gained control of the station. A similar, but more cautious, initiative was also underway at Swansea Sound during our research.

The BBC's provision is subject to the Welsh Language Act 1993 and the corporation has accordingly developed its own 'Welsh language scheme' (BBC Wales, 2003b). Even in the case of Radio Cymru, however, there have been continuing concerns as to whether the optimum usage of the Welsh language has yet been attained. Such concerns came to a head following the changes to the Radio Cymru scheduling in the mid-1990s. The perception of some campaigning groups, such as Cymdeithas yr Iaith Gymraeg or Cylch yr Iaith (the 'Language Circle'), was that the channel was becoming over-anglicized (Ellis, 2000: 192). The latter group was also highly critical of the standard of spoken Welsh used by Radio Cymru presenters, including their use of place names. Such protests thus carry a strong echo of those raised fifty years earlier to the Welsh Regional Advisory Council (as discussed above, p. 103). The BBC has actively sought to rebut such criticisms. It commissioned a survey in 2001, for example, that appeared to show that 82 per cent of listeners 'approved of the standard of language being used on RC' (BBC Cymru Wales, 2002).

More generally, a listening environment aimed at fostering consumption and maximizing numbers of listeners is not likely to reflect the full diversity of local communities. This is not only apparent in the reluctance of some stations to provide adequate programming in Welsh, but is further evidenced in the virtual absence of Wales's ethnic minorities from the 'airwaves' (Ellis, 2000: 197). This is also the case with television (K. Williams, 1997a: 24), an issue recently recognized by BBC Wales in their appointment of a diversity adviser (BBC Cymru Wales, 2002). Other segments of the community are also 'missing' on air. As most ILR services aim to attract listeners aged between the late teens and early fifties, the needs and interests of younger and older citizens are simply disregarded.

Conclusion

A historical perspective on the development of radio in Wales reveals a distinct shift in recent decades in the way radio audiences and services are viewed. In common with its commercial counterparts,

BBC Wales has recast its listeners and viewers as 'consumers' and 'stakeholders', and its television and radio services as 'brands' and 'brand-identities' (BBC Cymru Wales, 2002). Furthermore, the ever pervasive predilection of broadcasters to 'chase' ratings shapes the type and range of programmes being broadcast. In such an environment, notions of 'public good' and 'public interest' are displaced by the mantra of 'consumer choice', leading to a situation where '[c]onsiderations of what [people] need and what is needed to build a healthy and vibrant citizenship and community are downplayed' (K. Williams, 1997a: 29).

These patterns therefore bear out Bromley's contention that 'Whether public service or "independent", the mainstream media [in Wales] are all more or less market-driven – advertisers rather than people's media. They deconstruct communities into market niches . . .' (2000: 124; see also K. Williams, 1997a: 43). This is not to say that Wales is exceptional. On the contrary, the conclusions relating to ILR in Wales are broadly in line with those drawn in other geographical contexts (see Barnard, 2000; Hendy, 2000; Tacchi, 2001) in that they point to a sector in which a set of commercial imperatives ultimately encourage the stations to view listening figures and advertising revenue as the key indicators of successful engagement with their target communities, rather than any more thoroughgoing concern for genuine 'localness' and 'public interest'. More broadly, however, a common perception persists that Tunstall's view that the 'Welsh media are much less Welsh than the Scottish media are Scottish' (1983: 228) is at least as true of the radio in Wales as of other media sectors.

However, there may still be some grounds for optimism, bearing in mind Crookes and Vittet-Philippe's argument (1986: 4) relating to Europe's 'small nations' and regional media, specifically that regional and local radio can be harnessed as 'one of the main "region-building" tools, not only in traditional cultural terms (regional awareness, cultural identity, linguistic crystallisation), but also in terms of economy (provision of jobs, sensitisation of the public to communication technologies, dynamisation of local markets, etc.)'. In Wales, ILR rarely features in public debate about the nation's media. Given the role and reach of ILR and its potential as a local medium of communication, its 'invisibility' is somewhat surprising in the context of the policy developments initiated by the NAfW. The Assembly's vision for a 'new' Wales is, after all, guided by themes of 'sustainable development', 'tackling social disadvantage' and 'equal opportunities', with the aim of promoting active citizenship, social inclusion and rejuvenating democracy (National Assembly for Wales, 2000). There is arguably, therefore, a need for policy-makers in Wales to acquire a fresh awareness of the *potential* role of radio broadcasting – perhaps especially the ILR sector – in enhancing cultural identity, promoting community regeneration and developing a well-informed citizenry: This might involve, for example, the NAfW proactively establishing closer links with ILR stations, through liaison both with the stations themselves and with interested parties in their local communities, with the aim of raising awareness and expectations of ILR's potential contribution to Welsh life. It may also entail the NAfW's Culture Committee, as part of its monitoring of the relationship between OfCom and broadcasting in Wales, paying close attention to the regulator's responsibility to ensure the fulfilment of Welsh ILRs' stated commitment to serving the public interest of local communities.

Notes

1   See Crisell, 2002: 132; Schlesinger, 1987: xv. See also the conclusion of the OfCom Advisory Group (2003: 4.10), which argues that '[r]adio has not received the attention it deserves given its great popularity'.
2   It is worth remembering that Cardiff did not become the Welsh capital until the mid-1950s, and that at the time Swansea had the bigger population, while Bristol would have been a more logical choice on geographical and engineering grounds.
3   The BBC did not become the British Broadcasting *Corporation* until 1927, following the Crawford Report and the subsequent allocation of its Royal Charter (see Lucas, 1981: 39).
4   This took the form of a ten-minute talk on St David (Lucas, 1981: 22).
5   Reception in any case depended on whether a household had a valve set or a cheaper crystal set, the latter having a twenty-mile reception limit. This meant that 'transmissions from the Cardiff and Swansea transmitters could not be heard on inexpensive sets in mid and north Wales' (J. Davies, 1994a: 35).
6   See also Mackay, 1999: 5, and Scannell and Cardiff, 1991: 321.
7   K. Williams (1998: 108) notes that these protests were known in the BBC files as 'The Welsh Controversy'.
8   This imposition of a standardized approach also extended to assumptions about gender. J. Davies (1994a: 71) records how on one occasion during the 1930s 'the best applicant [for a radio newsroom post] was a woman, but she was turned down because she could not swear or be sworn at by London when things go wrong'.
9   See chapter 6.

[10] See chapter 6 for details of the effect of this report on television broadcasting in Wales.

[11] See J. Davies (1994a: 243), who makes the point that the significance of these party political broadcasts may easily be lost on a modern-day reader, unless we bear in mind that 'until the mid 1960s the BBC transmitted nothing of a political nature during election campaigns apart from [these] broadcasts'.

[12] The radio-specific licence fee was not abolished until 1971.

[13] It is worth pointing out that not all the protesting voices were in favour of more Welsh-language broadcasting. In the immediate post-war period, for example, 'about half the people troubling to write to the BBC demanded more programmes in Welsh, and about half demanded more programmes in English' (Briggs, 1979: 101; see also Lucas, 1981: 40, 143).

[14] Among these reasons were the economic recession and competition with other media (cassette-tape recording, teletext and breakfast television). See Crisell, 1997: 187.

[15] Cardiff had also had to lobby persistently (Anon, 1967; Anon, 1983; House of Commons, 1977b; Mansfield, 1978).

[16] A consensus was reached during the OfCom consultation process that Access Radio should in due course be redesignated as 'community radio'.

[17] See Barlow (2002) for illustrations of how community media organizations in Australia provide opportunities for citizens to own, manage and operate their own local communications medium.

[18] The 'Weekly Reach' is '[t]he number of people aged 15+ who tune to a radio station within at least 1 quarter-hour period over the course of a week' (Rajar, 2004).

[19] The '% Weekly Reach' is '[t]he Weekly Reach expressed as a percentage of the Population within the [transmission area]' (Rajar, 2004).

[20] The 'Market Share' is '[t]he percentage of all radio listening hours that a station accounts for within its transmission area' (Rajar, 2004).

[21] See also Briggs, 1965: 321.

[22] See for example Local Radio Workshop, 1983.

[23] It is worth noting that several ILR licences in Wales were allocated during the 1990s before the appointment of a national member for Wales to the Radio Authority Board.

[24] Similar arrangements applied to Welsh representation on the Broadcasting Standards Commission.

[25] This respondent was interviewed in December 2002 as part of the ESRC-funded project referred to on page vii and page 9. Interviews were granted on condition of anonymity. The information relating to Bridge FM in the preceding paragraph comes from interviews conducted for the same project.

[26] Scannell and Cardiff themselves make a similar point: 'whether the radio stations outside London operated by the BBC and the commercial stations in the Independent Local Radio network actually amount to a truly local service today is a matter of contention' (1991: 304).

[27] Interview conducted May 2002. See note 25 above.

28 Interview conducted December 2002. See note 25 above.
29 This similarity even extends to an end-of-schedule concentration on 'dance music'.
30 Interview conducted June 2002. See note 25 above.
31 Interview conducted May 2002. See note 25 above.

6

Television in Wales:
The Small Screen in Perspective

Television in Wales dates from the early 1950s. From a hesitant start under the BBC and then Independent Television, it grew remarkably quickly into the dominant medium of popular communication in the country. Television was the culmination of a series of technical innovations that went back to the nineteenth century. Its immediate predecessors were cinema and radio. Like these technologies its appeal lay in its immediacy, but also in its visual and aural impact and the multiple ways in which it could entertain people.

Building on the pre-existing organizational framework established for radio by the BBC, it gradually developed its own life. Television was framed by specific legislation. It developed its own system of organization and culture; it related to its audiences in particular ways. In Wales, like the press and radio, it was both part of wider developments in UK society and the focus of specific controversies over language, nationhood and culture, controversies that had been a feature of the other developments in mass communications addressed in this book.

In this survey we explore some areas of this complex social institution, examining its growth and development, the system of controls to which it was subject, aspects of its programming and its relationship with viewers and the ongoing issues of its connection with culture, language and the national question in Wales.

The BBC and television in Wales 1950–60

The BBC launched its first TV service in London on 2 November 1936. The service only ever reached a small number of middle- and upper-class Londoners able to afford the expensive sets before it was closed down for the duration of the Second World War (1939–45). Television services were resumed by the BBC in 1946. Thereafter the BBC began to roll out the service by building transmitters across the United Kingdom.

The arrival of TV in Wales was a slow process. Initially it came through overlap from transmitters serving England. Many Welsh households were able to pick up the signal from the Sutton Coldfield transmitter, opened on 17 December 1949; it reached parts of Monmouthshire, Glamorgan, Breconshire, Radnorshire, Flintshire, Denbighshire and coastal Caernarvonshire. By May 1950 there were over 1,000 holders of the requisite combined TV and radio licence in Wales. Reception in north Wales improved with the opening of the Holme Moss transmitter from northern England in October 1951. By May 1952 there were 10,048 licences in Wales. Complaints that the BBC was slow to set up a transmitter for Wales were common. The solution arrived at by the BBC, and one accepted by the BBC's Welsh Advisory Council, was a transmitter at Wenvoe, serving Wales and south-west England (J. Davies, 1994a: 171–5).

A Welsh Advisory Council had been established in 1947, and following the recommendations of the Beveridge Committee (1949–51), together with political pressure from Wales, the government inserted a requirement into the BBC's 1952 Royal Charter, establishing a Broadcasting Council for Wales, which would have responsibility for the BBC's 'Home' radio service in Wales and an advisory role in relation to TV. The Broadcasting Council for Wales met for the first time in January 1953 (J. Davies, 1994a: 175–81, 393). The demands for a Welsh voice in the BBC had, in part, been met. When in 1960 the Conservative government of Harold Macmillan (1957–63) appointed the Pilkington Committee to report on broadcasting in the UK, it had a Welsh member. He was Dr Elwyn Davies, a Welsh speaker, secretary to the Council of the University of Wales, and brother of the BBC's Welsh programme director, Hywel Davies (Briggs, 1995: 270).

The 1950s witnessed a steady growth of TV viewing in Wales. By 1958, in the UK, the number of TV and radio licences exceeded the number of radio licences. In Wales, by March 1959 half of Welsh households were licensed to receive TV. After the arrival of the Wenvoe transmitter in 1952, and up to 1957, cinema attendances in Wales dropped by 28.6 per cent. In 1960, 60 per cent of Welsh homes had a TV, a figure which had risen to 92 per cent by 1969. By 1961, the next stage in TV, colour television, was put on display at the Royal Welsh Show, to whet the public's appetite (Briggs, 1995: 185, 676; J. Davies, 1994b: 635; 1994a: 234, 259, 394).

Commercial television in Wales 1953–60

In 1953 the Conservative government under Winston Churchill, which had been elected in 1951, published plans for commercial TV in the UK. The Television Act became law in 1954. It established a system of regional commercial TV companies, funded by advertisements placed between programmes and in programme breaks. The licences were awarded by a new Independent Television Authority (ITA), based in London, whose members were appointed by the government. The Act had been the consequence of a period of intense political debate, pitting the supporters of non-commercial public service broadcasting against those who argued there was no contradiction between commerce and the public service goals of UK television (Briggs, 1979; J. Davies, 1994a: 206, 225; Sendall, 1982).

London's ITV service started in September 1955. In February 1956 the Birmingham service started, which could be received on the fringes of mid Wales. In May, Granada television started transmission from Manchester. This meant that most of the inhabitants of north-east Wales and many in north-west Wales could receive Granada if they had the right set (J. Davies, 1994a: 212, 394). Like the BBC, the ITA did not see establishing a specifically Welsh TV service as a priority. So, Welsh TV viewers gained access to commercial TV only in a piecemeal fashion.

The ITA advertised a contract covering only south Wales and south-west England. As with the early organization of the BBC radio services, and the placing of the BBC's transmitter at Wenvoe, these decisions were made from a London perspective. This perspective continued to treat Wales as a collection of regions, attached to parts of England, rather than as a distinct geographical and cultural entity.[1] The company that won the contract was Television Wales and West (TWW), which started transmissions in February 1958, almost three years after the initiation of the London service. Little of the investment in the company came from Wales. Its main investors were the UK impresario Jack Hylton (25 per cent), the *News of the World* (20.5 per cent) and, later, the *Liverpool Daily Post*, which acquired 14 per cent. The company was not required under the terms of the 1954 Act to provide programmes in Welsh. However, under pressure from the ITA's member for Wales, Alban Davies, TWW agreed to provide some Welsh-language programmes, but only if it could do so economically (J. Davies, 1994a: 225–6, 394; Sendall, 1982: 217).

Concern about the lack of an all-Wales TV service exercised the minds of Welsh broadcasters, educationalists and politicians. In 1958 the University of Wales set up a committee to inquire into the television services in Wales. In November 1959, the Lord Mayor of Cardiff convened a conference to look at ways of establishing a satisfactory TV service for Wales. Divisions emerged amongst those who wished to see the BBC and those who wanted a commercial contractor to provide the service. When, in 1961, the ITA invited applications for a service to cover west and north-west Wales a group emerged from those associated with the 1959 conference and made a bid for the contract. It was led by Hywel Williams, the director of education for Flintshire, and included Gwynfor Evans of Plaid Cymru.

Television Wales West North (TWWN) began broadcasting on 14 September 1962, before two of its key transmitters were operational. It initially provided eleven hours of Welsh and Welsh-interest programmes per week; this was a costly commitment for the company, imposed on it by the Post Office in London.[2] The weakness of the size of its advertising base, plus a lack of financial acumen and over-optimistic expectations by the company, plunged TWWN almost immediately into a series of economic crises. It survived for a short period, largely through subsidy from the ITA and its rival TWW. By September 1963 TWW had bought TWWN and their output was merged in January 1964 (J. Davies, 1994a: 217–18, 227–30; I. Evans, 1997).

The BBC from 1962 to 1977

The period between the publication of the Pilkington Report (Pilkington Committee, 1962) and the Annan Committee report (1977) on broadcasting witnessed the consolidation and expansion of BBC TV services in Wales. Pilkington was published on 27 June 1962, and, in its criticism of ITV's commercialism and praise for the BBC, it paved the way for the consolidation of TV broadcasting in the UK around a clearer public service orientation for the next twenty-five years. Pilkington had received a great deal of comment from Wales and recommended that a distinct BBC Wales TV be established. In July 1962 a government White Paper signalled its willingness to permit a BBC Wales TV service, with its output the responsibility of the Broadcasting Council for Wales (J. Davies, 1994a: 230–4).

BBC Wales was launched on 9 February 1964, functioning as a transmitter of London-based programming, but with a significant amount of output branded as BBC Wales. BBC2 was launched in 1964 and was meant to provide a distinctive alternative strain of programming to the main BBC and ITV channels. From September 1965 it became available in Wales. While BBC2 began its first colour transmissions in August 1967, BBC Wales's first colour TV transmission, a programme on the Llangollen Eisteddfod, was not broadcast until July 1970. By the early 1970s BBC2 was available to 90 per cent of the Welsh population (J. Davies, 1994a: 275, 282, 318, 395).

Commercial television in Wales, 1962–77

TWW, having taken over TWWN and merged their output from 1 January 1964, retained the Welsh commercial TV franchise until 1967, broadcasting to Wales and south-west England. From February 1965 it had the additional benefit of a new transmitter covering south Wales (Briggs, 1995: 1042; J. Davies, 1994a: 232, 394).

There had been much criticism of TWW's programming performance, and of the facts that its headquarters were in London and ten of its seventeen directors lived outside the area. So, when in 1967 a new round of contracts was awarded by the ITA, TWW became the first ITV company to lose its franchise. The contract went to Harlech TV, chaired by Lord Harlech, an ex-ambassador to the United States. Harlech continued to serve the two areas when it started broadcasting in March 1968, a population of 3,294,000 in the west of England and one of 2,174,000 in Wales. This made it a medium-sized ITV company, ranking sixth out of fourteen in order of size of the population it had in its catchment area (J. Davies, 1994a: 280–1; Potter, 1989: 16–17).

While it remained the commercial contractor for the next thirty years, Harlech TV suffered occasionally from cyclical drops in advertising revenue, as in 1969 when an average decrease of 5.5 per cent in revenue for the sector led it to cut programme budgets, and again in 1970 when its attempts to diversify its investments out of TV proved disappointing. In all of these cases, though, it retained the active support of the ITA, even though its programming bore no marked similarities to the plans it had outlined in its application (J. Davies, 1994a: 281; House of Commons, 1969; Potter, 1989: 80–2).

Criticism of ITV's programming had, by the 1970s, widened into criticisms of the range of programming and the accountability of the whole industry. When in 1974 the Labour government decided to set up a committee under Lord Annan, provost of University College London, a Welsh representative was appointed to serve on the inquiry. He was A. Dewi Lewis, chairman of the Dyfed Health Authority and a former grammar school headmaster (O'Malley, 1998; Potter, 1989: 224–5).

After Annan – satellites and markets

After Annan reported in 1977, the two most important developments affecting television in Wales were the arrival of Sianel Pedwar Cymru (S4C) and the change of UK broadcasting policy that occurred after 1979. Starting with the Conservative administrations of Margaret Thatcher (1979–90) and John Major (1990–7), and continuing under the Labour governments of Tony Blair (1997–2001, 2001–), official policy on broadcasting shifted towards the deliberate increase in commercial forces across the industry (O'Malley, 2001).

The *Report of the Committee on Financing the BBC* (Home Office, 1986), more generally known after the name of its chairman as the Peacock Report, argued that future policy should promote the market delivery of TV services, with public service provision operating as a relatively small-scale offering of services that the market could not supply. While the BBC remained intact and with its licence-fee funding relatively secure in the 1980s and 1990s, it was subjected to an intense period of reconstruction to make it more competitive internally and externally and to move it into the age of satellite and digital TV and the Internet. A series of laws, the 1990 and 1996 Broadcasting Acts and the Communications Act 2003, opened up the UK's TV market. It led to the rapid growth of an independent production sector, particularly in Wales, and the arrival of intense competition for ITV's advertising revenue from satellite providers such as Sky TV (Curran and Seaton, 2003; O'Malley, 1994).[3]

As a result, the duopoly that had emerged in Welsh TV after 1952 – BBC and ITV (Harlech) – was shaken. In 1984, BBC Wales became BBC1 Wales and BBC2 became BBC2 Wales. Under the director-generalship of John Birt from 1992, BBC Wales was part of a general restructuring of the corporation which involved the introduction of an internal market, known as 'producer choice'. John Birt was intent on making the BBC more competitive in the emerging digital age of satellite and Internet communications, and believed this could be done, in part, by importing practices from the private sector (J. Davies, 1994a: 373, 384; O'Malley, 2003).

The Broadcasting Act 1990 introduced the auctioning of ITV franchises. The Independent Broadcasting Authority was replaced by an Independent Television Commission, which oversaw the auction in 1991. It had to accept the highest bidder for a franchise, except where the quality of programmes offered was better than those offered by the highest bidder. HTV beat off three rivals, but at a high price. It had to pay £20,530,000 for the privilege of running the service (Bonner and Ashton, 1998: 421, 457).

So, in Wales, the 1980s and 1990s saw both the BBC and HTV working in a much more exacting financial environment. This included competition from cable and satellite providers. In the UK the number of homes receiving cable and satellite TV rose from 2,302,000 in 1992 to 10,278,000 in 2001 (BARB, 2003). A study in the 1990s commented that by the middle of the decade the take-up for cable in Wales was higher than in the UK as a whole (Mackay and Powell, 1997: 26–7). Multi-channel homes in Wales (served by satellite, cable and digital) continued to make considerable headway, achieving a much higher rate of take-up than in the UK as a whole, as Table 6.1 shows.

Table 6.1: Multi-channel penetration in
Wales and the UK, 2000–3

Year end	Multi-channel penetration in the UK (individuals) %	Multi-channel penetration in Wales (individuals) %
2000	45.1	49.2
2001	49.5	54.2
2002	52.0	63.4
2003 (Sept)	55.4	68.9

Source: S4C, 2004: 28.

By the late 1990s a new ecology of TV broadcasting had emerged in Wales. TV was no longer the preserve of the BBC and ITV, but included new terrestrial channels such as Channel 4 and Channel 5, S4C and hundreds of digital, cable and satellite channels (Curran and Seaton, 2003; Welsh Economy Research Unit, 2001: 8–9).

The emergence of Sianel Pedwar Cymru (S4C)

S4C emerged from a set of cultural debates in Wales from the 1920s onwards, which connected language, national identity, radio and television. The political background out of which the channel emerged provided a vital context for those debates, was itself part of those debates, and without it the development of television in Wales after 1952 cannot be understood properly.

Pressure for a separate TV service, in one form or another, existed in Wales from the 1950s. In 1957, Gwynfor Evans of Plaid Cymru joined the BBC's Broadcasting Council for Wales (BCW) and pressed the case for more Welsh programming on BBC TV. Within the BBC, the Controller for Wales, Alun Oldfield-Davies, wrote to the Director-General, Ian Jacob, in 1958, arguing for a separate BBC Wales TV channel, for, if not, he suggested, 'there are signs that other interested parties will do so' (J. Davies, 1994a: 217, 220–1).

Gwynfor Evans presented the case for a Broadcasting Corporation of Wales to the Pilkington Committee of 1960–2, and in 1961 the government rejected a request from the BBC for a separate BBC Wales network on the grounds that the ITA was developing plans for commercial TV in Wales (J. Davies, 1994a: 222–4; G. Evans, 2001: 99). These were the plans that resulted in the establishment of TWWN (see above, p. 130). Radio, which had been the focus of nationalist interest in the 1930s and 1940s had, by the late 1950s, been replaced by television.

It was the BCW which invited the playwright and founder of Plaid Cymru, Saunders Lewis to deliver the 1962 BBC Annual Lecture in Wales. He chose to concentrate on what he saw as the threat to Welsh language and culture then facing Wales, in his lecture 'Tynged yr Iaith'. The lecture stimulated the foundation of Cymdeithas yr Iaith Gymraeg (Welsh Language Society). This body embarked on a period of direct action to win official status for the Welsh language and also an intermittent campaign over almost two decades for a Welsh-language television service (J. Davies, 1994a: 253, 272, 394). The 1960s and 1970s in Wales was a period when Welsh nationalist sentiment played a key part in the formation of Welsh political and cultural life. This found expression in the establishment of the Welsh Office in 1964, the Welsh Arts Council in 1967, the Welsh Sports Council in 1972, the Welsh TUC in 1973 and the Welsh Consumer Council in 1975. Thus pressure for a distinctively Welsh TV service was part of a wider push for the establishment of distinctively Welsh cultural and political institutions (J. Davies, 1994a: 319).

In 1968, 200 members of Cymdeithas yr Iaith Gymraeg marched on the BBC buildings in Cardiff demanding more Welsh-language TV, and later in the year sit-ins were organized at BBC offices in Bangor and Cardiff. The following year the society published a pamphlet calling for a separate Welsh-language TV and radio network (J. Davies, 1994a: 289; Tomos, 1982: 39). Speaking in 1969, Gwynfor Evans summed up sentiments about the relative neglect of Wales in the planning of the UK's broadcasting structure:

> In discussing broadcasting in the future, a Welshman must be very much aware that in the past, at any rate, in the 1960s, '50s, '40s and '30s, no Government has ever attempted to devise a system of broadcasting in Wales suited to and adequate for the needs of Wales. They have not attempted to give priority to those needs.

He had in mind the government's plans to add an extra channel to the existing three channels (BBC1, BBC2 and ITV). He wanted a Broadcasting Corporation for Wales, funded by the licence fee and advertising, and running all four channels: 'One of these four channels should be devoted to the Welsh language, or at least, to the Welsh language and educational programmes. This is possibly the only way of securing fairness of treatment for our national language' (House of Commons, 1969).

During the 1970s the demand for a distinctively Welsh service gradually achieved acceptance at Westminster. This was, in part, due to the fact that the Labour governments of the period (1974–9) had very small majorities in the House of Commons. They therefore relied increasingly on the votes of the nationalist parties, Plaid Cymru and the Scottish Nationalists. It was also due to the continuance of political campaigning in Wales. In 1970 Plaid Cymru organized a non-political conference on broadcasting in Wales. Later in the year Cymdeithas yr

Iaith Gymraeg, submitted a document to the BBC's BCW arguing for two full TV services for Wales, one in English and one in Welsh. In 1971 the BCW agreed to look into the proposals, aware as they were that these ideas had sympathizers in the University of Wales and in Parliament (J. Davies, 1994a: 290–1).

In 1971 three language activists broke into Granada TV in Manchester causing limited damage to equipment. By June 1972, broadcasting in Wales was on the agenda of the Welsh Parliamentary Grand Committee, by which time many Welsh Labour MPs were in favour of a separate Welsh TV channel (J. Davies, 1994a: 293; Tomos, 1982: 42). The issue had by then gone to the heart of nationalist sentiment in Wales. In July 1972 magistrates in Bala 'gave absolute discharges' to a minister, two headmistresses and two teachers, who had refused to buy TV licences because the broadcasting system had too few Welsh-language programmes and as such was a threat to the language and culture of Wales (Fishlock, 1972).

In April 1973 a conference organized by the archbishop of Wales called on the Post Office to support a fourth channel for Wales, and in that month the Postmaster General, Sir John Eden, announced the establishment of a committee, chaired by Sir Stewart Crawford, which was charged with examining the Broadcasting Authorities' plans for coverage of television and sound broadcasting in Scotland, Wales, Northern Ireland and rural England. By the early 1970s then, there was a clear recognition at Westminster of the need to respond to the demands coming from Wales (J. Davies, 1994a: 296; House of Commons, 1973).

In February 1974 the Labour Party won the general election. In April, Home Secretary Roy Jenkins announced a committee of inquiry into the future of broadcasting in the UK, chaired by Lord Annan (J. Davies, 1994a: 299; House of Commons, 1974). Crawford reported in November, repeating the widely held view that there was a link between the decline in the numbers of people able to speak Welsh and the watching of English-language TV:

> It was put to us forcibly that if the young watch mainly English-language programmes the decline of the Welsh language will continue . . . The need for more programmes in Welsh is seen as urgent if the present decline is not to go beyond the point of no return. (Potter, 1989: 185)

In the allocation of a fourth channel, priority needed to be given in Wales to a separate Welsh-language service, even if this meant government subsidy (Briggs, 1995: 999–1000). The Welsh Language Society suspended its campaign of direct action as a result of Crawford's recommendations. In January 1975 the government responded by setting up the Siberry Committee 'to make proposals about the use of the fourth television channel in Wales' (House of Commons, 1975a; Tomos, 1982: 44). Siberry reported to the Home Office in July 1975, but the report was not published until November. While it provided a blueprint for implementing Crawford, in February 1976 the government announced that the general economic crisis which the UK faced meant it could not act immediately on the report. As a result, Cymdeithas yr Iaith Gymraeg renewed its campaign of direct action (J. Davies, 1994a: 329, 330; House of Commons, 1975b; Tomos, 1982: 45).

When it reported in 1977, the Annan Committee recommended the establishment of a Welsh fourth channel:

> The proposals of the Siberry Working Party for establishing a fourth television channel in Wales broadcasting in the Welsh language should be implemented as soon as the government can find the necessary finance. It should be operated jointly by the BBC and IBA at least until the new Authority is established. (HMSO, 1977: 483)

In 1978 the Labour government endorsed this recommendation (House of Commons, 1977a, 1978; J. Davies 1994a: 339). By this stage a general election was imminent. The Conservative Party went into the election on 3 May 1979 with a commitment to a single Welsh-language TV service, something which HTV was on record as opposing. The Conservatives won the election (J. Davies, 1994a: 337; Potter, 1989: 296). In September 1979, the Conservative Home Secretary, William Whitelaw, reneged on this commitment. A single Welsh-language service would not be attractive to advertisers and so he proposed that the ITV contractor and BBC Wales would each carry Welsh-language programmes. This may have been economically defensible, as a lack of advertising revenue would have meant government subsidy. Yet Crawford had recognized the need for subsidy, and Whitelaw's announcement overturned a consensus forged amongst opinion-formers and politicians in Wales and Westminster over the previous decade, and which prior to the 1979 election had embraced both main political parties (J. Davies, 1994a: 337; Potter, 1989: 296).

There followed an intensive campaign in Wales to overturn the decision. In November 1979, three prominent Welsh-language activists,

Ned Thomas, Pennar Davies and Meredydd Evans, switched off a TV transmitter at Pencarreg and were arrested. Subsequently, public meetings were held across Wales and more than 2,000 people refused to pay their TV licence. In the spring of 1980, the sixty-eight-year-old president of Plaid Cymru, Gwynfor Evans, announced that from 6 October 1980 he would fast to death unless the government changed its mind (J. Davies, 1994a: 395; Potter, 1989: 299; Tomos, 1982: 48–9).

In September 1980, the combination of the fear of widespread unrest in Wales and pressure from prominent figures in the Welsh political establishment, led by Lord Cledwyn of Penhros, a former Labour Secretary of State for Wales, resulted in the government's reversing its position. It agreed to set up a separate Welsh fourth channel. The Home Secretary would appoint a Welsh Fourth Channel Authority, which would acquire and schedule programmes for the new channel, but not produce any. It would take about ten hours per week of Welsh-language programmes from the BBC, free of charge, eight from HTV on reasonable commercial terms and about four hours from independent producers. A 'substantial proportion' of programmes had to be in Welsh, and these were to dominate peak-hour programming between 6.30 and 10 p.m. When programmes were not in Welsh, they were to come from the English Channel 4 service. The ITV companies were expected to pay a levy to the IBA to pay for the service, but in return the government would take this into account when deciding their level of taxation. Thus, in effect, the Conservative government had agreed to Crawford's view that a fourth channel for Wales would have to be subsidized (J. Davies, 1994a: 334–5; Potter, 1989: 296–303).

In order to meet its commitment to S4C, the BBC added another 350 people to its staff in Wales. The channel went on air in November 1982. In November and December 1982, 45 per cent of its Welsh-language programmes were from the BBC, 36 per cent from HTV and 19 per cent from independents. In its early months it attracted up to one-third of Welsh speakers (J. Davies, 1994a: 378–9). In retrospect, the emergence of S4C can be seen as the consequence of long-standing concerns in Welsh-language cultural and political circles about the impact of communications on the survival of Welsh-language culture. In addition, it was the result of concerted and focused political lobbying and direct action. It was a complex process, but what stands out is the extent to which no other development in broadcasting in the UK from 1922 onwards had been the product of such a prolonged and popular political campaign.

Controlling television in Wales

Television in Wales has been controlled from London since its inception. The House of Commons has established a legal framework governing almost all aspects of the organization, economics and content of Welsh TV. The BBC is controlled through a legal instrument known as a Royal Charter. Since 1926 this charter has been renewed at ten- or fifteen-year intervals by successive governments. Commercial TV in Wales has been regulated through a series of Acts of Parliament, the most important of which were passed in 1954, 1964, 1981, 1990, 1996 and 2003. The BBC, particularly since 1990, has had aspects of its activities directed by these statutes. The Communications Act 2003, for instance, placed some of the BBC's activities under the supervision of the Office of Communications (OfCom), the body which also thereafter regulated commercial radio and television (Curran and Seaton, 2003; J. Davies, 1994a).

Formal control over BBC Wales rests with the BBC's Board of Governors, which is based in London and which has always been appointed by the government. Commercial TV in Wales (TWW, TWWN, HTV) up to 1991 was controlled by the ITA and then by the IBA. The Independent Television Commission (ITC) had this task from 1991 until the end of 2003, and from 2004 onwards OfCom took over. The members of the governing boards of these bodies have always been government appointees. Since the 1950s the BBC has had a national governor for Wales on the BBC's Board of Governors. These have been chosen from amongst individuals prominent in Welsh public life, education, politics or industry. The first national governor, Lord Macdonald of Gwaunysgor (1952–60), had served the Labour government of 1945–50, and was a teetotal, Welsh-speaking Methodist lay preacher. Glanmor Williams (1965–71), Alwyn Roberts (1979–86) and Merfyn Jones (2002–) were all from the University of Wales (J. Davies, 1994a: 278, 340). A similar type of person was selected to represent Wales on the boards of the ITA and the IBA. Lord Aberdare (1954–6) was a former chairman of the National Advisory Council for Physical Training and Recreation; Mr J. Alban Davies (1956–64) was a businessman and former high sheriff of Cardiganshire; and Professor Huw Morris Jones (1972–82) was professor of social theory and institutions at the University College of North Wales, Bangor (Potter, 1989: 303).

Both organizations had advisory committees, which contained figures from cultural, political and business life in Wales. The BCW, for instance, played a prominent role from the 1950s onwards in pressing the interests of BBC Wales with the Board of Governors (J. Davies, 1994a). The IBA operated a General Advisory Council and individual ones for Scotland, Wales and Northern Ireland (Potter, 1989: 96). In 1977–8, for example, the authority's Welsh Committee met eight times, at Cardiff, Harlech, Wrexham, Newtown and Newport. It discussed the Annan Report, UHF reception in Wales, audience research and children's programmes (Independent Broadcasting Authority, 1978: 113–14). The Communications Act 2003 established a board for OfCom, without national representation for Wales, although Welsh interests were represented on its Advisory Committee for the Nations and Content Board. The BBC was not affected in this respect by the Act, and retained the BCW (OfCom, 2004a; Wales, World, Nation, 2003).

The system of control of Welsh broadcasting at a formal level has therefore always been centralized in London, and exercised through government-appointed bodies. This has provided the structures through which indirect supervision has been exercised over programme makers, and through which the opinion of the culturally and politically influential people in Wales could be canvassed on matters of programming and policy.

The government has also, historically, controlled the flow of resources to broadcasters. It has always set the level of the BBC's licence fee. It has set the economic framework in which HTV has operated, through taxation and the regulation of the number of hours of broadcasting and the amount of advertising allowed. It has also set the level of funding for S4C. This, as in the UK generally, means that the economic climate which structures Welsh broadcasting has always been profoundly influenced by government policy. Since the 1980s the UK government has increased the amount of commercial competition in UK broadcasting (O'Malley, 2001). This led to problems for all commercial TV companies in the UK, including HTV, who found their audience share decreasing. The extent of this competition has been particularly strong in Wales, as Table 6.1 above illustrates. Multi-channel homes in Wales meant more competition for viewing time and advertising revenue as a result of there being more commercially funded channels on offer to viewers.

Control in commercial broadcasting in Wales was also exercised through privately owned companies. Ownership of TWW, TWWN and HTV was in the hands of a few well-placed individuals. Like the IBA, ITC and BBC, membership of these companies was largely drawn from select groups of people, often already part of networks of association in the worlds of politics, entertainment and business. The ownership of TWW illustrates this. In 1952 Mark Chapman-Walker, who had been appointed Conservative Party director of publicity, helped to set up the Popular Television Association (PTA) to campaign for commercial TV. He did this on behalf of Lord Woolton, then chairman of the Conservative Party and a cabinet minister. The chair of the PTA 'which was actively assisted both officially and unofficially by the Conservative Central Office' was Lord Derby (Sendall, 1982: 21–2).

It was the then Conservative government which passed the Television Act 1954. The group which won the contract for Wales and the south-west of England, TWW, was a product of these connections. Woolton went on to become managing director of the *News of the World*. The TWW group was led by Lord Derby, included Sir William Carr, chairman of the *News of the World* and, when it won, it appointed Mark Chapman-Walker as its managing director. The links between the politicians promoting commercial TV (Woolton, Chapman-Walker and Derby) and the consortium were so blatant that Derby had to defend himself against criticism in the House of Lords in 1963. In a statement issued after criticism from Lord Ogmore, Derby claimed that when he had first joined the PTA, he had 'no intention of going into commercial television' (Sendall, 1982: 21–2, 181, 210–13). This combination of personal and political links amongst the social and economically powerful remained a key factor in the disposition of power in commercial TV. In this respect Welsh commercial TV did not differ from commercial TV in the rest of the UK; the BBC and IBA, too, were controlled in similar ways.

The most significant shift in controls over commercial TV in Wales occurred as a consequence of the 1990 and 1996 Broadcasting Acts. These unleashed a period of intensified competition for audiences and revenue, between the fifteen regional ITV companies in place at the end of the 1980s and their new competitors in the cable and satellite industry. The result was a period of pressure from the industry on government to allow the ITV companies to merge, so as to compete more effectively with their new rivals. In July 1997 HTV was taken over by the UK-wide newspaper and television company, United News-papers (Independent Television Commission, 1998: 84). Subsequently, HTV was bought by Carlton TV, and in 2003 the government agreed to a merger between Carlton and Granada, which left all the ITV companies in the UK, with the exception of Ulster TV, Channel TV

142 SECTORS AND INDUSTRIES

and the Scottish Media Group, under the control of one company (Competition Commission, 2003).

By 2004 the main ITV company in Wales had been subsumed under a UK-wide single company, ITV and was known as ITV1 Wales. The BBC retained control over BBC Wales from London, and the S4C Authority was appointed in London. Welsh TV was therefore characterized by centralized legal and administrative control, with devolved powers for Welsh broadcasting in the BBC and S4C, and a retreat, in the case of ITV, from a Welsh-focused commercial TV business (1958–97) to one owned by a UK-wide concern.

Aspects of programming and audiences

The majority of TV programmes produced for distribution in Wales have been in the English language. The majority of viewers have watched English-language programmes produced in or outside Wales. The production of programmes in Welsh has always played a significant role in Welsh television, even though the amount of English-language TV produced in Wales has mostly exceeded the amount produced in Welsh.

The first TV broadcast in Welsh was transmitted by the BBC on 1 March 1953. Between 1953 and 1955 the number of TV programmes produced by the BBC in Wales rose from two to seven per month. These could provoke hostile responses from some sectors of the audience. The broadcast of the first Welsh-language feature across the BBC network, on the bibliophile Bob Owen, between 7.40 and 8.20 p.m. on 6 March 1954, produced 'protests from England, although all that broadcast replaced was the test card' (J. Davies, 1994a: 203, 207, 394). Granada TV, the Manchester-based commercial contractor, started a series of hour-long Welsh-language programmes, twice a week, in 1957. By January 1959, TV Wales and West was producing 8 to 8.5 hours per week of programming, plus 1.25 to 1.5 hours of acquired film, just under 3 hours of which were in Welsh. Put in perspective, the total amount of originated programming by TWW at this point was only 15 per cent of its output. The other 85 per cent came via the ITV network arrangements and was in English (J. Davies, 1994a: 213; Sendall, 1982: 218–21).

The pattern thereafter was for growth in the number of hours of TV broadcast in the UK, and a steady development of programming produced in Wales. The BBC broadcast the first schools programmes in

Welsh in 1959. In 1963 the main Welsh-interest output of the BBC in Wales was *Heddiw* ('Today'), from 1.00 to 1.25 p.m., and *Wales Today* from 6.10 to 6.25 p.m.). TWW produced *Y Dydd* ('The Day'), a Welsh-language topical programme. From 1964 BBC TV programmes in Welsh began to be transmitted during network hours. Previously they had been transmitted when the UK-wide network was closed. They now replaced English-language programmes and provoked critical comment from monoglot viewers. This in turn provoked strong feelings in mid Wales, and opposition in Aberystwyth (J. Davies, 1994a: 262, 274). The Aberfan disaster of 1966, in which a school was submerged beneath a slag heap, posed a particularly harrowing challenge for the broadcasters. In spite of criticism of the coverage from the chairman of the National Coal Board, the corporation's governors agreed, on 3 November, with the views of Glanmor Williams that the coverage in English and Welsh had been of a 'high order of responsibility and sensitivity' (Briggs, 1995: 536).

Between 1964 and 1974, most people in Wales watched English-language programmes. This was a sensitive political issue. In 1971, with 20 per cent of Welsh people speaking Welsh, only 1 hour in 18 hours of programmes broadcast to Wales from Welsh transmitters was in Welsh. BBC Wales, in the early 1970s, was producing 6 hours in Welsh and 5 in English per week, mainly news and current affairs programmes. These were frequently accused of being trivial. While the bulk of drama produced by BBC Wales between 1964 and 1974 was in Welsh, the most popular programmes produced in Wales were sports programmes (J. Davies, 1994a: 288, 319).

In the 1980s the most popular programmes remained sports programmes, followed by news and topical magazine programmes. The arrival of S4C in 1982 relieved both the BBC and HTV of the responsibility of broadcasting programmes in Welsh. Thereafter the main TV channels in Wales were monoglot English (Bonner and Ashton, 1998: 141; J. Davies, 1994a: 359–60). Possibly the most successful Welsh-language production, *Pobol y Cwm* ('People of the Valley'), was first broadcast in 1974 on BBC Wales and transferred to S4C in 1982. It started going out on five days a week in 1988 (J. Davies, 1994a: 395–6).

By 1994 the BBC produced 10.25 hours per week of TV in English and HTV 9 to 11 hours. S4C transmitted around 35 hours per week in Welsh. Of the English-language TV the vast majority was news, rather than drama or music. Thus in 1998 HTV produced 5 hours 38 minutes of news, 1 hour 50 minutes of factual programmes, 1 hour 13 minutes of sport, 1 hour 2 minutes of education and only 11 minutes per week of drama (Independent Television Commission, 1999: 76). A sample of the analogue TV output in 2003 provides a 'snapshot' of the quantity of weekly provision of Wales-specific output (Table 6.2) and of the nature of its diversity (Table 6.3).

Table 6.2: 'Snapshot' of average weekly differentiated analogue TV output in Wales via S4C, BBC Wales, BBC2 and ITV1 (HTV), May–July 2003

	Total	% of total airtime
BBC Wales	7 hours 5 minutes	6
BBC2	2 hours 10 minutes	2
ITV1 (HTV)	8 hours 25 minutes	7
S4C	32 hours 45 minutes	26

Source: Barlow et al., 2005, based on data from *Radio Times*.

Table 6.3: Locally derived programmes by genre, May–July 2003 (weekly hours averaged over survey period)

	BBC Wales	BBC2	ITV1 (HTV)	S4C	Total
Children's programmes				8′ 45″	8′ 45″
News bulletins	2′ 55″		2′ 55″	2′ 25″	8′ 15″
Documentary	1′ 30″	10″	1′	1′ 35″	4′ 15″
Politics	30″	1′ 30″	30″	1′ 30″	4′
Drama	30″			3′	3′ 30″
Consumer affairs			1′	2′ 30″	3′ 30″
Arts	30″		30″	2′ 15″	3′ 15″
Sports (male)		55″		2′	2′ 55″
Comedy		30″			30″
Welsh-learning				30″	30″
Music		30″			30″
Religion				30″	30″

Source: Barlow et al., 2005, based on data from *Radio Times*.

Although the categories used in the ITC's 1998 figures and ours are different, the continuity in the amount and type of programming over the five-year period produced is notable. In addition, it is clear that drama, the arts and music were poorly provided for on Welsh TV. Thus, while the amount of programme production in Wales rose from the 1950s, it remained a negligible percentage of the total amount of programming transmitted via the BBC and ITV across our period (Mackay and Powell, 1997: 21).

The development of S4C's programming (Table 6.4) reflects not only the increase in the amount of Welsh-language programming, but also a bigger increase in the amount of English-language programming on S4C, due largely to the fact that Channel 4, like the other networks, moved after 1982 towards 24-hour broadcasting. The pattern of popularity of Welsh-language programmes on S4C also mirrored the longer-term pattern. In one week in September 2003 the most popular programmes were *Y Clwb Rygbi* (94,000), *Pobol y Cwm* (78,000), *Clwb Garddio* ('Gardening Club') (48,000) and *Newyddion* ('News') (45,000) (S4C, 2003).

Table 6.4: Weekly broadcast hours on S4C analogue

Year	Welsh	English
1983	22	47
1987	26	76
1992	32	104
1997	34	113
2002	38	120

Source: S4C, 2004.

Thus a fair assessment of television viewing in Wales since 1952 would stress two things. First, that there has been a considerable growth in the number of hours per week of Welsh-language or Welsh-interest programming on TV in Wales since the 1950s. Second, this increase has amounted to only a small percentage of programming transmitted in Welsh. The bulk of programming transmitted to and watched by Welsh audiences has always been in the English language.

Yet, the appreciation of TV produced in Wales amongst viewers is relatively strong. For instance, a survey by the ITC published in 2002 revealed that 68 per cent of respondents cited television as their main source of news about events in Wales, and 79 per cent for news about events in the UK. TV was the main source of local news in Wales for 49 per cent of respondents. In fact the ITC survey showed that in Scotland and Wales, in spite of concerns about the presence of too strong an English perspective on news, and in Wales too strong a Cardiff focus, nationally focused news was a valued form of programming. For one group of Welsh people whose views were examined in more detail by the researchers, Welsh TV was thought 'important in terms of educating Welsh people about their own country and reaffirming their national identity' (Independent Television Commission, 2002b: 5, 18, 37, 40, 73).

Television, language and identity

Television in Wales has been caught up in debates about the nature of Welsh identity, and questions about the survival of the Welsh language. Two of the most dramatic factors in Welsh life since 1900, the economic dominance and subsequent decline of the south Wales industrial belt, and the rise of the Welsh nationalist and language movements, with their stress on a link between the survival of Welsh and national identity, have generated strong views about the role of TV in society.

Welsh nationalists focused on broadcasting from the 1920s and won the establishment of a Welsh region of the BBC in 1936. Their concerns were also reflected in the establishment of the BCW in 1953 (J. Davies, 1994a: 393). From the outset, the council was committed to an idea of Wales, but it was one which, as its first chairman, Lord Macdonald of Gwaunysgor, pointed out in February 1953, had to be as inclusive as possible:

> Wales as we know it today, the Wales of song and sport, the Eisteddfod, of the drama and the Delyn, of the pulpit and the platform; the Wales of youth, the Wales of the aged, the Wales of the businessman and the financier in Cardiff, the Wales of industry and of the far-flung farming communities, Wales in its entirety, with all its variation and differences – that's the Wales the BBC must keep in mind. That's the Wales whose highest interests it must serve. (Briggs, 1995: 672)

The BCW's commitment to Wales was often perceived as a commitment to political nationalism. In January 1956 David Llewellyn MP complained of 'a distinct bias in the Welsh Region of the BBC in favour of Welsh Nationalism and Plaid Cymru'. The region was subjected to an inquiry, but was vindicated in a report published later that year (J. Davies, 1994a: 248–52). In fact, the BBC in London in the late 1950s was well aware of, and sympathetic to, the pressure from Wales for a wider range of programmes expressing national culture (Briggs, 1995: 652).

This belief that Wales had a distinct culture and as such should have a distinctive TV service fuelled the involvement of figures from across the political spectrum in Wales in projects such as TWWN and the campaign for a Welsh fourth channel. When in 1963 the ITA's Welsh regional officer, Lyn Evans, wrote a memo for the ITA's committee for Wales, he expressed the widely held view that TV was linked to the decline in the Welsh language and that ITV should have a role in promoting Welsh national identity:

> It is probably not too much to say that the coming of television to the Principality could mean the early disappearance of Welsh as a spoken language – the oldest in these islands. On the other hand, television could help to give it a new lease of life and, efficiently and sensibly organised, Welsh language programmes could help to promote and sustain a lively and progressively bilingual society. It is however imperative that the necessary steps are taken before it is too late . . . If a Welsh independent television service is to be of any real value to society and to the nation it should reflect that society, not only as it is but as it ideally has been and could be. (Butt Phillip, 1975: 255–6)

These assumptions about the relationship between TV, linguistic decline and nation building were the bedrock on which debates about TV in Wales rested in the 1960s and 1970s. They were shared by critics of the BBC and ITV as well as their defenders. In its 1969 pamphlet *Broadcasting in Wales*, Cymdeithas yr Iaith Gymraeg used these assumptions to attack the established broadcasters and assert the need for a Welsh-language TV channel. TV and radio programmes should 'reflect the spirit, civilisation and life of a nation' and 'should enrich that civilisation and enable the people to develop their own particular genius'. TV should therefore make full use of 'the national language of the Welsh people' and put 'forward a Welsh viewpoint'. Like the ITA official in 1963, the pamphlet feared the impact of TV and saw beneath its dominant Englishness a real threat:

English is the language of broadcasting in Wales and TV and radio sets are being used to Anglicise our home and kill our language. A Welshman is thus educated to look at life through English eyes. The few Welsh programmes cannot do more in emphasising the idea that Wales is a small insignificant province of England. (Tomos, 1982: 40)

This view was partly shared, but with an important difference of perspective on the role of established institutions, by the ex-broadcaster turned Tory MP Wyn Roberts, who in 1971 stressed 'the importance of radio and television to Wales in connection with the survival of the Welsh language. I pay tribute to the work already done by BBC radio and television and by ITV in the promotion of the language' (House of Commons, 1971). Indeed, one prominent commentator on Welsh affairs, Trevor Fishlock, argued in 1973 that the 'stronghold of spoken Welsh is now the radio and television set rather than the chapel. It has also contributed much to a greater sense of national identity' (Fishlock, 1973). In fact, as John Davies has pointed out, by the early 1970s about two-thirds of the BBC's production staff were required to speak Welsh, and at a higher level this was almost 100 per cent (J. Davies, 1994a: 285).

There was therefore widespread support for a stronger form of Welsh TV across the political spectrum by the early 1970s. It was the Crawford Committee (1974) which gave an official stamp of approval to the idea of a Welsh-language channel which it accepted was seen in Wales as 'the key to the preservation of Welsh culture' (Briggs, 1995: 998–1000; Potter, 1989: 185). The case for a Welsh channel was therefore accepted in Whitehall and Westminster by 1974, even though it took another six years of campaigning and lobbying to obtain final agreement. Underlying this case were the ideas that Wales was a distinct nation, that English-language TV was implicated in the decline of the language and that the remedy was to be found in the problem. In other words, by developing Welsh-language TV, national identity could be sustained and linguistic decline reversed.

Yet the issues were and remain complex. In 1977 Dafydd Ellis Thomas MP argued that

the media in Wales have made a fantastic cultural contribution to both consciousness and to the development of Welsh language culture. Through the medium of television national communications has been established in Wales. The history of the BBC and ITV in Wales shows that they have been able to establish a national culture and a national Welsh language culture which prevented such culture from becoming purely localised. (House of Commons, 1977b)

For, although TV in Wales contributed to debates about linguistic decline, it also made it more possible for people across Wales to engage simultaneously with a sense of Welshness that transcended locality and language, in a manner only equalled in the past by radio. Davies has argued that in the 1960s and 1970s 'the scarcity of programmes in their language was anglicising Welsh speakers' (1994a: 651). Yet he has also recognized that although TV helped to ensure that 'many cultural and social activities withered when faced with the competition of the box . . . the direct causes and effects are very difficult to establish' (J. Davies, 1994a: 258).

Challenges to the legitimacy of devoting so much time and money to a separate Welsh-language TV channel, when there was no English-language equivalent, continued to provoke debate. The south Wales MP Llew Smith was critical in 2001 of what he saw as the imbalance of investment in English-language as opposed to Welsh-language programming (Starling, 2001). A related perspective argues that the development of TV in Wales has been too heavily influenced by an identification of the Welsh language with Welsh identity, in a country which, since TV arrived in the 1950s, has had a majority of over 75 per cent of the population who were monoglot English speakers (J. Davies, 1999: 69–70; K. Williams, 1997a).

The links between language use and media use are part of a range of relationships that involve the family, school, peer group and locality, as well as factors like outward and inward migration, transport and the state of the economy (Delamont, 1987; G. Evans, 1997: 126, 146–7). Bearing this in mind, the assumption, common to all sides of the debates over television in Wales since the 1950s, that the language used on TV can have a significant effect on either the survival or the decline of Welsh, can be viewed as highly questionable. TV, arguably, cannot be abstracted, as it has been in these debates, from the wider social and economic changes. Specifying its exact role in linguistic change is difficult and the evidence does not suggest either that it caused the precipitous decline in Welsh speaking during the twentieth century, nor that the presence of Welsh-language programming or of S4C has had a dramatic impact on the marginal revival of the numbers speaking Welsh in the 2001 census. The point is not that television has no role in these issues but that, historically and in contemporary debates, it has perhaps been afforded too important a role. It appears to have functioned as the focus for much wider concerns about cultural change in Wales, as it has in the United Kingdom.

At another level, and in a similar vein to arguments developed by Anderson (1983) and Hobsbawm (1990), Bevan (1984) has made a link between the campaign for S4C and the nature of nationalist politics, both in Wales and in general. In Bevan's view the Welsh language has been seen as the focus of identity amongst sections of the Welsh population, but not the majority of people. Since many of these people have operated within the administrative, educational, political and broadcasting worlds, they have had, he argues, considerable success in influencing the attitude of the British state to communications policy in Wales. For Bevan, this

> focus on cultural identity and uniqueness has often served to obscure the more real issues of the economy, depopulation, deprivation and inequality. It has failed to recognise, as a result, the way these issues are related to economic and social formations as much within Wales as outside and across its boundaries. (1984: 114)

In this model, nationalist politics are the preserve of a self-selecting minority, whose concerns are focused on cultural issues to which they feel a particular affinity, but which do not necessarily address the wider causes of change in a given society. It is these groups, Bevan argues, that were mobilized to achieve the creation of S4C.

For some, this focus on cultural identity, so characteristic of those who fought for a Welsh-language channel, has gone hand in hand with a rejection of industrialization and its culture. In this rejection the cultural life of the English-speaking working classes, by far the majority in Welsh society for most of the twentieth century, was sidelined. In spite of Lord Macdonald's promotion of an inclusive Welsh identity and of S4C's commitment to promoting a cultural identity 'not restricted to a narrow interpretation of culture' (S4C, 2004: 41), the fact remains that critical energy in post-war Welsh broadcasting politics was focused on the link between the Welsh-language Welsh culture and its relationship with television. Another vision has been articulated by Dai Smith, who has argued for Welsh broadcasting to 'stress the achievements and tradition of the majority experience in twentieth century Wales, in the language of that majority, the English tongue that has become our principal Welsh means of communications' (D. Smith,

1999: 35). In defence of the Welsh-language activists' position it should be noted that no comparable campaign for an English-language TV service for Wales emerged out of the organized Labour movement in the post-war years, and it was the very existence, arguably, of the pressure for a Welsh-language channel, that focused people's minds on the wider question of the need for a distinctive English-language service. In fact it was Plaid Cymru who had argued for a separate English-language TV service for Wales since the 1950s.

So, TV in Wales has been and remains at the centre of wide-ranging debates about changes in Welsh society and culture. The power of these debates has rested on the force of the real changes in Welsh society since 1900 that have dominated people's experience. It is not surprising, therefore, that such a highly visible medium as TV should take on such a prominent role in these debates. The fact that television's role in these long-term changes in Welsh society is as yet imperfectly understood, and that therefore much of the public and political debate has not been founded on strong evidence either way, only adds depth and interest to a complex and enduring problem.

The experience of Wales in this respect foreshadowed many of the arguments that were to face England in the 1990s with the advent of satellite TV and the breakdown of audiences for its major 'national' channels. It is therefore of profound significance for our long-term understanding of the way societies in the twentieth century responded to the challenges posed by television.

Conclusion

Like the other forms of mass communications covered in this book, television was embedded in the shifting history of politics and culture and the economy of post-war Wales. As an institution, its organization and control raised questions of political accountability, paralleling those raised about broadcasting as a whole in the UK (Curran and Seaton, 2003). In Wales, though, this was complicated by the national question and, as in Scotland, this led to television occupying a particularly important position in Welsh political and cultural life. This chapter has outlined some of the key issues, but much research remains to be done to illuminate the history of TV in Wales, in relation to the cultures, history and contemporary experiences of the Welsh people.

Notes

1. See chapter 2.
2. The General Post Office was the government department responsible for broadcasting at this point.
3. See chapter 8 for a discussion of policy developments in general.

Does Wales have a national newspaper?
The Daily Post shop in Rhyl; Broncoed Stores in Mold

Remote control: What's local about local radio?
Red Dragon, Cardiff; MFM 103.4, Wrexham

Storm clouds after the Communications Act 2003: w[h]ither local production?
ITV1 Wales, Culverhouse Cross, Cardiff; BBC Wales, Llandaff, Cardiff

Cinemas urban and rural: accommodating culture and commerce?
Chapter, Cardiff; Pola Cinema, Welshpool

Bayside power: differing models of accountability
National Assembly for Wales, Cardiff Bay; Office of Communications
(OfCom), Cardiff Bay

A place for Welsh-language broadcasting in a multi-channel era?
S4C, Cardiff; 'Planed Plant' mobile

The Welsh press: open for business!
North Wales Newspapers, Mold; Western Mail and Echo, Cardiff

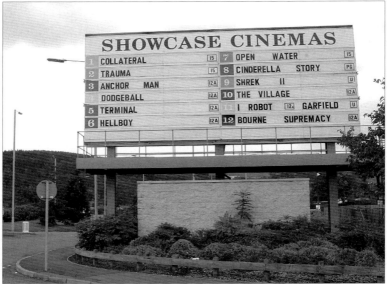

Hollywood glitz on the Trefforest Industrial Estate
Showcase cinemas, Nantgarw

7

Bridging the Digital Divide:
Wales and the Internet

The development and expansion of the Internet[1] in Wales calls to mind Raymond Williams's contention (1974) that the advent of a new media technology is a potentially critical moment in any society's history. The expectations many communications theorists place on the Internet as a potential vehicle for the fomenting of active citizenship and for the creation of a reinvigorated public sphere, even for a degree of genuine community regeneration, do have a particular resonance for the Welsh situation. These expectations apply not only to the sites – and sounds – of the World Wide Web, but also to the interactive resources of e-mail, Usenet newsgroup bulletin boards and chat rooms. The cultural impact of such expectations extends to the rest of the Welsh media. The launch of S4C's website, for example, was hailed by the organization's chief executive as being of comparable significance to the first translation of the Bible into Welsh (Mackay, 1999: 9).

Such optimistic thinking has also been embraced by Welsh political leaders. The declarations of intent by the National Assembly for Wales (NAfW) in this regard could scarcely be more emphatic:

By exploiting the opportunities of the e-economy, in particular the Internet, Wales can achieve sustainable growth, increased global competitiveness, enhanced employment opportunities and a better quality of life for all . . . These technologies have the potential to transform society and the economy in Wales; they are . . . crucial to the future of Wales . . . integral to our strategic plan . . . and our National Economic Development Strategy. (National Assembly for Wales, 2003)

Bearing in mind that this strategy for economic growth is predicated on the Welsh economy's managing to grow 1 per cent faster than the UK average over the first decade of the twenty-first century (Downing, 2002: 4), it is clear that a great deal rests on the development and deployment of this new media technology.

Here as elsewhere, however, there is a need to untangle the rhetoric from the reality. As a first caveat, careful consideration needs to be given to the extent to which a 'small nation' can realistically aspire to a viably discrete and separate information and communications technology (ICT) policy (see Selwyn and Gorard, 2002: xi). It is also worth bearing in mind that as a media sector the Internet is in several respects different in kind from the others under scrutiny in this book. For example, it does not constitute a media *industry* in the same way as film, broadcasting or the press, in that there is a far less readily identifiable set of owners and of professionals. Moreover, there is a less tangible media–audience relationship. As has frequently been pointed out by the Internet's main prophets, the technology is a 'many to many' as opposed to a 'few to many' means of communication. In the words of Poster (1997: 211):

> The 'magic' of the Internet is that it is a technology that puts cultural acts, symbolizations in all forms, in the hands of all participants; it radically decentralises the positions of speech, publishing, filmmaking, radio and television broadcasting, in short the apparatuses of cultural production.

Regulatory issues are also rather more nebulous.[2] The current chapter is organized so as to reflect these constraints and complexities. In contrast to the other media sectors reviewed in this volume, the Internet in Wales, by virtue of the fact that it is a new development, has as yet a relatively undeveloped academic literature. Rather than seeking to build a historical narrative, this chapter therefore begins by outlining the key areas of wider – indeed, global – debates regarding the Internet's emancipatory potential, and summarizes arguments about the benefits of political and public intervention in this paradigmatically 'control-free' sector, while sketching a preliminary account of the relevance of these controversies to the post-devolutionary Welsh context. The chapter then examines the problems which have beset attempts to initiate a full deployment of public and domestic Internet access throughout Wales, despite the growth during the 1990s in domestic and institutional Internet usage.

It then proceeds to evaluate the policy-makers' response to such difficulties, in particular the NAfW's Cymru Ar-Lein/Online for a Better Wales initiative. Following on from this, the next section assesses the contemporary situation in more detail, paying particular attention to Internet use by existing media, from on-line journalism to its exploitation by educational, cultural and political institutions. This section also analyses a range of issues arising: the role of Usenet newsgroups; the use of the Welsh language on the Internet; the technology's potential role in enhancing a sense of identity at regional and local level, as well as amongst the Welsh diaspora; and its role as a forum for mediated public debate.

The final section looks forward to the supposedly imminent era of 'convergence' of new media and information technologies, and evaluates the case for firmer state intervention in facilitating a more penetrative implementation of the Wales-specific Internet access policies, against the backdrop of the new UK-wide regulatory framework.

'Spinning' the web: competing definitions of the Internet's role

Where does the NAfW's optimism, outlined above, originate? In one sense, it is a surprising viewpoint, given historical patterns and other sets of constraints:

> Lower average incomes in Wales could mean that Welsh consumers are less likely to be able to afford the hardware . . . necessary to access the Internet. They may also be unable to pay for Internet access. In addition, due to its lower Gross Domestic Product and geographical structure, Wales has often tended to lag behind the rest of the United Kingdom in infrastructure developments of the past, such as canals, railways, roads and electrification. (Downing, 2002: 3–4)

Clearly, political and cultural debates surrounding the Internet in Wales have not developed in a vacuum. A set of competing debates and theories surround this technology and its social role. This section sets the contemporary Welsh situation, in particular the Internet-related policy and manifesto commitments of the NAfW and of the leading political parties, within a wider context of competing theories about the Internet's role – potential and actual – and about the nature of new media autonomy.

'Internetphilia'

A whole body of literature has emerged over the last two decades, originating mostly from North America, extolling the civic virtues of the Internet and assigning the new media technology a unique position in terms of its democratizing and emancipatory potential.[3] 'Internet-philia' is a term coined by Patelis (2000) to refer to this perspective and to its hopes and expectations of the Internet.[4] An initial summary of this literature reveals a focus on the new technology's potential for enhancing active citizenship in three main senses: first, by improving the dissemination and sharing of knowledge via the expansion of public information services and libraries (Liff et al., 2002), and also via an optimized use of the media's educative role (Crooks and Light, 2002). Second, by fostering a keener sense of civic engagement via the creation of virtual communities (Rheingold, 1995) and of civic networks (Schuler, 1996; Tambini, 1999), as well as by facilitating various strands of political activism (Foot, 2002; Stromer-Galley, 2002), and by instilling a reinvigorated sense of identity amongst the diaspora (MacKay and Powell, 1998; Tsaliki, 2002). Third, by facilitating public interaction with various societal elites, in that it may permit a freer interactivity between citizens, political parties and elected representatives (Greenough, 2002; Hagemann, 2002; Oblak, 2002), and also an enhanced public interaction with media professionals (Dahlgren, 1996); this can lead in turn to a blossoming of 'alternative' and community-based journalism (McQuail, 2003: 58; Slevin, 2000). Overall, such views are typified by Negroponte's seminal distinction (1995) between 'pushing' and 'pulling' technologies[5] and by Poster's (1997) heralding of the dawn of a second media age characterized by user choice and by a blurring of the lines between sender and receiver.

Positive versus negative Internet freedoms

The Internet's relative 'independence' from political control, regulatory restrictions and proprietorial interference is often taken as axiomatic. However, such thinking arguably betrays a conception of 'freedom' which is either simplistic or politically motivated: 'Freedom is what the virtual frontier stands for; the value that is prioritised over any other. However the freedom in question is the negative idea of freedom, meaning freedom from external restrictions' (Patelis, 2000: 85). In other words, discourses about Internet freedom tend to focus on issues such as censorship and other forms of content control (or on their relative absence); on the lack of restrictions on mergers and takeovers; on cross-media ownership; or on the absence of legal sanctions against publishing dissident opinions. The emphasis, then, is on freedom *from* rather than freedom *to*. Hence the acclaim bestowed on the US Supreme Court's much quoted 'Communications Decency Act' ruling (1997) that '[a]s the most participatory form of mass speech yet developed, the Internet deserves the highest protection from government intrusion' (cited in Naughton, 1999: 193).

Conversely, a perspective which prioritizes a more 'positive' sense of media freedom lays more emphasis on a given media technology's potential for empowering its users (see, for example, Collins, 1996; McQuail, 2003). The concept of freedom is, from this perspective, more appropriately reformulated as one of 'communicative entitlements', to use the term favoured by, for example, Forgan and Tambini, who refer to 'the range of services to which citizens should have guaranteed access', a range which should expand with the arrival of Internet technology, so as to include 'government services, (e.g., education) and government information [via] a government portal' (2001: 11).

Free market versus public service model

A third area of debate of direct relevance to the development of the Internet in Wales is the question of whether the technology is best nurtured and protected as a public service (BBC Wales being the obvious model and reference point), or whether it is best developed as a free-market enterprise. During initial developments of Internet technology in the United States, an inevitable reference point and influence for Europe, early political debates centred on the possible creation of a National Research and Education Network, to be set up in accordance with strongly public service principles (Naughton, 1999; Underwood, 2002), only for the Telecommunications Reform Act 1996 to enshrine a firm commitment to open-market principles for the Internet and related technologies. In the wake of this move, a number of critics of the West's media have seen this as a further illustration of a set of media-related policies which ostensibly privilege the 'free exchange of information' principle while in practice favouring corporate interests in general and those of the transnational media corporations in particular (see, for example, Schiller, 1996).

A crucial and parallel development in Europe was the publication in 1994 of the Bangemann Report to the EU.[6] This highly influential document marked a decisive move away from any idea of the deployment of public service principles in governmental approaches to Internet technology. Among the report's rallying cries are the following:

> This report urges the European Union to put its faith in market mechanisms; . . . it means fostering an entrepreneurial mentality . . . [and] developing a common regulatory approach to bring forth a competitive, Europe-wide market for information services; . . . it does NOT mean more public money, financial assistance, subsidies, *dirigisme* or protectionism. (Bangemann, 1994: 3)

The influence of such thinking can be discerned in the EU's *E-Commerce Directive* (European Union, 2000), which established a new regulatory framework for on-line services in Europe, and was designed to stimulate competition, partly by limiting the liability of Internet service providers (ISPs). The Bangemann Report also appears to have been influential in the UK government's 2002 policy paper *In the Service of Democracy* (HM Government, 2002), and has led to a widely accepted view that 'the Internet and the market are . . . essentially similar entities, inseparable and self-regulatory' (Patelis, 2000: 86).

The view from Wales

In Wales, as elsewhere, there are fears regarding the extent to which the technology may be developing as a corporate-driven rather than a citizen-based phenomenon. Moreover, there are related concerns that freedom of access is dependent, perhaps more than with any other current medium (with the possible exception of satellite-TV reception) on the citizens' own financial outlay.

Where has the NAfW stood on such issues? As signalled above, the Assembly's public rhetoric on the technology's implementation (National Assembly for Wales, 2003) is one that has placed a firm emphasis on its participative and regenerative functions. More than this, however, it explicitly invokes the Internet's potential for enhancing and fostering a set of what it sees as Welsh society's core characteristics. It is seen as a protector of Wales's 'unique and diverse identity' and of 'the benefits of bilingualism'. It can help the nation become 'more prosperous, well-educated, skilled, healthy, environmentally and culturally rich'. The nation's public services may become more 'modern, effective, efficient and accessible'. Moreover, the technology will be used 'to combat social exclusion and reduce existing social divisions' and 'to help remove physical, geographical and linguistic barriers'. Such pronouncements are strongly in line with those expressed by UK-wide policy-makers, of course. Even more tellingly, perhaps, they also echo the discourse of regional and local governments elsewhere (see the examples from Canada and Italy discussed by Tambini, 1999).

In relation to the debates summarized above, therefore, the interim conclusion – thus far in the Welsh context, at least – is that the NAfW has tended to (a) embrace Internetphilia; (b) place a strong emphasis – at least if its policy statements are taken at face value – on its positive freedom potential; and (c) incline towards a free-market model, with certain nods towards a public overseeing role, whether at local or at national (that is, Wales-wide) level.

A further indication of Welsh political thinking on such issues can be gauged from the published policies of the leading parties at the time of the 2003 Assembly elections. The Welsh Labour manifesto, for example, gave great prominence to its record of establishing, when in government, that 'Wales now has the largest public sector investment programme in super fast "broadband" Internet services anywhere in the UK' (2003: 19), and makes a strong commitment to increasing broadband availability to '310,000 extra homes in Wales'.

Plaid Cymru's 2003 manifesto placed even greater importance on broadband development, 'particularly in a country of dispersed settlements such as Wales', and the specific goal of the creation of 'new knowledge-based industries' (2003: 25). Plaid Cymru goes further, in fact, in arguing that inadequate use had been made of EU funding and that the 2007 target for broadband development would 'leave Wales even further behind the rest of the UK and Europe' (2003: 31).

Similarly, the Welsh Conservative Party's manifesto's emphasis is on the potential of Internet broadband connectivity to 'greatly increase economic productivity' and to make use of the public sector network to reduce connection and running costs for the business community, arguing also, as did Plaid Cymru, for the creation of a 'wireless broadband network to meet the needs of rural Wales' (2003: 41).

All of these documents appear to conflate broadband provision with actual Internet access. In other words, none of them allude directly to the problem of facilitating wider domestic ownership of personal computers (PCs) and of improving the wider affordability of ISP access charges. By the same token, they all share a similar set of assumptions regarding the beneficial effects of an expansion of such provision in tackling the difficulties presented by Wales's geographical, economic and socio-cultural peculiarities.

Widening access in Wales: a problematic expansion

The gap between rhetoric and reality in the deployment of the Internet is arguably seen at its clearest in the statistical indicators of the new technology's presence in Wales. As revealed by the information summarized below, Wales is doubly problematic, in that it lags behind almost all UK regions in providing domestic Internet access to its citizens, while also showing a variety of internal imbalances and inequities, notably between suburban and rural areas of Wales, but also in terms of gender, age and socio-economic group.

In undertaking its post-devolutionary initiatives for the expansion of public provision and exploitation of the Internet, Wales is starting from a remarkably low base. As a general, contextualizing indication of this, comparative figures for the development of knowledge-based indus-tries, as defined by the Organisation for Economic Cooperation and Development (OECD), reveal Wales to be lagging significantly behind the United Kingdom average (see Courtney and Gibson, 1999: 8, who define the Welsh economic framework as one 'weighted against high-growth, knowledge intensive activities'). The NAfW's ambitious plans for broadband expansion (see the next section) are particularly hampered by these low levels of economic activity and by the low usage by Welsh small and medium enterprises of other new information and communication technologies. UK government statistics show that Internet penetration in both homes and businesses in Wales has consistently been among the lowest anywhere in the UK, while the Department of Trade and Industry's Connectivity Indicator also places Wales in a highly disadvantaged position.[7] There is also evidence that Wales has one of the least developed regional software development sectors (Courtney and Gibson, 1999: 19–20).

This particular 'information gap' has been ascribed to various factors: cultural, political, technological[8] and, above all, economic – specifically, a chronic lack of venture capital and a resultant gross domestic product (GDP) growth which has run conspicuously behind its Welsh Development Agency-set targets.[9] Some researchers have also identified shortcomings in education and training which have resulted in a shortage of relevant skills (see Chaney et al., 2000). Taken together, such factors have severely compromised the competitiveness of Wales's wireless and wired communication networks, especially outside the main industrial areas (see Hargreaves, 1999: 1).

More encouragingly, a clear political and commercial post-devolutionary consensus would appear to have emerged regarding the need for concerted action aimed at improving Internet access and usage in Wales. While the driving force for this is fundamentally commercial,[10] the concern has clearly spilled over into the reconfigured political arena, to the extent that, in Courtney and Gibson's phrase, '[i]t may be no over-statement to suggest that the credibility of the country's new political institutions is at stake' (1999: 9).

**Figure 7.1: Percentage of adults with home
Internet connections in Wales**

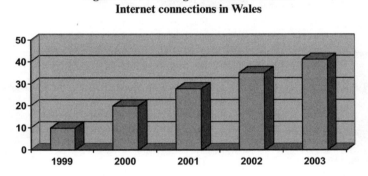

Sources: Conflated from data from Tuck,[11] 2003, and from the Office for National Statistics, 1999–2003.

On one level, the statistics about Internet access in Wales reveal some positive signs. Figure 7.1, for example, shows a markedly steady increase in domestic access since 1999. However, such figures need placing within a UK-wide perspective. By comparison with most English regions, for example, Wales lags well behind, as shown by Figure 7.2 below. In Tuck's apt phrase, 'it would be fair to say that Wales is in the wrong half of the digital divide' (2003: 6). Table 7.1 compares the period between 2001 and 2003 in more detail, and emphasizes that around the UK only Northern Ireland has a lower domestic take-up of Internet connections than Wales. Although this table also shows that Wales's current rate of growth is among the fastest in the UK, there is even some evidence that, in the light of the figures for Internet access, PC manufacturers have shown a certain reluctance to advertise to the Welsh market (see, for example, Courtney and Gibson, 1999: 14).

Figure 7.2: Percentage of UK households with Internet access

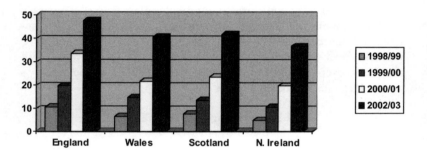

Source: *Family Expenditure Survey*, Office for National Statistics, 2003.

Table 7.1: Percentage of UK households with home access to the Internet (September 2003)

Region/UK country	% 2001/2	% 2002/3	Change
North east	36	43	+7
North west	41	43	+2
Yorkshire and the Humber	39	43	+4
East Midlands	46	48	+2
West Midlands	34	46	+12
East of England	52	48	-4
London	50	52	+2
South east	50	53	+1
South west	41	47	+6
England	44	48	+4
Wales	**31**	**41**	**+10**
Scotland	40	42	+2
Northern Ireland	30	37	+7
United Kingdom overall	**43**	**47**	**+4**

Source: *Family Expenditure Survey*, Office for National Statistics, 2003.

It is not only UK-wide comparisons that yield grounds for concern. As Downing comments, 'a digital divide persists *within* Wales' (2002: 13; emphasis added). In other words, homes in Cardiff, the south-east and the mid-west of Wales are clearly in an advantageous position, in terms of both current level of access and rate of growth, with respect to other parts of the country, which include the more isolated rural zones and other areas of relative socio-economic deprivation (see Table 7.2).

**Table 7.2: Percentage of adults in Wales with home
Internet connections, by region**

Welsh region	2000	2001	2002
Mid/west Wales	22	25	42
Cardiff and south-east Wales	20	29	41
West/south Wales	21	29	34
North Wales	18	30	28
The Valleys	22	25	27
Total	21	28	35

Source: Tuck, 2003: 9.

Such patterns confirm the regional biases discernible in other sectors of the media in Wales (see, for example, Bromley, 2000: 125). In the specific case of the Internet, the imbalance can partly be ascribed to the investment made by BT and NTL in their prioritizing of fixed infrastructure provision in industrialized south Wales (see Courtney and Gibson, 1999: 9).

**Table 7.3: How consumers from different regions of
Wales access the Internet (%)**

	Home and outside	Home only	Outside home only	Do not access the Internet at all
North Wales	11	18	13	58
Mid/west Wales	20	23	8	49
West/south Wales	13	21	9	57
The Valleys	8	17	10	65
Cardiff and south-east Wales	15	26	11	48

Source: Tuck, 2003: 13.

While it is true that the disparities exposed in Table 7.3 are not huge, the figures nonetheless support the view that the population in the less affluent and less urbanized areas are less likely to access the Internet from home and also less likely to have access overall. This point reinforces, of course, the importance of the question of whether public policy intervention should focus on the provision of public access support or, conversely, on maximizing *domestic* access. This point will be assessed at the end of the chapter.

In Wales overall, the situation by 2002 was that 'members of the DE socio-economic group were still three times less likely to have home Internet access than those in the AB socio-economic group' (Downing, 2002: 31). This ties in closely with research findings carried out on a UK-wide basis which reveal a marked correlation between household income and access to new ICTs (see Golding, 1994; Underwood, 2002). Golding's gloomy mid-1990s prediction that we are destined for a 'misinformed society' (rather than the information society heralded by Rheingold and others) perhaps has a special relevance for Wales:

> The mundane arithmetic of domestic economy places huge barriers between large sections of the community and the turnstiles through which the information paradise is gained. For those with the spending power to enjoy the communications bounty, the future beckons enticingly. For others, such goods and services remain luxuries displaced by the pressing needs of food, clothing and shelter. (1994: 475, cited by Underwood, 2002)

Moreover, there are some intriguing differences in usage of the Internet which reflect socio-economic variation (see Table 7.4). Of particular interest here is the evidence that the lower socio-economic groups are far more likely to use the Internet for game-playing, but much less likely to communicate by e-mail or to use the Internet for general information gathering. The Internet's potential for social interaction would therefore seem to be far more exploited by the higher socio-economic groups (except for any interaction – whether unmediated or electronic – as part of on-line game-playing).

More generally, the cost of computer hardware, on the one hand, and Internet access fees, on the other, seem to be having a very clear effect in terms of the evident disparities in Internet take-up across the various income brackets. Similarly, the lower social classes are least likely to access the Internet from outside home. This would appear to challenge the apparent triumphalism expressed by the UK e-envoy regarding the adequacy of public access points (UK Online, 2003; see also Blair, 1999). Tuck makes the related point that 'given the social and economic deprivation that tends to be associated with social tenants in the post Right to Buy era, this group was far more likely than any other to make no use of the Internet at all' (2003: 13), as illustrated in Table 7.6.

Table 7.4: Social class variations in use of the Internet by consumers in Wales

Types of activity	Percentage of Internet users in Wales	
	ABC1	C2DE
Sending/receiving e-mail	63	45
General research	58	38
Obtaining holiday information	35	27
Buying goods and services	26	22
Playing games	2	28
Obtaining travel information	26	17
On-line banking or other financial services	21	16
Paying bills	3	5
None of these	11	21

Source: Downing, 2002: 18.

Figure 7.3: Percentage of adults in Wales with home Internet connections , by social class

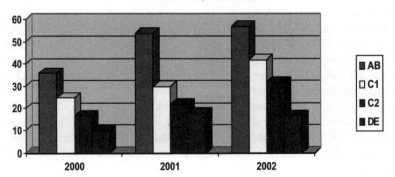

Source: Tuck, 2003: 8.

Table 7.5: How different social classes access the Internet (%)

	Home and outside	Home only	Outside home only	Do not access the Internet at all
AB	25	31	12	32
C1	18	24	15	43
C2	10	22	8	60
DE	5	12	6	78

Source: Tuck, 2003: 13.

Table 7.6: How consumers from different housing tenures access the Internet (%)

	Home and outside	Home only	Outside home only	Do not access the Internet at all
Owner	16	26	10	48
Social tenant	5	7	7	81
Private tenant	15	12	21	52

Source: Tuck, 2003: 13.

Overall, then, there is abundant support for Downing's suggestion that imbalances in home access across different socio-economic groups may constitute the clearest evidence of a lingering digital divide in Wales (2002: 9). Such imbalances also extend to the age of those using Internet technology. UK-wide trends are reflected in Wales in that access is significantly higher in younger age groups. As Downing comments (2002: 9), '[a]s government services are increasingly available online it is ironic that some of the heaviest users of these services, including the 65+ age group, will be unable to access them at home by using the Internet'.

However, it will be seen from Figure 7.4 that, in 2002, up to the age of 54 the proportion of users of the Internet in fact increases with age, although it then falls sharply. Nevertheless, as Tuck (2003: 7) points out, use by the post-65 group is rising faster than any other. Table 7.7 shows the link between access outside the home and age range. There is clearly an association between non-domestic access and those still in full-time education and the younger age group are more likely to frequent public access points. As Downing points out, '[t]hese age differences may reflect the increased relevance of Internet access to people with children of school or university age' (2002: 8). Gender imbalances are also somewhat apparent in such figures. Figure 7.5, for example, shows how male users are more likely to be connected to the Internet at home than female users, though this particular disparity is shrinking (Downing, 2002: 8).

**Figure 7.4: Percentage of adults with home
Internet connections in Wales by age**

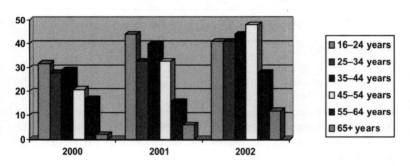

Source: Tuck, 2003: 8.

Table 7.7: How different age groups access the Internet (%)

Age	Home and outside	Home only	Outside home only	Do not access the Internet at all
16–24	25	17	24	34
25–34	17	24	16	43
35–44	21	24	15	41
45–54	18	29	4	48
55–64	5	24	6	66
65+	1	12	1	86

Source: Downing, 2002: 9.

**Figure 7.5: Percentage of adults in Wales with home Internet
connections, by gender**

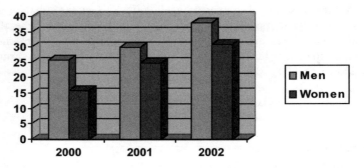

Source: Tuck, 2003: 7.

A crucial factor relating to the Welsh and UK-wide ICT policy-making
is the disparity between access from home, on the one hand, and from
work or from Internet cafés, libraries and other public access points, on
the other. It is especially revealing, perhaps, that it is those users who
already have home access who are far more likely to use the Internet
outside the home, as shown by Table 7.8. Such data would appear to
call into question the confidence with which the UK government has
drawn positive conclusions regarding the use of public access points
and their impact on the digital divide. Relatedly, figures also reveal that
in total only one in ten of Welsh citizens currently accesses the Internet
from outside the home (see Table 7.9).

**Table 7.8: Internet access of users (%) with and without
a home connection (2002)**

	Have home Internet connection	No home Internet connection
Use Internet outside home	40	16
Do not use Internet outside home	60	84

Source: Tuck, 2003: 10.

What of Welsh citizens' stated reasons for not using the Internet?
Research carried out to date presents the picture shown in table 7.10.
Such figures suggest that the benefits of using new media technologies

are not perceived as widely as the e-envoy's Annual Reports imply. As Tuck comments, 'Education and public access points may tackle issues of knowledge and access, but the high "don't want to" figure suggests real resistance to the Internet in some quarters' (2003: 15). The figures also provide a salutary reminder that there are other factors to take into account besides issues such as the socio-economic inequalities discussed above. The same survey indicates that a disturbingly small proportion – approximately one in ten – of such sceptical non-users have stated any desire to become Internet users in the future. Significantly, this group of current non-users who are intending to become users also displays the same discrepant patterns as the group of current users. In other words, they are skewed by region (those outside Cardiff and south-east Wales being less likely to declare any future intention) and by age (older age groups also being less likely).

Table 7.9: Where people access the Internet (%)

	Percentage of consumers
Home and outside the home	14
Home only	21
Outside only	10
Do not access the Internet at all	55

Source: Tuck, 2003: 10.

**Table 7.10: Reasons given why people do not want
to access the Internet**

%	Reason
3	Do not need it
7	Have not got round to connecting at home
13	Cannot afford it at home
17	Do not know how to use it
43	Do not want to use it
9	Other reasons
9	None of the above
6	Not answered

Source: Tuck, 2003: 15.

Such patterns are in line with UK-wide trends which, as observed by Curran and Seaton, indicate that

> lack of confidence and skills (given as a reason by 20% in a recent survey), as well as limited disposable income, are likely to remain serious obstacles to net use, especially among the elderly and poor. Their continuing exclusion from the online world will reinforce other forms of social and economic marginalisation. (2003: 280)

To summarize, then, substantial sectors of the Welsh citizenry are on the wrong side of the digital divide, and these patterns of inequality in the virtual Wales are closely in line with those in the real nation. This parallel is in turn typical of those found in the UK overall (Curran and Seaton, 2003: 260, 280) and indeed worldwide (Patelis, 2000: 89). What response has this state of affairs received from Welsh policy-makers, and from the wider media industry in Wales?

Highway construction: From nation to e-nation

Wales's first fully fledged Internet-related policy initiatives were developed by the 1997 decision of the Welsh Development Agency (WDA) to establish its Wales Information Society programme. This consisted mainly of a series of funding mechanisms for discrete small-scale projects around Wales. Since this project's inception, much debate, at both policy-making and academic levels, has centred on Welsh citizens' physical access to Internet resources. The relative scarcity and poverty of such access, resulting from the resource issues outlined above, have drawn criticism from those focusing on the Welsh situation.[12] These criticisms may be fruitfully considered alongside wider polemics calling for large-scale public investment in public Internet access in libraries, community education facilities, cultural centres and so on (see Liff et al., 2002: 83–7; Tang, 1998: 199–200). In the absence, hitherto at least, of such public investment in Wales, the financial barrier to equality of user access (perhaps more pronounced than any other medium) has been a very tangible one, and it is arguably exacerbated by other forms of barrier to full participation: cultural, educational, gender-related, generational and linguistic.[13]

Cymru Ar-Lein

The flagship of the Welsh Assembly Government's ICT strategy, approved by the NAfW in July 2001 and launched in November the same year, is Cymru Ar-Lein/Online for a Better Wales. Building on the WDA's late 1990s Wales Information Society project, this consists of development programmes – via mixed funding sources – in community regeneration and a whole battery of 'e-initiatives'.[14] In addressing the shortcomings summarized above, the framework makes explicit claims that the investment will foster cultural and linguistic diversity and enhance active participation in local communities, 'where the voice of local people is heard' and 'where everyone is valued and [given] an opportunity to play a full part' (National Assembly for Wales, 2003).

Specific initiatives relevant to the issues considered in this chapter include: a full database of ICT facilities across Wales; connection of all Welsh schools to the Internet; other educational initiatives such as the establishment of the National Grid for Learning Cymru, which supports the development of the Curriculum Cymreig. Perhaps crucially, several programmes are aimed at developing and exploiting broadband provision, notably the Broadband Lifelong Learning Network, to which all public libraries in Wales will eventually be connected, and the Broadband Wales scheme, trailed as the biggest government investment of its kind in broadband in the UK and funded via the earmarked aggregating of funds already allocated to ICT development by the NAfW government, the WDA and Objective One monies.[15] This aggregating of funds is a very deliberate policy strategy, partly designed to increase demand, but partly also with the aim of 'influencing the UK government and other UK institutions such as Oftel' (National Assembly for Wales, 2003).

Clearly, these initiatives will be a key priority for any critically informed monitoring of devolved democracy in Wales, given the large claims they stake towards empowering local activism and enhancing public accountability. Initial public responses indicate that a degree of scepticism is already apparent with regard to at least some aspects of Cymru Ar-lein.[16] Nonetheless, the fact that such criticisms are being voiced on the NAfW's own web-based discussion fora (in addition to Usenet news groups such as www.wales.politics.assembly and the CompuServe Wales Forum) might itself be interpreted as an encouraging sign, perhaps symptomatic of a genuine embracing of the technology's scope for citizens' feedback.

Similarly encouraging is the NAfW's publicly expressed awareness of the very constraints, shortcoming and future dangers summarized in this chapter:

> [M]any people in Wales face physical, social or linguistic barriers to accessing online services and information. Rapid technological change could lead to people already facing barriers becoming increasingly disadvantaged . . . ICT is only a tool. Applied poorly, it has the potential to increase social divides, inequalities and environmental damage. (National Assembly for Wales, 2003)

It should also be emphasized that the NAfW's policy initiatives have met with a significant amount of praise. Mackay and Powell (1998: 213), for example, commend the successive initiatives of the Welsh Office, the WDA, the Development Board for Rural Wales and a range of local authorities for the cumulative establishing of what amounts to 'a publicly funded electronic infrastructure'. Downing (2002: 32) lauds the education-related policies in particular. Similarly, Selwyn and Gorard's generally more sceptical view is nonetheless appreciative of the way in which Wales-wide initiatives have been allowed to complement 'community-level collaboration between public sector and private-sector organizations' (2002: 46) and also of the priority given to education-related ICT policies (2002: 196).

Moreover, there is also a widespread recognition that, in the specific Welsh context, some of the market mechanisms these policies have exploited may have, in Talfan Davies's words, 'efficiency and [an] undoubted relationship to freedom and democracy' (1999: 47). Perhaps most significantly, an EU-funded audit,[17] carried out in April 2003 and designed to investigate 'whether the CAL [Cymru Ar-Lein] strategy is complementing, or conflicting with, the Welsh Assembly Government's duty to deliver sustainable development, taking into consideration that ICT policy in Wales is still in its infancy' (Digital Europe, 2003: 2), lavished praise upon the Cymru Ar-Lein scheme; it commended the 'visionary approach and use of non-technical, accessible language' and suggested that the programme's attempt to harness technology for 'economic, social and environmental progress should be applauded and replicated in other regions' (2003: 5).

Within the constraints and shortcomings outlined in the preceding section, the key question remains of how successfully attempts have been made to construct a fully fledged e-nation. Notwithstanding problems of access, in other words, has the Internet thus far been exploited to anything like its full extent?

Internet content in Wales

The most common use of Internet technology in Wales in 2001 was sending and receiving e-mail and 'general research'. This latter category subsumes the accessing of news and on-line journalism sites, as well as of the World Wide Web pages of Wales's public institutions, including the NAfW's own site, into which significant resources have been invested (National Assembly for Wales, 2003).

Table 7.11: Use of Internet by consumers in Wales (2001)

Types of activity	% of Internet users in Wales
Sending/receiving e-mail	56
General research	50
Obtaining holiday information	32
Buying goods and services	25
Playing games	24
Obtaining travel information	22
On-line banking or other financial services	19
Paying bills	4
Other	15

Source: Downing, 2002: 15.

The increasingly interactive nature of the usage of Internet-related technologies by public bodies and elected representatives (though under-exploited in some areas, notably by the elected AMs, see Greenough, 2002; Walker, 2001) is encouraging. Specifically, as this usage includes experiments in formal and informal electronic consultation, it embodies the hope that concerns about accountability such as those expressed to the Welsh Affairs Select Committee on Broadcasting in Wales (see Mungham and Williams, 1998) have not been ignored. The NAfW's site offers discussion boards for public participation with headings such as 'Citizen and Community', 'Infrastructure', 'Welsh and ICT' and 'Sustainable Development and ICT'. The hope, therefore, is that such initiatives in accountability will help to bridge what Hagemann (2002: 61) identifies as 'the gap between institutionalised public discussion that exists within the party élite and the uninstitutionalised, informal public discussion that transpires in other public and private domains'. The difficulty, however, and the necessary focus for ongoing critical scrutiny, is whether this ostensibly most 'unaccountable' of media can indeed demonstrably contribute towards making governance more accountable.

As with broadcasting, the web-based public service provision offers a useful indicator of whether a sufficient Wales-specific differentiation is being incorporated. In this context, BBC Wales's launch of on-line bilingual news sites has been hailed as a key exponent of public service broadcasting's response to the post-devolutionary situation (Talfan Davies, 1999: 28–9, 49). The web has thus allowed an expansion and enhancement of the BBC's definitions of Welshness and Welsh national identity, leading to a more differentiated set of news values, as well as more interactivity. John Davies goes on to assert that such on-line provision 'will also allow [the BBC] to reach the Welsh diaspora which, because smaller than that of the Irish or Scots, is more difficult to reach but, nevertheless, sizeable' (1999: 51).

By 2003 this investment was showing a remarkably rapid growth. In March of that year BBCi Wales had achieved 5.1 million monthly page impressions (increased from 1.8 million in March 2002). The rise in the Welsh-language mini-site BBC Cymru'r Byd, while encouraging, was not on the same scale, with a total of 490,000 page impressions (up from 390,000) (BBC Wales, 2004). From 2001 BBC Wales has also widened this policy by introducing live audio webcasts from both the National and Urdd Eisteddfodau, as well as 'Welsh-only' on-line discussion fora with Welsh-speaking writers, artists and musicians (the Super Furry Animals were early participants in this scheme).

In addition to developing its own content, BBC Wales's website increasingly acts as a portal to, or directory of, other Wales-based websites. The usefulness of such resources bears out the claims made by the Institute for Public Policy Research (IPPR) that access to sites fulfilling a definite public service remit should be earmarked for special funding initiatives or for more onerous regulatory content rules (see, for example, Tambini, 2000; Forgan and Tambini, 2001).

The use of the Welsh language on the Internet

In 2003 the NAfW's Culture Committee published a self-evaluative report on its first four years. Among points it highlighted was the Assembly government's support in adopting the committee's vision of a bilingual Wales (Culture Committee, 2003: 3). This support has had an impact on its Internet policy, as reflected in the Cymru Ar-Lein project, which emphasizes a number of statements of intent in this regard:

[the NAfW will] ensure that cultural and linguistic information relating to Wales is collected, preserved and made available in an electronic format and raise the profile of Wales on the international stage by providing a focus for bilingual, Welsh content and services; . . . encourage the development of bilingual educational and training materials that are relevant to needs in Wales to enable lifelong learning and support the Welsh National Curriculum; . . . develop a synergy between ICT and the Welsh language so that Welsh speaking organisations are not disadvantaged and bilingual working is made accessible for all business in Wales. (National Assembly for Wales, 2003)

The UK government's e-envoy has also published a clarification of the legal ramifications for Internet use of the Welsh Language Act (UK Online, 2003), aimed at reminding public, local authority and educational websites of their statutory obligations. There is some preliminary evidence that such institutions have taken this responsibility seriously for some time; see, for example Mackay and Powell (1998: 215) whose evidence in fact indicates that 'the Internet . . . has been using the Welsh language extensively from the outset' (1998: 214). A case in point would be the site of the Bwrdd Croeso Cymru/Welsh Tourist Board.

BBC Wales describes its Cymru'r Byd mini-site, launched in March 2000, as 'the first ever "daily" newspaper in the Welsh language' (BBC Cymru Wales, 2002). As part of its Welsh-language commitment it has also integrated its *Catchphrase* Welsh tuition course, a long-standing component of Radio Wales's provision, into its Internet operation, via another designated mini-site.

On-line journalism

The opportunities afforded by web-based publishing and journalism should, in theory, help Wales to overcome some of the economic and geographic problems which have restricted the setting up of a wider variety of news outlets. Prominent among these problems have been notoriously high distribution costs, tight profit margins, and the lack of the substantial AB audience which is crucial to newspaper advertising revenue (Talfan Davies, 1999: 19). More difficult to overcome will be the cultural and demographic difficulties presented by entrenched readership patterns. Similarly, the web's provision of a greater diversity of sources of information should in time lessen the Welsh audience's dependence on mainstream broadcast media and information providers and provide a platform for alternative voices.

A useful case in point in this regard was 'Wales Watch' a satirical website set up in 1999, somewhat in the manner of North American sites such as *The Onion*, consisting of spoof news stories – including mock-ups of BBC Wales's own on-line news pages[18] – and semi-investigatory political exposés. Tellingly, the site's stated aims were to counteract the perceived lack of diversity and critical awareness in Welsh journalism, and its satire was aimed as much at Wales's mainstream news media as at its elected representatives.[19]

More generally, there are initial indications that on-line journalism is increasingly seen as a means of overcoming ownership constraints, and is already showing signs of augmenting existing publishing initiatives in 'alternative' and community-based journalism and information provision (see Dahlgren, 1996). Against this must be set the recognition that mainstream on-line journalism is underdeveloped by Welsh journalists, in that by early 2004 none of the main Wales-based newspapers had established a clearly defined web presence, just as local and regional radio in Wales have been slow to develop a thoroughgoing Internet presence (as discussed in chapter 4). UK-wide developments in on-line journalism during the 1990s were greatly influenced by the 1994 European Commission *Report on New Media*, which in effect warned editors and proprietors that a secure financial footing could not be guaranteed for a print-only press. This led to the *Daily Telegraph*, the *Financial Times* and the *Irish Times* all becoming fully fledged on-line papers by the end of that same year. In such a context, the slow pace of on-line journalism developments in Wales is striking. The nearest Welsh equivalent to such UK-wide ventures has been the ic Wales website ('the national website of Wales'), set up by the Trinity Mirror Group which, as owner of the *Western Mail, South Wales Echo* and over two dozen other newspapers across Wales, dominates the Welsh newspaper press (see chapter 3).

In due course, positive outcomes may be anticipated from the opportunities web-based journalism provides for changes in the nature of news provision: multi-modal presentation; enhanced interactivity, including direct e-mailing; greater multiplicity of sources; more decentralized and less hierarchical news-gathering; wider professional and public access to databases and archives; and so on (see Hall, 2001; Harper,

1998; Pavlik, 2001). These changes are all ones which tend towards changing the relationship between media and audience, in that as owner-ship becomes less of a determining factor the audience begins to be seen less as buyers and consumers and more as co-assemblers of their own news texts. The new Welsh media's main task thus becomes 'to present [the audience] with information in ways that allow them to build nar-ratives of their own' (Talfan Davies, 1999: 36), while the on-line journalists' role adjusts to that of 'guide and guarantor of quality information' (p. 22).

A genuine flowering of Welsh on-line journalism would be important not least as regards the reporting of the Welsh political process itself. As Talfan Davies emphasizes (1999: 67), the NAfW's processes differ in some significant ways from those of Westminster,[20] and require an imaginative and innovative coverage which makes full use of new ICTs. This would help achieve the crucial aim of 'the new processes becoming an inextricable part of our conscious and sub-conscious daily narrative' (1999: 9). Moreover, it would help balance out the tendency identified by John Davies (1994) for contemporary Wales to be defined as an artefact produced by broadcasting.

Talfan Davies also cautions, however, that 'the exclusion of any part of the population from that daily narrative flow should be of concern to anyone anxious to create a more healthy democracy' (1999: 9). Much will therefore depend on the extent to which the UK-wide trend towards subscription-only access to on-line journalism (another po-tential form of cyber-exclusion) becomes reflected within Wales.

On-line discussion fora

There is a certain amount of evidence already that the Usenet newsgroup bulletin boards are beginning to serve as an electronic meeting point for the Welsh diaspora (see MacKay and Powell, 1998), and to provide an opportunity for a tentative sharing and shaping of a common sense of national identity. The limited nature of what has thus far been achieved needs to be stressed, however. For example, Mackay and Powell's study of on-line discussion fora found a number of worrying trends. One was an overemphasis on stereotypical views of Welsh society and culture (1998: 212). Another concerns the low number of people using the Wales-related Usenet groups. In fact, Mackay and Powell (1998: 212–13) explicitly see the Welsh case as a salutary illustration of the unrealized nature of the theories developed by Rheingold (1995), in particular, regarding the Internet's potential for the creation of a new electronic public sphere and go so far as to question whether such discussion groups can meaningfully be classed as communities: 'our study of Internet usage gives little support to the notion that it is sustaining democratic, inclusionary, progressive politics . . . the fora can scarcely be seen as communities' (1998: 213). This reference to on-line political activism is especially telling, in view of Rheingold's highly influential expectations that: 'the technology that makes virtual communities possible has the potential to bring enormous leverage to ordinary citizens at relatively little cost – intellectual leverage, social leverage, commercial leverage and most important, political leverage' (1995: 84). Mackay and Powell's findings in fact bear out the reservations expressed by Poster (1997) and by Schudson (1997) on the lack of genuine rational debate in such on-line fora. In Curran and Seaton's words (2003: 265) 'the net is no different from most other media in that it marginalises politics'.

Discussion fora such as those available on Trinity Mirror's ic Wales site are often specifically aimed at 'ex-pat' communities. This site, for example, has a newsletter written especially for the Welsh diaspora and summarizing developments in Welsh commerce, urban planning and the tourism industry. It also has a message board which is mainly used for tracing old school and university friends, typical messages being: 'I've been living in Brazil for five years and if any of my friends back in Brynmawr reads this message please drop me a line.' and 'I think the new stadium name should be St David's stadium. Any one agree?' A similar function appears to be served by several of the discussion fora on the BBC Wales website, known as its 'TalkWales message board'. The 'I love Wales' board, for example: 'Tell us what you love about Wales. Maybe you're an ex-pat or just love being Welsh?' These public service website discussion fora provide an insight into the BBC's conception of its Welsh audience: they are mostly devoted to sport (rugby, football, cricket and surfing) and general interest topics (including one earmarked for 'quirky banter').

Many areas of contention revolve around the definition and application of the concept of 'community'. On the one hand, notwithstanding the reservations summarized above, there is evidence from these bulletin boards that, as Stromer-Galley has found in a Dutch context (2002: 23), '[t]he Internet may provide a new context for those who would not normally engage in face-to-face political conversations, thus bringing new voices into the public sphere'. In this sense, also, the gap is thereby reduced between the institutionalized and uninstitutionalized public discussion (identified by Hagemann, 2002). A role is therefore emerging for electronic 'mediated publicness' (Slevin, 2000), the development of which Oblak contends is crucial for 'the process of normalisation of cyberspace' (2002: 7).

On the other hand, there is also evidence to bear out the view propounded by some critics that only when a greater assiduity and inclusiveness is registered in Internet usage will real progress have been made. In Tsaliki's words,

> unless netizens test their opinions in public systematically, the notion of the Internet as a tool for democratic deliberation is seriously undermined . . . In that respect, cyberspace resembles the familiar world of everyday politics as an arena for the ongoing struggle for power and influence, despite the hype surrounding it. (2002: 95)

In the Welsh context, Mackay and Powell make a related point when arguing that 'usage of the Internet cannot be seen as constituting an extension of civil society unless its use ties in with civil institutions' (1998: 213).

Towards full convergence?

It is anticipated that we will eventually witness a full convergence of ICTs on digital format (see, for example, McQuail, 2003: 113; Underwood, 2002). Such a convergence would lead, among other consequences, to the long-heralded 'switching-off' of analogue TV and radio provision. There is a growing body of opinion that it could also be significant for the Internet in general, and for its development in a nation such as Wales in particular. After all, despite its problematic position on most UK-wide indicators relating to the Internet, by 2003 Wales was actually far above average in its take-up of digital television, with a presence in over 50 per cent of Welsh homes (BBC Wales, 2004).[21] To put this at its simplest, 'Access to the Internet via the television set in front of the sofa rather than through the computer on the desk might be the way ahead in Wales' (Gower, 2002: 1). In addition, as Downing points out (2002: 2), '[t]his route also has the potential benefit of removing lack of computer literacy as a barrier to Internet access'.

Similarly, over 70 per cent of the Welsh population have mobile phones, enabling the BBC's introduction of an SMS text service for

Welsh learners in March 2003. Given such developments, one optimistic view is that Wales will in effect go from a period of so-called 'cyber-exclusion' (paralleling the existing patterns of wider social exclusion) towards a subsequent stage when media convergence will usher in a more inclusive period of more equitable access to on-line content of various types.

The consequences of convergence

Some controversy surrounds such a view, however. Firstly, some critics dispute the reality of the convergence process. Curran and Seaton (2003: 282–3),[22] for example, argue that the technical and logistical complexities inherent to such a process have been underestimated, and while they do not cite Wales directly, some of the geographic and infrastructural difficulties to which they allude are known to be especially problematic in the Welsh context.

The second controversy is that, surrounding the deregulatory impact of this convergence, 'what is put forth is that telecoms, a liberalised industry, and broadcasting, more or less regulated, are converging into one technology . . . In short if different applications are to co-habit on-line then only a liberalised regulatory regime can deal with them' (Patelis, 2000: 86, 88). In fact, the UK government's e-envoy explicitly invokes this process in applauding the creation of OfCom and suggesting that further deregulation will ensue:

> The creation of OfCom will bring a more strategic overview to the whole sector and will instigate a flexible regime that will support a dynamic and flexible market-place while protecting consumers and citizens. As this convergent market matures and develops, we expect that further de-regulation may be appropriate in some areas and that self-regulation should be further encouraged wherever possible. (UK Online, 2003: 21)

While some voices have defended the importance of differential regulatory regimes (Campaign for Press and Broadcasting Freedom, 2001; Huston, 2002), the principle of a single regulator seems to be accepted even by some who are critical of the way in which the Internet is conceived and handled by the UK government; witness the pragmatic argument of the Institute for Public Policy Research (IPPR):

As the Internet's capacity to deliver video, audio, text and pictures improves, audio-visual services delivered over the Internet may displace audience share of other platforms . . . If Internet services are delivered to digital television it may eventually be difficult for consumers to distinguish between television and Internet services, and radically different regulatory environments may be difficult to defend. (Forgan and Tambini, 2001: 5)

Much of this debate can be reduced to a single key question: how can we best create a situation in which Welsh Internet users are allowed to behave as fully fledged on-line citizens, as *netizens* to use Tsaliki's formulation (2002: 95), rather than being treated as consumers?

From on-line consumers to 'netizens'

While it may be true in some senses that 'the state loses its legitimacy in the online world' (Patelis, 2000: 85–6), its intervention is nonetheless crucial for a realistic hope that universal access will be attained. If there does exist a distinctly Welsh 'Internetphilia', at least among the political class and policy-makers, then further public investment and the widening of home access – rather than merely the fomenting of e-commerce – seem inevitable. The alternative may be that laudable initiatives such as Cymru Ar-Lein will be condemned to operate 'in the margins of mass communications, linking the interested with the interested, rather than with the public at large' (Barlow et al., 2005).

It is here, therefore, that the ideas of the Institute for Public Policy Research (IPPR) may be relevant (as outlined in Tambini, 2000). Though intended for UK-wide application, they also have a particular resonance for Wales, given the extent of the 'digital divide' discussed above. In dissenting from the European Commission's view, one which is highly favourable to corporate Internet network developers and providers, the IPPR advance the counter-argument in favour of the creation of a Universal Service Fund (USF), to which all network owners would contribute and whose overarching objective would be to facilitate universal domestic access to the Internet, based on the idea that this USF would also expect contributions from general taxation; from an access fee (analogous to the existing television licence fee); from a national e-lottery; and from the sale of advertising space on public service Internet portals. This argument also extends to the proposed creation of a discrete department within OfCom with specific responsibility for promoting universal access, and for adjudicating on

Internet access rights claims. Such a move would clearly involve a radical re-evaluation, on the UK government's part, not only of the relationship between the new regulatory system and Internet technology, but also of the role in these matters – actual and potential – of the Assembly. In the meantime, the hope remains that the Internet's potential can eventually be instrumental in addressing a long-standing failing of the Welsh media – to provide a coherent, differentiated sense of Welsh identity (K. Williams, 1997a: 8–9). In Talfan Davies's words, this technology might thus create 'the possibility of a new kind of national conversation' (1999: 22).

Notes

[1] Throughout this book we have followed the widespread typographical convention of capitalizing the first letters of both 'Internet' and 'World Wide Web'. It is worth acknowledging, however, that such usage is not uncontroversial and has a bearing on wider debates. For example, Curran and Seaton (2003: 237), in eschewing this usage, posit a historical parallel with the now obsolete use of an initial capital for 'Press', and argue that such conventions betray society's tendency to display an uncritical 'awestruck . . . wonderment' before new media technologies, symptomatic of their wider critique that 'so much current discussion of the net is naïve and credulous'.

[2] See chapter 9 for further discussion of regulatory issues relating to the Internet.

[3] For a detailed – if highly critical – review of the literature in question, see Patelis, who distinguishes between 'a liberal-populist approach concerned with individual freedom and the Internet as the marketplace of ideas' and 'a more postmodernist approach, analysing how Internet communication frees the subject from the ontological curse of modernity' (2000: 86).

[4] Nettleton et al. (2002) suggest the term *cyberbole* as an appropriate neologism for this arguably widespread tendency to enthuse too readily over the Internet's perceived freedom of operation and emancipatory potential. See also the scepticism expressed by Haywood (1998) regarding the Internet's capacity for alleviating social exclusion, and the specific caveats voiced by Mackay and Powell (1998: 204) regarding the technology's future development in Wales.

[5] See Curran and Seaton (2003: 248) for further discussion.

[6] Patelis also cautions, however, that the development of infocommunication policy in the EU and in the US cannot be too closely equated, since the EU policy is characterized by 'a tension between social and economic prosperity' (2000: 100).

[7] The DTI's connectivity figures take into account indicators such as number of websites, frequency of external e-mail use and so on; see DTI Policy Action Team (2000).

8   See Courtney and Gibson (1999: 9), who point out that in many parts of Wales these problems relate to the sheer distance between exchange and subscriber.

9   The target, set by the WDA in the 1990s, was to reach 90 per cent of the UK average by 2010 (see *www.wda.org*).

10 In Courtney and Gibson's words (1999: 3), 'Wales' future prosperity depends upon its ability to exploit knowledge for commercially profitable ends'.

11 The surveys were carried out by Beaufort Research on behalf of the Welsh Consumer Council (see Tuck, 2003: 5).

12 See, for example, Courtney and Gibson, 1999; Mackay and Powell, 1997 and 1998.

13 For example, the Welsh Language Board has compiled a comprehensive list of computer resources available in Welsh. This begins to address widespread concerns regarding minority language use in the western European media (see Cormack, 1998).

14 These include 'e-learning', 'e-procurement' and 'e-democracy', in addition to the appointment of an 'e-Minister'. Collaborating organizations include Education and Learning Wales (ELWa); the National Library of Wales; the NHS Wales; the Welsh Development Agency (WDA); the Welsh Language Board; and the Welsh Local Government Association (WLGA).

15 The scheme aims to increase the affordable availability of terrestrial broadband services in Wales by 30 per cent, bringing the services to an extra 310,000 homes and making 67,000 business lines available.

16 For example, some who post messages on these bulletin boards claim to detect a certain glib populism in, for example, the labelling of the connection programmes in public libraries as 'The People's Network'. Others have expressed initial mistrust of the emergence of what are perceived as new 'quangos', such as the ICT Advisory Panel.

17 This audit was a case study by the 'Digital Europe' project funded by EC under the Information Society Technology Programme.

18 A typical spoof headline was: 'As part of its new Youth Policy, the Welsh Assembly today announced that the A470 would be reserved for skateboarding from 1 September'.

19 The site closed in 2002.

20 The NAfW's setting and procedures are seen as differing from Westminster's in, for example, the rounder shape of the debating chamber; the designated seats with PCs; the committee membership; and so on (Talfan Davies, 1999: 67).

21 Use of video conferencing is also significantly higher in Wales than in most parts of the UK, or indeed of Europe (Digital Europe, 2003: 3).

22 See also the political-economy perspective of Patelis (2000: 92), who argues that in essence the process known as convergence would more accurately be defined simply as one of *vertical integration* within and across the media industries. See also Goldberg et al., 1998.

III

*Wales and the Assembly:
Communications and
Cultural Policy*

8

Policy Matters!

In the lead-up to the renewal of the BBC Royal Charter in 1946, Gwynfor Evans (1944) called for the establishment of a Welsh Broadcasting Corporation that would take responsibility for determining broadcasting policy in Wales. He was unimpressed with the practices of a BBC driven from London and sceptical about the impending introduction of commercial broadcasting, doubting that the 'merchants and industrialists of Britain, the United States and other countries . . . would respect the life and language of Wales' (G. Evans, 1944: 11). Evans argued that control of broadcasting should rest in Wales, as it did for institutions such as the University of Wales, the National Museum, National Library and National Eisteddfod (G. Evans, 1944: 6).

There were other calls during the twentieth century for the introduction of measures that would make the media in Wales accountable to its people, particularly when the prospect of devolution became a possibility. Anticipating such an outcome, Kevin Williams (1997a; 1997b) extended the debate beyond broadcasting, arguing that Wales needed a media policy – not one repatriated from London, a process likened to the 'badge engineering' associated with the motor industry (Talfan Davies, 1999: 12), but one developed through wide public consultation in Wales.

The development of a media policy was suggested because the mass media would be key players in developing support for a future National Assembly for Wales (NAfW or Assembly); it would also assist broadcasters in their 'cultural mission' and help challenge misrepresentations by London-based media (K. Williams, 1997a: 61). A media policy was also seen as a way of mitigating the impact of contemporary patterns of ownership in Wales which, it is argued, have rendered the media a 'weak' element of Welsh civil society (Paterson and Wyn Jones, 1999: 176).

Matters such as these act as a reminder of why the mass media are key institutions in contemporary society. Moreover, as a result of the economic, political and socio-cultural dimensions of mass communications, it is generally accepted that some degree of state intervention, in the form of public policy, is required: 'To inform, to discuss, to mirror, to bind, to campaign, to entertain, and to judge – these are the important functions of the media in any free country. The purpose of public policy should be to enable the media to perform them more effectively' (Curran and Seaton, 1997: 319). This chapter examines the ways in which the public authorities have shaped, or tried to shape, the structure and practice of the media in Wales. As these policies have been and continue to be developed at the state – rather than sub-state – level, the situation in Wales can be considered only in the context of the wider United Kingdom, which is itself subject to European legislation.

The chapter includes four sections. The first of these examines the context in which policy emerges, paying particular attention to the reasons given for policy initiatives and to the economic, social, political and cultural forces to which policy responds. Here, attention is focused on the period from 1979 onwards following the election of the first Thatcher government, a time when media policy in Britain is judged to have entered a new phase (Garnham, 1998: 212). The second section takes as its focus New Labour's reformulation of the UK communications environment with the introduction of the Communications Act 2003. The third section teases out some of the key issues arising from the Act and considers the likely implications for Wales. The final section takes its direction from New Labour's White Paper on devolution, *A Voice for Wales/Llais dros Gymru* (Welsh Office, 1997), to explore the extent to which Wales, through the Assembly, has acquired a 'voice' and how it has been used.

Shaping policy: in whose interests?

Until the emergence of the Thatcher government, it was generally accepted that the British state had a key role in organizing industry, including broadcasting. Moreover, radio and television services were imbued with specific civic functions and were not simply seen as vehicles for selling programmes or commodities to the listening and viewing public. Both these premises were destabilized in the late 1970s. Changing economic circumstances, in the form of a downturn following the post-war economic growth, coincided with the emergence of right-of-centre 'neo-liberal' governments in the US and Britain (Goodwin, 1998: 8; O'Malley, 1994: xi). The Thatcher-Reagan project redefined the relationship between government and economic activity. In Britain, the government extolled 'free' markets, small government, minimal state intervention, reduced public expenditure and the privatization of public assets. Public services, such as British Rail and British Airways, and public utilities, such as water, coal, gas and electricity, were dismantled and transferred into private hands. Market-based mechanisms also impacted on health and education. With ready profits awaiting entrepreneurs keen to take on previously publicly owned services and under-priced shares and tax cuts awaiting the citizen, 'free' – rather than regulated – markets were hailed as a more attractive proposition (D. Hutchison, 1999: 157).

The emergence of large conglomerates, or transnational corporations, is seen as instrumental in this unravelling of regulation by governments in Britain and elsewhere. Four key trends in world communication have contributed to this process: digitization, consolidation, deregulation and globalization (Hamelink, 1994, cited by Boyd-Barrett, 1995: 191). They are interrelated in the sense that digitization – the extension of the binary language of computer communication to all electronic communication – enables technological and institutional convergence, allowing large conglomerates to expand their global reach. Once this is achieved, and in order to maintain and expand their commercial power, these organizations rely on governments throughout the world to relax regulation and bring about the privatization of media and other goods and services. Such developments have been seen as an advanced form of cultural imperialism and described as 'transnational corporate cultural domination' (Schiller, 1991: 15).

Until the Thatcher government, no official reports on broadcasting had questioned the need for public regulation, although unease had been expressed about the relationship between broadcasters and governments and campaigns had been organized for more openness, diversity and democratic control of broadcasting (Curran and Seaton, 1997: 324; O'Malley, 1994: xi). Similarly, although not subject to regulation in the same way as broadcasters, the British film industry was also reliant on certain forms of state intervention, such as the

Cinematograph Act 1927, the Eady Levy and the National Film Finance Corporation. The removal of these measures, all of which had helped maintain a British film industry in the face of Hollywood domination, was seen as a defining moment for film in the UK (Hill, 1996: 102).

Thatcher's ideological challenge to public service broadcasting was influenced by ideas developed by a number of right-of-centre 'Think Tanks' during the 1970s and 1980s, such as the Centre for Policy Studies, the Conservative Philosophy group, the Institute of Economic Affairs and the Adam Smith Institute (O'Malley, 1994: 15–21). In effect, the reforms being countenanced were intended to move broadcasting to a footing similar to that of the press in the twentieth century, self-regulating and part of the market (Curran and Seaton, 1997: 319).

The opportunity to reshape British broadcasting was significantly strengthened by developments in computer, satellite, video and fibre-optic technologies. These developments, plus the emerging possibilities of digital technology, helped undermine the scarcity argument which had been used to justify the regulation of electronic communications in the public interest, and they also called into question the future of terrestrial broadcasting services (Curran and Seaton, 1997: 333). The potential for 'media plenty' via a multitude of channels delivered by a variety of means provided neo-liberals with the grounds for deregulation.

The rhetoric associated with the technological possibilities of 'new' media is voluminous and somewhat overstated. For example, the 'promise' of cable communications has never been realized, but there might have been a different outcome if public funding had been committed to create the sort of 'wired society' that was being envisaged (Goodwin, 1998: 62–6; Hutchison, 1999: 59–60). Referring to cable developments in Wales, Mackay and Powell (1997: 27) argue that, without a public service ethos and a commitment to universal coverage, 'cable is likely to exacerbate the divisions in Wales – between urban and rural, or south-east and the rest'. It is now digital developments that preoccupy broad-casters, policy-makers and the communications industry, following the government's commitment to replace the analogue transmission of television and radio services with a digital network. While the benefits of these developments continue to be 'talked up', take-up will be influenced in Wales by access factors such as affordability and topography.

Economic factors played a key role in influencing government intervention in media and communications during the 1980s. At a time of economic slowdown, the communications industries provided opportunities for economic growth and employment through the production and export of audio-visual goods. Additionally, in what has been variously referred to as an information, communication or knowledge society, the retention or development of industries that require highly skilled and creative personnel was seen as essential to a country's economic competitiveness. This view still retains currency. The British government and the NAfW categorize broadcasting, film and 'new' media as 'creative industries', a sector earmarked as a key driver of economic, cultural and social renewal in Wales (Welsh Assembly Government, 2002; C. Smith, 1998). Aside from the hoped-for economic benefits, concerns about cultural self-determination also influence such developments. There is still a widely held view that expanding the communications industries will reduce the possibility of American imports and mitigate against the 'creeping "coca-colanization" of European culture' (Curran and Seaton, 1997: 341).

Pressures on the nation state to reduce regulation continue, with the rationale now well rehearsed. Whether in North America, Europe or Asia, the argument is that media conglomerates must be allowed to 'achieve the financial resources, distribution muscle and multi-media synergy' that will enable them to compete in a global marketplace (Curran and Seaton, 1997: 365). As well as the media owners themselves, industry associations, advertisers and groups representing shareholder interests also pressurize government and regulators.[1] The same argument was used as a means of generating support for the merger in 2003 of Granada and Carlton to form an integrated ITV company in Britain, completely overshadowing concerns about the potential impact on regional production at HTV, now ITV1 Wales.

Making policy: for whom?

On coming to government in 1997 New Labour chose not to reverse the policies of the previous Tory administration. It had 'courted right-wing publishers' while in opposition (Curran and Seaton, 1997: 339–40), and, at a meeting in Australia with senior managers of Murdoch's News Corporation in July 1995, Tony Blair made the following remark: 'There is an obvious requirement to keep the system of regulation under constant review. The [communications] revolution taking place makes much of it obsolete' (cited in G. Williams, 1996: 10). Blair's thinking on communications policy was informed by pro-business organizations, so much so that New Labour ditched the party's earlier opposition to the intrusion of commercial values, favouring 'the spread of privately owned market driven media' (O'Malley, 2002a: 3). This position is reflected in the policy instruments and narratives that culminated in the Communications Act 2003.

The 'new' communications era

Three key documents preceded the Communications Act 2003: the 1998 Green Paper, the 2000 White Paper and the 2002 draft Communications Bill.[2] Each is considered briefly.

The Green Paper
Published in 1998, *Regulating Communications – Approaching Convergence in the Information Age*, set out the government's views regarding the likely impact of digital convergence on the 'legal and regulatory frameworks covering broadcasting and telecommunications' (Department of Trade and Industry/Department of Culture, Media and Sport, 1998: 1). It outlined the principles that would inform future changes:

> the promotion and protection of the consumer interest as the overriding objective of regulation; coherence in the treatment of economic issues; the removal of overlaps and gaps in regulation; minimum effective regulatory intervention (regulation should be the minimum necessary to achieve clearly defined policy objectives); transparency and accountability, and clarity with flexibility. (Department of Trade and Industry, 1999: para. 3.48)

While stressing that the government favoured an 'evolutionary path' to regulatory reform, the Green Paper flagged the possibility of replacing the then current multi-sectoral approach with a single, fully integrated regulator. The interests of the consumer dominate the policy narrative. In a published summary of the Green Paper, 'consumer' is mentioned on at least eleven occasions, while 'citizen' is referred to only once (Department of Trade and Industry/Department of Culture, Media and Sport, 1998). The Green Paper generated seventy-nine responses of which seventy-two were from organizations and seven from individuals. Only three submissions emanated from organizations with an obvious Welsh connection: the Catholic Bishops' Conference of England and Wales, the Welsh Advisory Committee on Telecommunications and S4C.

The White Paper

Published in 2000, *A New Future for Communications* (Department of Trade and Industry/Department of Culture, Media and Sport, 2000), reflected long-standing tensions over 'broadcasting as commerce' and 'broadcasting as culture' (Barnett, 2000a: 7). The policy narrative is driven by a predominantly technological determinist discourse. A sense of transformation prevails, with readers reminded that, '[a]s railways transformed the economy and society in the 19th century, so telecommunications will transform them in the 21st' (Department of Trade and Industry and Department of Culture, Media and Sport, 2000: para. 2.10.4), and that '[t]he communications revolution is creating a new economic and democratic landscape' (para. 1.1.1).[3]

Economics and the primacy of the market are at the forefront of the White Paper. It confirms media and communications as a major and growing industry in the UK and notes how consumer spending on such services now exceeds what is spent on beer (para. 1.1.18)! A future regulatory framework, it argues, must deliver the goals that 'we seek as a society' (para. 1.1.25), that is, 'to make the UK home to the most dynamic and competitive communications and media market in the world' (para. 1.2.1). Therefore, the degree of regulation required would be minimal, with the prospect of it being rolled back even further at a later stage (para. 1.3.9).

Portraying the then regulatory system as cumbersome, inflexible and insufficiently responsive to the needs of the new communications environment, the White Paper concretized the idea flagged in the earlier Green Paper for an Office of Communications, or OfCom (para. 1.3.6). As the centrepiece of a new regulatory structure, OfCom would replace the existing regulators, with the exception of the BBC Board of Governors and the S4C Authority (paras 8.1–3). OfCom would be expected to make links and consult with the NAfW, but Wales would not have representation on its board of directors. The restructuring of regulatory responsibilities is outlined in Table 8.1.

The White Paper confirmed that public service broadcasting would have a key role in a digital environment and that public service television channels would continue to be free at the point of consumption after the digital switchover (para. 3.2.1). However, it also flagged changes in the way it would be regulated (para. 5.1). This would be achieved through the introduction of a three-tier structure, the lower level requiring certain standards of all broadcasting services with the upper tiers only applicable to public service broadcasters (paras 5.5–8).

For instance, at the second-tier level, OfCom would be charged with ensuring the more quantifiable public service obligations, such as compliance with targets for independent production and regional programming. At the third-tier level, a self-regulatory regime would be introduced in order to reduce 'box-ticking' – a complaint often expressed by the ITV companies – allowing public service broadcasters to decide for themselves how best to deliver their public service remit. The remit of the BBC and S4C would remain unchanged. However, ITV1 Wales (and the other ITV franchisees) would be subject to less prescriptive regulation, with the likelihood that their obligations would be further eased as competitive pressures increased in the digital era.

Table 8.1: Overview of planned regulatory changes

Current regulators of electronic communications sector	Regulatory bodies after White Paper proposals are implemented
Broadcasting Standards Commission Independent Television Commission Oftel Radio Authority Radiocommunications Agency	OfCom
BBC Board of Governors British Board of Film Classification Office of Fair Trading Sianel Pedwar Cymru (S4C)	BBC Board of Governors* British Board of Film Classification Office of Fair Trading Sianel Pedwar Cymru (S4C)*

*but with modified responsibilities

Source: Department of Trade and Industry and Department of Culture, Media and Sport, 2000: 78.

The White Paper also signalled the government's intentions to amend the regulations on ownership (paras 4.6–11). For instance, the ownership rules for television would be relaxed, thereby enabling a further concentration in ownership of the ITV companies. There were similar plans to relax the ownership rules pertaining to commercial radio. Cross-media ownership rules would also be examined with a view to relaxation and the White Paper canvassed the idea of a 'lighter touch' approach to newspaper mergers.

The NAfW response to the White Paper centred on three issues (National Assembly for Wales, 2001a). First, it stressed the need to ensure that digital communications would be available and accessible throughout Wales. Second, it underlined the necessity to maintain high-quality public service broadcasting services in both languages and to ensure that all Welsh viewers would have access to Welsh broadcasting signals, and it requested that OfCom be required to set targets for television operators in respect of local production and for the UK-wide networks. Third, it argued for the inclusion of a member from Wales on the board of OfCom, with the appointment to be made by the Assembly.

The Communications Bill
The draft Communications Bill (the Bill) was published in May 2002. The Bill reiterated the government's plans to simplify the regulatory framework by establishing OfCom; to liberalize controls on media ownership, including the abolition of rules barring foreign ownership; to maintain and secure a role for public service broadcasting, albeit with greater reliance on self-regulation; to clarify the regulations relating to telecommunications; and to introduce a regime for trading radio spectrum (Department of Trade and Industry/Department of Culture, Media and Sport, 2002: 2–3).

In setting out the case for change, the Bill identified potential benefits for consumers and citizens – in that order. Consumers, it argued, would benefit from the choice enabled in an increasingly global and competitive market, as would local businesses if the UK continued to be seen by communications companies as a good place to do business. In prioritizing competition over regulation, the Bill argued that citizens would benefit from a diverse range of services and plurality of voice in a multi-channel digital era. Regulation would, therefore, be reduced, but safeguards would be maintained through the retention of public service broadcasting.[4]

Following some public disquiet over the Bill, a joint committee of the House of Lords and House of Commons (the Joint Committee) made numerous recommendations on how and why it should be amended and, in doing so, prioritized the interests of citizens. Central to the Joint Committee's proposals was a 'Plurality Test': '[a]t the heart of our conclusions and recommendations about media ownership is the proposal for a new plurality test to be used in connection with mergers and takeovers across all the media' (Puttnam, cited in Campaign for Press and Broadcasting Freedom, 2002a: 2).

The Assembly's response to the draft Bill identified the same three issues that formed the basis of its response to the White Paper, but reversed their order of priority (National Assembly for Wales, 2002b).[5] On this occasion, the need for Welsh representation on the OfCom Board and in other parts of the new regulatory framework was prioritized. This was followed by a further assertion that identifiable and enforceable regional production and programming targets for television were required, the particular concern being the future performance of HTV. The Assembly also argued that HTV should be required to have a managing director for Wales as well as one for the west of England, because the existing arrangements – where the managing director lived in England – were not considered satisfactory.

The Assembly's final concern related to access, and four points were made. First, that the government must ensure that no Welsh viewers would be disadvantaged by the analogue 'switch-off' and, if necessary, should provide financial assistance to ensure universal access. Second, measures were suggested to try to increase the numbers of Welsh viewers watching television from Wales. Third, the Assembly argued that the 'must carry' requirement demanded of public broadcasting services on cable and terrestrial providers be applied to the satellite platform before switch-over, because some Welsh viewers would only be able to receive digital television by way of satellite (National Assembly for Wales, 2002b: 5). Fourth, with the risk that Welsh channels would be lost in a multi-channel era, the Assembly argued that Wales's public service channels should receive 'due prominence' on electronic programme guides (National Assembly for Wales, 2002b: 5).[6]

The Communications Act 2003

The Act received Royal Assent on 17 July 2003. It confirmed that the principal duty of OfCom is: '(i) to further the interests of citizens, and (ii) to further consumer interests in relevant markets, where appropriate by promoting competition' (HMSO, 2003: 6). Both the chairman and chief executive of OfCom expressed their dismay about the decision to prioritize the interests of citizens over consumers (Barnett, 2000b: 7). The key principles underlying the Act are: '[e]nsuring access to a choice of high quality services; [e]nsuring that public service principles remain at the heart of British broadcasting; [d]eregulation to promote competitiveness and investment' (Department of Culture, Media and Sport, 2003b: 2).[7]

The Joint Committee's Plurality Test, now known as the Public Interest Test (PIT), will be administered by OfCom on the direction of the secretary of state if further investigation is required in proposed mergers involving newspaper enterprises, broadcasting enterprises, or between broadcasting enterprises and newspaper enterprises (OfCom, 2004b: 1). In any such merger three criteria will need to be satisfied:

> Is there a sufficient plurality? Secondly, will the merger or acquisition so affect the broadcasting ecology that 'taken as a whole' there is an appreciable risk of detriment to range and quality? Thirdly, will the new owner 'demonstrate a genuine commitment' to the standards Codes, in particular to the impartiality and accuracy that the UK media market has come to expect? (S. Carter, 2003: 7)[8]

OfCom will provide advice on whether such a bid will be accepted, rejected, or allowed subject to certain conditions, but the final decision will rest with the secretary of state. While the PIT inserts an additional hurdle into the decision-making process over certain mergers or acquisitions, the criteria are sufficiently loose as to allow the government's preferred outcome. Moreover, it is unclear which secretary of state – Trade and Industry, or Culture, Media and Sport – will have the final word.

Polic[y]ing Wales?

A number of points might be made about the potential impact of the Act in respect of Wales and on its process to statute.[9] Four areas are singled out for attention: OfCom's constitution and powers; the immediate prospects for public service broadcasters; the ramifications of a more liberalized ownership regime; and the place of citizens, as stakeholders, in the legislative process.

OfCom's constitution and powers

The board of OfCom is appointed by the government to oversee the implementation of its policy.[10] It is not constituted in a way that resembles or even attempts to represent the interests of the wider society. For example, there are no places for representatives from Wales or the other nations or regions, neither are there places for those representing other sectors of society, such as education, non-government organizations and trade unions. In fact, the issue of representation is almost belittled. The Bill states that the OfCom board will be 'small and lean' and will 'concentrate on effectiveness and function rather than representation of particular interests' (Department of Trade and Industry/Department of Culture, Media and Sport, 2002: 3, 15). This rankled in Wales. Jenny Randerson, the then Assembly minister for culture, sport and the Welsh language, said 'I still believe there is a need for national representation on the main Board' (Randerson, 2002b), and expressed her frustration in evidence to the Richard Commission:[11]

> it has proved very difficult to get the UK Government to take account of Assembly Government policy interests, and to get these reflected in the Bill. The Assembly Government has found itself in the position of having to lobby hard to ensure that Wales secures the same degree of representation within the new regulatory body as it currently has on the existing regulatory broadcasting bodies. (Randerson, 2002a: 7)

Wales is, though, represented on a content board. The content board is a committee of the main OfCom board and is charged with the regulation of television and radio quality and standards, its primary role being to 'examine issues where the citizen interest extends beyond the consumer interest' (OfCom, 2003). The content board offers advice to the main OfCom board, except in matters that have been delegated to it by the parent body. The content board comprises thirteen members, four of whom are appointed to represent the interests of Wales, Scotland, Northern Ireland and the English regions. All members of the content board are appointed by OfCom. The first member for Wales on the content board was Sue Balsom.[12]

An additional channel for Wales's voice is provided through the establishment of an OfCom external relations team and an Advisory Committee for Wales. In 2004 the director for Wales, Rhodri Williams, was a member of the external relations team. He was based in Cardiff and chaired the Advisory Committee for Wales. This committee is made up of nine members, all appointed by OfCom, and met for the first time in March 2004.[13] Its brief is to advise OfCom 'about the interests and opinions, in relation to communications matters, of persons living in Wales' (OfCom, 2003).[14]

A consumer panel is also in place to advise the main OfCom board. Appointed by OfCom, the panel focuses on consumer concerns as they relate to service delivery within the communications sector, but it will not address issues of content. The panel held its first meeting in February 2004. The membership of eleven is required to be sufficiently diverse in order to be in a position to represent the interests of consumers throughout the UK, including those in rural communities, older people, people with disabilities and those who are on low incomes or who are otherwise disadvantaged. Wales's representative on the consumer panel in 2004 was Simon Gibson.[15] Both Sue Balsom, from the content board, and Simon Gibson were expected to work closely with the Advisory Committee for Wales.

OfCom's executive group comprises members from the commercial sector, previous regulatory bodies and government.[16] It includes three policy groups: strategy and market developments; competition and markets; and content and standards. Given OfCom's mission and the make-up of its board and executive, 'regulatory capture' will be a real possibility, resulting in industry interests taking precedence over those of the wider public. In fact, the public interest might be better served if complaints, content and consumer issues became the responsibility of another body independent of OfCom.[17] The blurring of boundaries and responsibilities within OfCom is another issue that has prompted disquiet. The former Radio Authority cautioned about the relegation of radio-related matters to a 'Friday afternoon job' (Stoller, 2001: 1).

Prospects for public service broadcasting
Despite government assurances that public service broadcasting will remain a key plank in the UK's broadcasting ecology, there are real concerns that the requirements for the commercial channels are too vague or too light (Barnett and Seaton, 2002: 3). In light of this observation, HTV's response to the Bill was pertinent: 'we [HTV] have argued for clear but non-prescriptive public service remits to be set and are pleased to see their inclusion in the draft Bill' (HTV, 2002: 4). This brings into question the future of regional programming by ITV franchisees. While the Bill commits to quotas for ITV's regional pro-grammes and for regional production on Channel 4, it is not explicit on the number of programming hours involved. Regional production, it is argued, should also constitute different types of programmes and not simply be restricted to news and current affairs. Furthermore, 'quotas' do not guarantee quality and cynics will justifiability ask who will enforce such measures.[18]

Of concern in the longer term are signs that the commercial channels will seek to reduce, or simply 'shrug off', their public service obligations as competitive pressures increase in a digital multi-channel environment (Tambini, 2002: 8). In light of this, a more forceful way of embedding public service broadcasting in the UK would have been to strengthen such requirements on channels 3 (ITV), 4 and 5, and require the same of all non-terrestrial services (Campaign for Press and Broadcasting Freedom, 2002b: 6.4). In the current scheme of things, the likely outcome is that the BBC and S4C will become the sole providers of wide-ranging public service programming in Wales. In 2003, S4C, aware of the challenges it will face in a digital environment once the analogue network is switched off, initiated an internal review of its performance and role. This was timed to feed into a process which included OfCom's first review of public service broadcasting and the Department of Culture, Media and Sport's review of the BBC's charter, due for renewal in 2006 (Department of Culture, Media and Sport, 2004; S4C, 2004).

In terms of the BBC, there are doubts in some quarters about whether it will be able to remain outside the scope of OfCom in the longer term.[19] However, the decision to maintain the roles of the BBC board of governors and the S4C Authority and not subject them to control by OfCom might be seen as a fillip for democracy and a safeguard against a further diminution of diversity and plurality. This is despite ongoing concerns that neither institution is accountable to the people of Wales. OfCom does, however, have oversight of the BBC and S4C in respect of aspects of their remits and, irrespective of whether it eventually exercises greater control over them, its impact on the former is likely to be significant. Charged with promoting economic competition while safeguarding the interests of licensees and the public interest, OfCom is likely to pressurize the BBC into justifying why it should produce programmes that could otherwise be produced profitably by commercial operators, hence the concern about regulatory capture. Some commentators see intrusion extending to 'interfering with strategic decisions – such as moving the peak-time news – which have potentially negative repercussions for commercial rivals' (Barnett and Seaton, 2002: 3).

Liberalization of ownership

The liberalization of ownership is unlikely to increase diversity and plurality. By rolling back the regulatory safeguards, the government is simply continuing the shift begun by Thatcher whereby the interests of large companies take priority over those of the public. McChesney (2002: 2) cleverly captures the sleight of hand taking place, noting that the term 'deregulation' would more accurately be rendered as 're-regulation' because what is occurring is 'unabashed and unacknowledged regulation on behalf of powerful self-interested private parties'. By relaxing ownership rules, the government not only provides the opportunity for non-European companies to acquire media in Wales and the UK, but also gives the green light for greater cross-media ownership (see, for example, Freshfields Bruckhaus Deringer, 2003). This is likely to exacerbate the already concentrated and distant ownership of the press and commercial radio and television in Wales, further diminishing the overall diversity and plurality of its media.

Citizen participation

The tendency to marginalize 'citizen' and favour 'consumer' in the policy narratives symbolizes the reality of public participation in the legislative process. Despite a widely acknowledged view that the Act radically reshapes the regulatory framework for broadcasting and communications in the UK, the journey from Green Paper to statute involved the wider public only partially. As one of the supposed key 'actors' in the policy process – along with politicians, civil servants, regulatory bodies and media organizations – 'ordinary' people were all but excluded from the event until publication of the Bill in 2002. Essentially, it was as a result only of the activism of bodies such as the Campaign for Press and Broadcasting Freedom, Voice of the Listener and Viewer, Public Voice and various trade unions, that (some of) the public became involved in a debate which until that point had been the preserve of power elites.

This is not to suggest that the government set out deliberately to exclude the public. Nonetheless, setting very limited time-frames for public consultation – sometimes spanning key holiday periods – does not suggest a genuine attempt to procure public participation.[20] In Wales, although the NAfW did consult widely on its review of arts and cultural policy, it had insufficient time to do so in respect of the White Paper and made no concerted attempt to seek wide public consultation on the draft Bill. As Hutchison (1999: 139) notes, while most people may not want to be involved in consultations over media policy, 'a surprisingly large number of citizens might well take the chance to express their views if the opening were there'.

Policy on the margins

In July 1997 New Labour's proposals for a Welsh Assembly were published in the form of a White Paper, *A Voice for Wales*. In a preface to the White Paper, Tony Blair outlined how the new Assembly would enable the people of Wales to have 'more control over their own affairs' by providing the opportunity for 'many more matters that affect Wales to be decided in Wales' (Welsh Office, 1997: 3). Responsibility for the following areas passed to the Assembly: economic development; agriculture, forestry, fisheries and food; industry and training; education; local government; health and personal social services; housing; environment; planning; transport and roads; arts, culture, the Welsh language; the built heritage; and sport and recreation (Welsh Office, 1997: para. 1.7). The Assembly would be empowered to 'set policies and standards' in respect of its designated areas of responsibility; to 'reform and oversee the work of unelected bodies' – the notorious quangos; and to 'make detailed rules and regulations, through secondary legislation, within the framework laid down in Acts of Parliament' (Welsh Office, 1997: para. 1.1).

The White Paper was also explicit about areas of responsibility that were not to be devolved: foreign affairs; defence; taxation; macroeconomic policy; policy on fiscal and common markets; social security; and broadcasting (Welsh Office, 1997: para. 1.9). A concordat, devised by the Department of Culture, Media and Sport (DCMS) to guide relationships between individual UK government departments and devolved administrations, set out the position in respect of broadcasting in Wales:

> The subject matter of the Broadcasting Acts of 1990 and 1996 and the British Broadcasting Corporation is an area in which no functions have been devolved. The ITC, Radio Authority, Broadcasting Standards Commission [all now replaced by OfCom], S4C and BBC Cymru/Wales will however make their Annual Reports available to the Assembly for information to facilitate debate. The Secretary of State [for Culture, Media and Sport] will consult the First Secretary on broadcasting matters of special relevance to Wales. (Department of Culture, Media and Sport, 2000, para. 32)

The concordat did, though, acknowledge that matters such as broadcasting and film – another area where no specific functions had been devolved – could be considered by the Assembly in respect of its responsibility for arts, culture and the Welsh language (Department of Culture, Media and Sport, 2000: paras 31, 33). The secretary of state for culture, media and sport would also continue to make appointments to public bodies such as the BBC board of governors and the S4C

Authority (Department of Culture, Media and Sport, 2000: paras 44–7). These and other related matters became the subject of an inquiry by the Welsh Affairs Select Committee, almost guaranteeing that while powers relating to broadcasting were 'reserved' to Westminster, this subject would be addressed by a future Assembly.

The Welsh Affairs Select Committee

The committee launched its inquiry in August 1998. Its report, *Broadcasting in Wales and the National Assembly*, was published in May 1999 and listed thirty-seven recommendations and conclusions. The committee's terms of reference encompassed plans for covering the Assembly elections and the work of the Assembly, problems with television reception, the impact of digital broadcasting and what role the Assembly should play in respect of broadcasting in Wales (Welsh Affairs Select Committee (WASC), 1999: 1).

Evidence, in the form of submissions, was sought from a wide range of sources, including broadcasters, regulators, trade unions and politicians, and these were supplemented with oral sessions in London, Cardiff and Newtown. In thanking contributors, the committee noted that broadcasting had always been a sensitive subject when raised with politicians, but was 'doubly sensitive' in Wales due to issues relating to the Welsh language. The committee was generally satisfied about plans to broadcast Assembly elections and its proceedings, and it was also cognizant of the importance of broadcasting and allied sectors to economic development in Wales. As a result, the more substantive and potentially controversial elements of the inquiry centred on television reception and digital broadcasting, but in particular on the Assembly's role in relation to broadcasting.

Accountability
A key theme of the inquiry was the issue of accountability. The committee did not agree with the decision that appointments to public bodies such as the BBC board of governors and S4C Authority should be made by the DCMS. It rejected the government's view that 'constitutional niceties' required that such appointments be responsible to the government as a whole and that to do otherwise could risk unbalancing the BBC's independence. With not one broadcasting body wholly regulated in Wales, the committee believed that direct appointments by the Assembly, or their approval of such appointments, would clarify

issues of independence and make it clear that the appointees were accountable to the people of Wales (WASC, 1999: para. 18).

Turning to S4C and the BBC, the committee rejected the idea of devolving responsibility for the former to the Assembly and accepted the view that to break up the latter would be unwise due to the potential negative impact on public service broadcasting in Wales. Nevertheless, aspects of accountability were raised in respect of both organizations (WASC, 1999: paras 19, 21). S4C's accountability was described as 'somewhat weak' and this was seen to be particularly problematic at a time when the organization had embarked on new commercial initiatives and expanded its digital services. This judgement was premised on the fact that S4C was self-regulating, that it was not obliged to consult on service changes and that there was no formal means of reviewing the organization on a regular basis, unlike the BBC's charter process (WASC, 1999: paras 19–20). However, this will now change following plans by the DCMS to review the performance of the S4C Authority on a regular basis (S4C, 2002: para. 2.1).

As regards the BBC, the committee reflected the strength of the submissions it had received in arguing that BBC Wales should have more autonomy (WASC, 1999: paras 22–3). The committee argued that the independence of the Broadcasting Council for Wales (BCW) was compromised because it was chaired by the BBC's national governor for Wales and its members were appointed by the board of governors (WASC, 1999: paras 22–3). The BCW was, therefore, part of the BBC, rather than being independent of it. As a result, the committee recommended that the national governor for Wales should no longer chair the BCW (WASC, 1999: para. 22). The committee was also sensitive to the possibility that S4C and BBC Wales could become distracted from their prime role as public service broadcasters due to the increasing pressure to raise revenue from commercial activities. This prompted the idea of establishing a Welsh body, independent of the political process, to regulate, or monitor, both broadcasters. The committee envisaged a revamped BCW taking on such a role, if 'extracted' from the BBC (WASC, 1999: paras 23–4).

In respect of the Independent Television Commission (ITC) and HTV, the committee again argued for greater accountability in Wales, noting that the post of national member for Wales on the ITC was vacant and had been so for some time (WASC, 1999: para. 25). As a means of strengthening accountability within Wales, the committee raised the possibility of splitting the HTV franchise for Wales and the west of England and creating separate 'regional' ITC offices, but the idea was rejected because it would duplicate costs (WASC, 1999: para. 25). Although the committee was hopeful that devolution would eventually result in broadcasters in Wales being more accountable to the Assembly, it acknowledged that the regulation of broadcasting now occurred in a UK and European context (WASC, 1999: para. 27).

Television leakage

Not surprisingly, with poor television reception in parts of Wales a long-standing problem, the committee received detailed and wide-ranging submissions on this matter (WASC, 1999: paras 38–9, 44). It was also evident that the broadcasters would not correct this situation because analogue transmission was now viewed as a dying technology and not worthy of further investment. Furthermore, there was a realization that the introduction of digital television would not necessarily overcome these problems (WASC, 1999: paras 40–3). Issues of affordability were also raised by the committee, with many viewers reported to be unwilling, or unable, to pay for the equipment needed to access digital television and particularly for those services that they currently received free of charge (WASC, 1999: para. 41).

The committee was also informed that, in addition to those viewers who were unable to view Welsh television, up to 330,000 people living within the overlap area of English transmitters watched television from England, either through choice or from a lack of awareness of Welsh options (WASC, 1999: para. 44). This data, coupled with the realization that up to 87 per cent of the Welsh population read newspapers published in London, prompted the idea of an 'information deficit' which, the committee argued, the Assembly and the broadcasters needed to address (WASC, 1999: para. 46).[21] One of the submissions that raised this issue outlined the potential implications:

> If this 'information deficit' is not addressed seriously – and quickly – the result may well be the creation of a sizeable minority increasingly alienated from the political process in Wales. Lack of information not only effectively precludes active participation in the democratic process, but breeds mistrust and misapprehension. (Wyn Jones, 1998: 2)

In terms of both its process and end product, the inquiry was highly significant. First, the report authorized the new Assembly to address a non-devolved matter and one with long-standing significance in Wales.

Second, the consultation process undertaken by the enquiry required
broadcasters and broadcasting bodies to put their views on the public
record and to be accountable, albeit in a limited way, to the people of
Wales. It also provided an opportunity for key elements of Welsh civil
society to launch – or relaunch – familiar debates that would inevitably
gather pace.

The Assembly

The Assembly held its first plenary on broadcasting in November 1999,
six months after the official opening ceremony (National Assembly for
Wales, 1999). Most of the issues raised in the report by the Welsh
Affairs Select Committee featured in this debate. As a result, the Post-
16 Education and Training Committee (Post-16 Committee) was asked
to meet with the broadcasters to discuss the report's recommendations.
Already committed to undertake a wide-ranging policy review of arts
and culture in Wales, in which BBC Wales, S4C and HTV were
expected to participate, the Post-16 Committee would now meet with
broadcasters and broadcasting bodies to discuss two separate but
related matters.

Post-16 Committee
In pursuing its policy review of arts and culture in Wales the Post-16
Committee met with representatives of BBC Wales, HTV and S4C in
May 2000. In wide-ranging discussions the broadcasters were asked
whether the Assembly should have a role in relation to broadcasting
and whether there might be value in establishing a minister for culture
with a corresponding subject committee – a Welsh equivalent of the
DCMS at Westminster (Post-16 Committee, 2000b).

   In November 2000, after a six-month period of consultation, the
Post-16 Committee published its report, *A Culture in Common*, an
extensive document with over 100 recommendations (Post-16 Committee,
2000a). The report articulated a vision for Wales and set out principles
to guide future policy development (Post-16 Committee, 2000a: 58).
Over a period of ten years, the ultimate aim of policy was to achieve five
ends:

   a rich culture in support of stronger communities;
   a confident diversity – making the most of our positive distinctiveness and
   identity;

a learning country supported by a vibrant artistic and cultural activity;
enterprising industry, and a creative culture;
national ambition, and international reach. (Post-16 Committee, 2000a: 16)

To help in achieving these goals the committee recommended the
establishment of a Cultural Consortium/Cymru'n Creu in order to
encourage open communication, to provide a forum for discussion and
to demonstrate a partnership approach to the culture portfolio (Post-16
Committee, 2000a: 58). This latter body was established in February
2001 and included amongst its membership representatives from Sgrîn,
S4C, BBC Wales and HTV (Welsh Assembly Government, 2002: 64).[22]
In line with its own recommendations in *A Culture in Common*, the Post-
16 Committee would later be replaced by a Culture Committee.

In June 2000, taking its direction from the Assembly's first debate on
broadcasting, the Post-16 Committee met separately with representatives
from the ITC, Channel 4, S4C, BBC Wales and HTV to discuss the
recommendations made by the Welsh Affairs Select Committee. It set
two objectives for these meetings: 'to gain an understanding of key issues
in broadcasting, and where the broadcasting bodies stand on them; and
to identify issues of significance to Wales, and any areas where there
could be a case for seeking to influence the UK government' (Post-16
Committee, 2000c: 2). Essentially, these meetings focused on: 'missing'
Welsh viewers; the introduction of digital television, terrestrial, satellite
and cable; potential changes to the UK's regulatory framework; and
whether responsibilities for broadcasting should be devolved. Responses
to the latter two issues are worth noting.[23] The ITC rejected the idea of
a Welsh system of regulation on the basis that broadcasting did not
respect national boundaries, and advised that the most appropriate
model for Wales was one that would enable 'adjunct advice' on broadcasting (Post-16 Committee, 2000c: 4). Representatives from HTV chose
not to respond to questions about the devolution of powers relating to
broadcasting because of their dual-franchise status which spanned
Wales and the west of England. They did, however, argue for a looser
form of regulation on the basis that the current system was overly
prescriptive and required 'too much box ticking'.

Representatives from S4C acknowledged the eventual possibility of a
Broadcasting Authority for Wales, but raised questions about how the
BBC and the (now defunct) ITC could be federalized and whether
broadcasters such as Channel 4 and BSkyB would be represented on
such a body. Anticipating changes to the UK's regulatory system and

unhappy about the lack of a Welsh presence on the government's expert panel which advised on communications reform, members of S4C were adamant that Welsh representation on any new structure was essential and should not be limited to a single voice. Channel 4's response to questions about devolution was somewhat less heartfelt but nonetheless amusing, its representative noting how peculiar it was that there had been 'devolution of health, but not *Casualty*'! (Post-16 Committee, 2000c: 7).

Culture Committee
In October 2000 the Assembly announced the appointment of a minister for culture, sport and the Welsh language. It also established a corresponding committee to be known as the Culture Committee, with a remit that included broadcasting and media. This resulted in the dissolution of the Post-16 Committee. The Culture Committee met broadcasters in November and December 2000 to seek their views on the government White Paper, *A New Future for Communications* (Culture Committee, 2000a; 2000b). The information gleaned from these meetings provided the basis of the Assembly Cabinet's response to the White Paper. It was tabled at a plenary session of the Assembly in February 2001 where it was endorsed with some minor amendments (National Assembly for Wales, 2001b).[24]

The Culture Committee inherited, but did not adopt, *A Culture in Common* (Culture Committee, 2003: 1), the intention being to transform this extensive and detailed overview of arts and culture in Wales into a coherent and achievable strategy for cultural development. The outcome, *Creative Future: Cymru Greadigol*, a culture strategy for Wales, was published in January 2002 and launched officially the following month (Randerson, 2002c). Taking its cue from *A Culture in Common*, this first ever cultural strategy for Wales was underpinned by a broad understanding of 'culture' and was envisaged as a 'cross-cutting' initiative that would feed into and respond to other portfolios in the Assembly, particularly economic development and community regeneration:

> [O]ur cultural life cannot be parcelled up separately from the rest of living. Rather it infuses everything. It follows that the task of creating a 'culture in common' and a truly creative society is a task for the whole administration. It will be a test of our capacity for 'joined-up thinking', across the whole range of government. The full development of our cultural potential should be an over-arching theme. (Welsh Assembly Government, 2002: 2)

Creative Future: Cymru Greadigol is built around eight themes to guide the work of cultural bodies. It includes over 100 recommendations and highlights the importance of 'cultural professionals'. Its cross-cutting intentions in respect of broadcasting, film and new media – all now incorporated under the banner of creative industries – are apparent in a section on 'culture and the economy', and premised on the view that 'culture can be a springboard to a more prosperous society' (Welsh Assembly Government, 2002: 48).

Digital developments are seen as a way of opening up opportunities for both languages and a further means of promoting the cultural diversity of Wales locally and globally (Welsh Assembly Government, 2002: 50). Local radio also receives a mention, with suggestions that Wales has been 'let down' by the broadcasters and regulators, particularly in respect of radio formats and coverage (Welsh Assembly Government, 2002: 50). This development is noteworthy because in all previous debates about broadcasting in the Assembly, and in its subject committees, local radio had received barely a mention. Neither were the owners of such stations, nor the regulating body, invited to join other broadcasters at the Assembly to discuss impending technological and legislative developments. Film also receives attention. Despite a recognition that levels of production and distribution in Wales fail to match those in Scotland and Ireland, there is a determination to 'transform the film industry in Wales into one of the most active in Europe' (Welsh Assembly Government, 2002: 50). Action plans have been created as a means of 'correcting' or 'redirecting' these media, such as:

To ask the Radio Authority and other regulators [all now subsumed by OfCom] to investigate ways of making the audio-visual environment in Wales a leader in the field not an afterthought.

Establish a Cymru'n Creu sub-group on ICT to develop proposals for a Welsh 'Culture on Line' concept.

To restructure the work of film commissioners in Wales to ensure the most simple, efficient and effective service to the film industry and to increase the total inward investment.

In partnership with UK wide authorities, encourage new broadcasting initiatives based in Wales and increase the number and range of TV and radio channels covering the affairs and interests of Wales. (Welsh Assembly Government, 2002: 52–3)

While action plans such as these demonstrate the Assembly's intentions to harness broadcasting, film-making and new media to its cultural strategy, its powers to do so are limited. The Assembly has no role in shaping the policy framework in respect of broadcasting or film at the wider UK level, neither does it have any formal role or responsibilities in respect of the mass media operating within its borders. Moreover, while the then minister for culture, sport and the Welsh language, Jenny Randerson, has argued that Wales needs a 'strong Welsh voice in communications' (Randerson, 2002b: 1), its powers and numerical presence at OfCom suggest a diminished rather than strengthened role in the regulatory arena. It is also noteworthy that no major concerns were raised in plenary sessions at the Assembly about the thrust of the Communications Act 2003, in particular the implications for Wales following the loosening of rules on ownership and cross-media ownership.

Conclusion

The case has long been made for a media policy for Wales based on the uniqueness of its features within the wider UK, in particular its two languages, culture and topography. Furthermore, specific suggestions have been made on the range of responsibilities that could be devolved to Wales at some stage (see, for example, Osmond, 1998; Mungham and Williams, 1998). However, certain events have worked to undermine such possibilities. During a period in which there was much discussion about Wales being given a 'voice' in the form of a devolved Assembly, the UK government introduced radical legislation in the form of the Communications Act 2003 which impacts on Wales's communicative space. There has also been a consolidation and centralization of regulatory arrangements in the form of OfCom. When compared to the previous system of regulation, this has reduced the numerical presence and power of representatives from Wales.

The so-called 'new' future for communications merely marks a continuation of the direction set by Margaret Thatcher. That is, a preference for market-based mechanisms of service delivery and a view that media and communications remain a key driver of economic growth in an information society. It is, therefore, not surprising that media policy becomes subordinated to industrial and economic policy (Garnham, 1998: 214). As a result, it is a cultural – and not a media –

policy that has emerged in Wales; one which sees 'old' and 'new' media being harnessed to policies whose prime aim is to achieve economic outcomes which in turn will, it is hoped, achieve cultural goals. McIntyre (1996) has questioned the validity of cultural agencies using public funding to subsidize industry and industrial development, querying who are the prime beneficiaries of such arrangements. Strikingly, he observes that,

> There has been a general historical drift that has seen regional arts agencies with responsibility for film and video [previously the ACW and now Sgrîn] increasingly moving away from culturally and aesthetically autonomous arts practices and embedding themselves and their work within a general rhetoric of 'cultural industries' while simultaneously increasingly successfully brokering co-funding deals with broadcasters in order that regional film and video production secures high production values of mainstream industry and therefore can be seen to validate those rhetorical claims. (McIntyre, 1996: 215)

Such developments do little to address the wider structural issues that have shaped the media in Wales and brought about a situation where concerns about ownership and accountability are seen to impact on issues such as democracy and national identity. Neither do they help in 'correcting' another mismatch between rhetoric and reality. That is, the almost universal failure of politicians and those who serve them in the policy arena to make connections between 'active citizenship' and greater public participation at all levels of the mass media. Moreover, devolution has barely impacted on a situation that allows mass-media organizations in Wales to remain unaccountable to the people through their democratically elected representatives at the Assembly. Nonetheless, the advent of the Assembly has provided an important arena for the public discussion of communications and cultural policy in Wales, one which hitherto had not existed on such a scale or at this level of national legitimacy.

Notes

[1] Examples of this type of activity are described by O'Malley (1994: 22–7) and Williams (1996: 6, 9).

[2] A further document, *Consultation on Media Ownership*, was published in 2001.

3   The White Paper was informed by the work of an 'expert' panel. This group
    did not include a Welsh representative, nor anyone who had relevant or
    recent experience of working or living in Wales (Barlow, 2001).
4   This view might be contrasted with that of the Campaign for Press and
    Broadcasting Freedom. It argues that the regulation of communications
    must be organized differently from other areas of the economy because a
    diverse media enabling a plurality of views and opinions is essential for the
    process of citizenship and the interests of citizens and consumers (Campaign
    for Press and Broadcasting Freedom, 2001: 1). See also Barnett (2003c: 22),
    who responded to the Bill by saying: 'What lies behind this Bill is a blind,
    almost theological, conviction that – against all global evidence to the
    contrary, against the warnings of experts, against the pleas of those at the
    creative coalface – markets and competition will deliver more and better
    creativity.'
5   The Richard Commission (see n. 11) was critical of the fact that the NAfW
    had not made representations to the Joint Committee (see Randerson, 2002a).
6   Leighton Andrews AM discussed all the changes raised by the NAfW and
    the responses from the UK government at a conference, Communication in
    Wales after the Communications Act, held at the University of Wales,
    Aberystwyth, on 29–30 March 2004.
7   In contrast, the Campaign for Press and Broadcasting Freedom (O'Malley,
    2002b: 6) argues for a more accountable form of regulation where regulators
    are elected rather than appointed and that they be required to represent the
    public at large rather than the industry.
8   Stephen Carter is the chief executive of OfCom and formerly chief operating
    officer of the debt-laden cable company, NTL.
9   Some such matters are also considered in chapter 9.
10 The OfCom Board is chaired by Lord David Currie, dean of the Business
    School at London's City University. Also on the board is Ian Hargreaves,
    director of corporate and public affairs for the international airport group
    BAA, and professor of journalism at Cardiff, who has previously canvassed
    the idea of scrapping the BBC licence fee, privatizing the organization and
    introducing advertising (G. Williams, 1996: 12).
11 Under the stewardship of the Rt Hon. Lord Richard QC, the 'Commission
    on the Powers and Electoral Arrangements of the National Assembly
    for Wales' was established in 2002 and reported in March 2004 (see
    www.wales.gov.uk).
12 Sue Balsom was a member of the Broadcasting Council for Wales. Her CV,
    along with those of other content board members, was made available on
    the OfCom website when she was appointed (www.ofcom.org.uk).
13 Yet again, critics will raise questions about the appointment, rather than
    election, of these people and the extent to which they are representative of
    the wider citizenry.
14 Support for an advisory structure of this nature emerged as a result of a task
    group appointed by Jenny Randerson. This group – small, select and hardly

representative – was chaired by Geraint Talfan Davies. The two options it considered were: 'i) That an OfCom Wales Communications Council should be established to advise and assist the executive team in Wales, ii) That no advisory structure be created by OfCom, and that the executive team in Wales should be reliant instead on a structured relationship with the National Assembly and the Welsh Assembly Government' (OfCom Advisory Group, 2003: 18). It recommended the former. This document can be located at: *www.wales.gov.uk/subiculture/content/ofcom-report-e.pdf*.

[15] Simon Gibson's CV and those of the other members of the consumer panel were included on the OfCom website (*www.ofcom.org.uk*).

[16] One member of the executive is Ed Richards, a former media adviser to the New Labour government, whose role is senior partner, strategy and market developments.

[17] See Campaign for Press Broadcasting and Freedom (2002b: para. 3.3) on this issue.

[18] Equity (2002: 2), the actors' trade union, refers to an earlier period when HTV's proud announcement to the Welsh Affairs Select Committee that it intended to increase its drama output from 11 to 20 hours was abandoned almost immediately after its take-over by Carlton Communications. This resulted in a reduction of jobs and a further diminution of indigenous programming.

[19] The National Union of Journalists (2002: 2) asserts that 'the BBC will increasingly be drawn into [OfCom's] orbit'.

[20] For instance, the White Paper was released on 12 December 2000, with submissions required by 12 February 2001. Likewise, the *Consultation on Media Ownership* was released on 26 November 2001, with responses required by 25 January 2002.

[21] This idea of an 'information deficit' is addressed in chapter 2.

[22] The work of Sgrîn, the Media Agency for Wales, is discussed in chapters 4 and 9.

[23] While sources are cited in respect of evidence provided at this hearing, one of the authors of this book, Barlow, also attended. His own notes of the proceedings add additional points not included in the formal record.

[24] Between its submission on the White Paper and its response to the draft Communications Bill, the Assembly held a 'minority party debate' on broadcasting initiated by Plaid Cymru (National Assembly for Wales, 2002d).

9

A Voice for Wales?

This final chapter has two overall aims. First, following on from the preceding chapter's examination of the background to media and communications policy in a UK-wide context and cultural policy in the Welsh context, it presents a sector-by-sector review of the salient policy issues which relate specifically to the press, film, broadcasting and the Internet. This review includes an account of historical developments, where relevant to policy-making, and an evaluation of the actual and potential role of the National Assembly for Wales (NAfW or the Assembly) in each of these areas. The second half of this chapter then puts these considerations in the wider context of a summative assessment of the media in Wales. This latter section draws together the main themes which have been developed in the course of this book, with particular emphasis on a set of key issues, relating especially to economics, technology, geography, language, national identity and diversity.

Media and communications policy

Policymaking and the press

The press in the UK has been regulated by economic and legal instruments. The period from the early sixteenth century to the 1860s was characterized by a variety of legal measures designed either to censor or to restrain publications. From the late nineteenth century onwards, the emphasis shifted away from legal and towards economic regulation.

While the state continued to legislate in relation to the press, the factor which influenced its development most significantly was the development of large-scale, private ownership, a factor which successive governments have, with minor qualifications, allowed to dominate the industry.

In England and Wales the state retained the right to censor prior to publication and to punish severely those writers and publishers who evaded regulation, until the lapse of the licensing laws in 1694. Thereafter, from the early eighteenth century until the 1860s the state used a battery of laws to restrain the publication of newspapers, by making the legal publication of newspapers an expensive business. These measures were eventually described by critics as the 'taxes on knowledge'. They included the imposition of duties for the official 'stamp' necessary for legal publication, paper and advertisement duties. As the nineteenth century progressed these became politically indefensible and difficult to police. By the end of the 1860s most of these economic controls had been repealed (O'Malley and Soley, 2000).

From then onwards the legal position was, and remained, that articulated by Blackstone in his famous legal *Commentaries* of 1765. The law would not prevent publication, but if publication resulted in the infringement of another law, such as libel, then the consequences had to be faced: 'The Liberty of the press is indeed essential to the nature of a free State; but this consists in laying no previous restraints on publications, and not in freedom from censure for criminal matter when published' (Robertson, 1991: 255). While governments have, since the late nineteenth century, generally adopted this position, this has been accompanied by measures which qualify or restrain freedom of the press. The Official Secrets Act 1911 was widely criticized as a way of curtailing legitimate criticism of government policy. It was replaced by the Official Secrets Act 1989, which tightened up the law. Yet it still leaves informants whose main offence has been to embarrass the government liable to prosecution (Curran and Seaton, 2003: 410). The libel laws and legislation such as the Contempt of Court Act 1981 combine further to restrict press freedom (Robertson, 1991: 289–93).

Successive governments have also left the regulation of press standards in the hands of the industry. Throughout the twentieth century the press in the UK has been subjected to recurrent bouts of public criticism about its low standards of accuracy, its constant misrepresentation of people and issues, and grossly unacceptable intrusions into privacy and private grief. The owners therefore established the Press Council (1953–1990) and then the Press Complaints Commission (1991–) to deal with these issues. The Press Complaints Commission receives complaints from the public about breaches of the industry's code. The code covers matters such as privacy, inaccuracy, the reporting of minors and questions of race. Both of these bodies have been subjected to sustained criticism for lacking the power to enforce their decisions. A combination of the relative complexity of establishing satisfactory statutory regulation of standards and the reluctance of politicians to pass legislation that would be fiercely opposed by the press owners has left self-regulation intact. The Human Rights Act 1998 has incorporated the European Convention on Human Rights into UK Law. This guarantees the rights to privacy, respect of family life and freedom of expression, amongst others. Yet it will take some time before the cumulative effects of this Act in the form of case law impact on the industry and the practice of self-regulation (O'Malley and Soley, 2000).

Economic instruments have been the other major tool of press policy. The 1947–9 Royal Commission on the Press was established by the 1945–50 Labour government in response to political concern about the impact of concentration of ownership on diversity (O'Malley, 1997). This concern about ownership remained a source of controversy, but very little was done by successive governments to seriously address the issue (Curran and Seaton, 2003). The two major instruments designed to limit concentration have been the Fair Trading Act 1973 and the Competition Act 1998. These measures have largely been ineffective, for, as Curran and Seaton point out, 'out of the 172 transfers of news-paper ownership to major press groups between 1980 and 2000, only three applications (all involving minor papers) were refused, and a further five approved subject to conditions' (Curran and Seaton, 2003: 354). This relaxed attitude to press ownership was endorsed by the Communications Act 2003 which placed competition law at the centre of media ownership regulation, leaving the Competition Commission and the Office of Fair Trading with responsibility for mergers, in consultation with OfCom (Doyle, 2002: 130). Given the current degree of concentration of ownership in the press in Wales, these developments point towards further, rather than less, concentration of ownership in the future.

The newspaper press in Wales has been subjected to the UK-wide policy framework outlined here. The press in Wales has, as a con-sequence, and in general, become part of UK-wide media companies. The Assembly was not given powers in these areas and is unlikely to acquire them. The most the Assembly could do would be to find ways of funding systematic research into the nature of the press in Wales and, on that basis, intervene. This intervention could take the form of submissions to the Competition Commission, the Office of Fair Trading and OfCom when changes in ownership that affect Wales are planned. The Assembly might also set up a research unit to measure the extent to which self-regulation on matters of standards served the public interest in Wales. In addition, through liaison with other agencies, the Assembly could help to promote initiatives designed to diversify the types of newspapers in Wales. It could also play a role in bringing together owners, trade unions, community interest groups and members of the public to monitor and discuss these issues on a regular basis. The existence of the Assembly therefore provides an opportunity for informed public research, debate and intervention to promote the public interest in this industry in ways which do not exist in England.

Policymaking and film

The development of film in Wales has been constrained by a number of factors. In particular, a limited domestic market has been subject to policy developed for the wider UK, itself overshadowed by the pervasive influence of Hollywood.

The Welsh Arts Council (WAC) began life as part of the Arts Council for Great Britain (ACGB) and was dependent on this body for its finance. Critics argue that the ACGB's meagre funding of the WAC 'retarded film development' in Wales (Berry, 1994: 315). In addition, the Welsh arts establishment was not enamoured of film, preferring to support artists and musicians (Berry, 1994: 312–13; M. Ryan, 1986: 183–4). It was not until 1970 that the WAC established a film committee and made some funding available for film; this after a period of twenty years when no films were made in Wales outside television (Aaron, 1979: 304).

Early beneficiaries of WAC funding included the Newport Film School and Cardiff Street Television. The WAC was later instrumental in helping to establish a film and video workshop sector at the Chapter Arts Centre in Cardiff and Wales's first film archive at Aberystwyth. It also helped to catalyse initiatives to rejuvenate cinemas in the south Wales valleys and other ventures aimed at promoting a greater awareness of Welsh film (Berry, 1994: 312–13, 351, 429–30).

As a measure to try to 'correct' the dearth of Welsh-language films, a Welsh Film Board (WFC)/Bwrdd Ffilmiau Cymraeg (the Bwrdd) was established in 1971, funded by the North Wales Arts Association and the WAC. The WFB/Bwrdd produced a number of features, short films and other productions made especially for children, substantially increasing the number of Welsh-language films that were available for hire (Aaron, 1979: 305–6). Once S4C was established in 1982 the role of the WFB/Bwrdd became less important and it ceased operations in the mid-eighties. However, it is widely acknowledged that the WFB/Bwrdd played a key role in helping to develop and sustain film-makers working in Welsh during a period when few other opportunities were available (Berry, 1994: 331).

Recognition that Wales needed a more coherent and strategic approach to film eventually led to the creation of the Wales Film Council (WFC) in 1993. This was a joint venture by the WAC, S4C and Ffilm Cymru, the latter body having been set up in 1989 by the BBC and S4C to boost film production, its major success being *Un Nos Ola Leuad* (1991) (Berry, 1994: 417, 430, 457). The WFC evolved into Screen Wales in 1994 before Sgrîn Cymru Wales (Sgrîn), the Media Agency for Wales, began operations in 1997. This initiative was driven by the major broadcasters in Wales, the Welsh Development Agency (WDA) and what is now the Arts Council for Wales (ACW).

Following its election in 1997, New Labour initiated a review of film policy and introduced a tax-relief scheme for film production in the UK. In 1998, the Film Policy Review Group published its report, *A Bigger Picture*, which the government adopted as its overarching policy for film (Department of Culture, Media and Sport, 2003a: 5). *A Bigger Picture* set out an action plan to address five problem areas (Film Policy Review Group, 1998: 4–5). First, taking its direction from the US, it recommended that the British Film Industry become 'distribution-led' rather than 'production-led'. Second, it highlighted the need for more investment in training. Third, it stressed the need for an improvement in the commercial viability and quality of British films. Fourth, it argued that work was necessary to increase cinema attendance and bring about a better appreciation and understanding of film. Fifth, the business environment, it was argued, needed to be improved in order to encourage investment from overseas, support British exporters and ensure a lead role in the European film industry.

Following recommendations in *A Bigger Picture*, the government established the UK Film Council in 2000, amalgamating four organizations: British Screen Finance, the British Film Commission, *bfi* production and the Arts Council of England Lottery Film Department. The Film Council is controlled by a government-appointed board of directors drawn from the commercial film industry and film education. As the key body for film in the UK, the Film Council develops film policy and strategy and administers Lottery and government grant-in-aid funding. Public monies are directed to three areas – creativity, industry and education – on the basis that the return will enable 'lasting cultural and economic benefits' (Film Council, 2003: 2).

While no specific functions relating to film are devolved to the NAfW, the Film Council is obliged to make its annual reports available to the Assembly and its UK-wide brief involves establishing a close working relationship with Sgrîn (Department of Culture, Media and Sport, 2000: 6). Within this framework, Sgrîn is expected to develop policies in response to local needs. Unlike the Film Council, but in common with other regional and national film agencies in the UK, Sgrîn places greater emphasis on working with television and new media as well as film (Film Council, 2002: 9). Funded by the ACW, the British Film Institute, BBC Wales, S4C, Teledwyr Annibynnol Cymru (TAC) and the WDA, Sgrîn is the 'lead body' for film in Wales, its brief being to achieve economic and cultural outcomes (Rowlands, 2002–3: 3). Sgrîn's action plans encompass exhibition, production and education.

In terms of exhibition, Sgrîn aims to ensure that all parts of Wales have access to mainstream and cultural cinema; to promote Welsh productions; and to facilitate linkages between exhibitors and other interested parties (Sgrîn, 2002–3: 10). In this regard, it organizes, on an annual basis, an exhibition forum, a Wales Cinema Day and a tour to promote Welsh short films. The Cinema Exhibition Support Fund is used to support 'cultural programming'. This has provided funding for film festivals and subsidies for commercial cinema operators in order to encourage the exhibition of films produced in Wales and other international films (Sgrîn, 2002–3: 10–11).[1] Sgrîn also provides financial support to the Chapter Cinema in Cardiff and the Cardiff Screen Festival.[2] Chapter is expected to screen a range of world cinema and be accessible to a wide range of audiences; to help achieve these goals it received £39,250 in both 2001–2 and 2002–3 (Sgrîn, 2001–2: 12; 2002–3: 11).

To support its goal of increasing film development and production in Wales, Sgrîn now has control over the allocation of Lottery money, a role previously undertaken by the ACW (G. S. Jones, 2001–2: 2). Under its Lottery film production programme thirty-two projects were supported in 2002–3 and another twenty-four received assistance under a 'short film' category, three of which involved Black and Asian film-makers under a programme, 'Digital Visions', an initiative to reflect the diversity of Wales (Sgrîn, 2002–3: 20–1). Sgrîn also provides support services for screenwriters and emerging Welsh film producers.

Sgrîn's education policy has its roots in *A Bigger Picture*, which recommended that attention be given to creating a more ' "cineliterate" population, through education', but with an emphasis on culture rather than vocation (Film Policy Review Group, 1998: para. 6.8). Sgrîn has set itself two aims; the first relates to training and the second to education:

> To facilitate the provision of quality training for the moving image industry in Wales, with particular reference to film.
>
> To encourage audiences to broaden their experience of the moving image by developing and ensuring the provision of formal and informal education activities within the bilingual context of Wales. (Sgrîn, 2002–3: 8)

To meet these aims Sgrîn has developed a 'cross-cutting' education policy that aims to underpin its activities in exhibition and production. Its educational initiatives include: supporting festivals such as the Urdd Eisteddfod in Cardiff and the National Eisteddfod at St Davids; funding Media Education Wales; sponsoring students to attend industry events; and supporting Ffresh, an annual student moving image festival held at Aberystwyth (Rowlands, 2001–2: 5; Sgrîn, 2002–3: 9). Sgrîn's duties also extend to other areas. Through its 'Media Antenna' section Sgrîn provides advice and assistance to film-makers in Wales seeking to access Media Plus, a European Union programme committed to the development of audio-visual industries (Sgrîn, 2002–3: 14–15). A Wales Screen Commission, coordinated by Sgrîn, is now in place to promote Wales as a 'film friendly nation' and attract more film-makers to Wales (Sgrîn, 2002–3: 24). A member of Sgrîn's new media section sits on Cymru'n Creu, a group established by the NAfW to advise on the implementation of cultural policy in Wales (Sgrîn, 2002–3: 19). Although there has been much discussion about the creation of what is variously referred to as a 'Welsh Film Fund', 'Film Fund for Wales' or 'Film, Television and New Media Fund', this has yet to materialize (German, 2001: 1; Randerson, 2003: 2; Sgrîn, 2002–3: 20).

Among the Assembly's priorities at the start of the twenty-first century was the need to find an adequate response to calls by Welsh film-makers for additional 'spaces'. One such space could be the provision of a fifth television channel for Wales, which may become feasible in a digital environment. However, a second and equally challenging proposition is that, because of the idiosyncratic nature of BBC Wales and S4C, an infrastructure separate from television is needed if Wales is to develop a truly independent film sector (Evans, cited in Blandford, 2000c: 86). A further issue is the need to ensure that 'cultural' – as well as commercial – films are produced and exhibited on a regular basis in venues throughout Wales and not just in the major urban centres (see, for example, Morris, 1998: 27–8). Although the now diminished BFI Regional Film Theatres (RFTs) network previously assisted with this goal,[3] the responsibility for extending and expanding access to film in Wales rests with Sgrîn (2002–3: 10–11).[4]

Policymaking and broadcasting

Like press and film policy, broadcasting policy in Wales has been set within a UK framework. Unlike press policy, Welsh political and cultural concerns have had an impact on policy development. The UK policy on broadcasting has been characterized by two major phases. The first phase, from 1922 to the late 1980s, can be described as the public service broadcasting phase, the second, since 1990, the market phase.

The public service broadcasting phase
In the first phase, policy was driven from London, from the government and civil service in Whitehall, and to some extent, by the Houses of Parliament in Westminster. The central instruments – the BBC's Royal Charter, the successive Acts regulating commercial TV and radio (1954, 1964, 1972, 1981) – were designed to ensure centralized state regulation of broadcasting. Unlike the press, broadcasting policy was understood as a matter in which the public interest had a central place. In addition, especially after 1945, wider political tensions within the UK state led to challenges to Whitehall and Westminster's right to speak for Scotland and Wales on political and cultural issues (Weight, 2002). These two factors helped to shape Welsh involvement in the development of broadcasting policy.

The pressure from Welsh political elites resulted in, first, the establishment of a BBC Wales region in radio in 1936 and increasing levels of support for Welsh-language programming. The Broadcasting Council for Wales was a consequence of the critique of the centralizing tendencies of the BBC enunciated in the 1951 Beveridge Report. ITV's regional structure, established after the Television Act 1954, reflected this desire for a less London-centred broadcasting system across the UK. In fact,

Wales benefited from a UK-wide growth in interest about questions of broadcasting accountability amongst political parties and society at large after 1945 (O'Malley, 1998).

Under the public service framework the voices of public interest groups and of nationalist pressure were increasingly taken into account by policy-makers. The creation of commercial TV in Wales, the creation of BBC Wales, Radio Cymru and Radio Wales and eventually of S4C were all responses by London-based policy-makers at the BBC, the IBA, Westminster and Whitehall to political pressure from Wales. Indeed, as we pointed out in chapter 6, Welsh popular politics seems to have played a uniquely influential role in UK broadcasting policy formation.

Yet, within these boundaries, policy-making was top-down. In spite of the developments listed above, policy remained controlled firmly from London. The evolution of a Welsh system within the general system could be viewed as a form of co-option by the centre of critical voices from the periphery. It is significant that the concessions fell far short of the establishment of a Broadcasting Corporation for Wales, for which Plaid Cymru and others had argued.

The market phase
The second phase was characterized by the reorientation of aims in UK broadcasting policy towards the market. Starting with the Broadcasting Act 1990, government policy gradually prioritized the notion that the primary purpose of a broadcasting system was to mimic a commercial market place. Within this emerging framework, public service broadcasting was viewed as a major player, but as one which would increasingly act as a provider of quality services which the market could not provide, but to which the government chose to allocate resources (O'Malley, 2001). Consequently, the rules governing new entrants, such as Sky TV and new and existing commercial radio operators, were significantly more liberal than those which continued to apply to the BBC, ITV, Channel 4 and S4C. Promoting competition and efficiency became the guiding principle underpinning the Communications Act 2003. OfCom's main aim was to promote competition in all areas of commercial electronic communications, including ITV, satellite, commercial radio, digital services, and telecoms. The BBC, S4C and Channel 4, continued to have significant public service responsibilities and, like the press, remained independent of OfCom. The exact nature and the implications of this shift has been the subject of controversy about the extent to which it does, or does not, signal the ultimate

demise of public service broadcasting and its replacement by a largely commercially driven system of communications (O'Malley, 2001; Curran and Seaton, 2003).

In the Welsh context, the most obvious change was in the representation of Welsh interests at the highest level of regulation. Until 2003, the Independent Television Commission and the Radio Authority had a Welsh representative on their main boards. While these people were not democratically accountable to the Welsh public, they were appointed with a view to representing specifically Welsh interests on these bodies. The OfCom board had no such representation. Welsh representatives were included at important – though lower – levels of the organization and OfCom is required to establish National Advisory Committees. The BBC also retained its national governor for Wales. In addition, the increasingly competitive environment within Wales took its toll on S4C's audience, as outlined in chapter 6.

The NAfW appears to be the body best placed to act as a force for greater accountability in Welsh broadcasting. The creation of OfCom was essentially an act of administrative centralization – drawing together bodies that regulated different sectors (commercial TV, commercial radio, telecoms, etc). The creation of the Assembly was a decentralizing measure. The two measures then pulled in opposite directions. While some compromise on OfCom's internal structure was reached in the negotiations around the Communications Act 2003, the fact remained that the Assembly did not have strong powers in relation to the communications industries in Wales. The regime established in the 2003 Act looks set to remain in place for many years.

Whether the Assembly should have more powers over broadcasting in Wales is a matter of debate. On the one hand, it might give too much influence to a body as yet uncertain of its overall role in relation to the Welsh public. On the other, stronger measures might help create a real space for the voices of the communities that make up Wales to have a meaningful influence over the communications which envelop their everyday lives. Whatever the short-term outcome of the changes set in motion by devolution and the 2003 Act, the tension between centralization and devolution that is represented by these two developments will provide material for ongoing debate over the regulation of broadcasting in Wales in the next decades. This, as in press policy, is an area where the Assembly can intervene, promoting research, discussion and policy development, as well as more formal lobbying.

It is impossible to foresee how broadcasting will develop in Wales in the next decades. Yet there can be no doubt that broadcasting policy, unlike policy on the press, film and the Internet, has always provided a vehicle for Welsh voices to be heard and to have influence. The question is whether the influence of those voices will diminish or whether the Assembly can act as a stimulus for a new phase of Welsh involvement and success in policy-making.

Policymaking and the Internet

The development of an integrated set of Internet polices for Wales has proved consistently problematic. As with broadcasting, any Wales-originated policy initiatives in this arena have been circumscribed by and dependent on UK-wide policy-making. This is not the case simply with the Internet, of course; there is also a wider constraint on the development of policies aimed at harnessing the full potential of a range of new-media technologies and thereby constructing a viable 'National Information Infrastructure' (NII). Some have argued that, because of the fact that ICT (information and communication technology) policies have been a particular priority of New Labour, the Assembly's hands have been tied even more tightly in this regard, a problem exacerbated by the conspicuous absence within Wales of the transnational IT firms likely to wield influence on UK-wide and pan-European policy.

Notwithstanding these constraints, however, the Assembly policy-makers may still have some room for manoeuvre, as Selwyn and Gorard have argued: 'Whilst Westminster continues to be directing ICT implementation and establishing a form of "NII" in Wales, the very least that the National Assembly can be attempting to do is to act as effective local "reconstructors" of that NII' (2002: 196). Precisely such a process of 'reconstruction' has, it would appear, been attempted in Wales by a range of NAfW policy initiatives relevant to the Internet, channelled under policy areas which *have* been devolved, the chief examples being industry and training; culture; education; Welsh language; and economic development. Much of the post-devolutionary policy thinking in this regard has emerged from the Welsh Development Agency's 'Wales Information Society' project, which benefited from European Union backing and was designed to 'accelerate the introduction of an information society in Wales' (Welsh Development Agency, 1998: 15).

There are ongoing strategic policy debates concerning both Wales's enforced subservience to UK-wide policy-making and the NAfW's attempts to operate within these constraints. A number of these debates are carried out against the backdrop of pan-European Union (EU) policy developments from the European Commission.[5]

The UK-wide policy perspective is itself far from straightforward, however. The New Labour government took a deliberate and strategic decision to omit the Internet from the scope of the Communications Act 2003, other than its references to 'associated facilities' and 'electronic communication networks' (Collins, 2003). The overall policy approach implies that the government sees this medium as one which can be self-regulated through an open market or through self-regulating network institutions. Collins (2003) points out that this approach may lead to a set of potentially anomalous situations in which identical or overlapping content services, such as video streaming, are governed by disparate regulatory approaches.

Nevertheless, a further and clarificatory indication of the UK government's perspective on Internet regulation can be observed in the role of its UK Online Office, a discrete government department set up in 1999 and overseen by an e-envoy with the specific remit of developing and monitoring policy initiatives, including those initiated by post-devolutionary governments in Wales, Scotland and Northern Ireland. This office's approach to Internet policy is encapsulated in its 2003 annual report. The consistent discourse presented here is one which consists of 'pro-competitive policies', a 'light touch regulatory framework' in debt to a beneficent 'early deregulation of the telecoms market', and which is guided by the overall policy goal of 'us[ing] technology to fit government around customers, not customers into government' (UK online, 2003: 4, 20, 6 and 36). Such thinking pervades successive annual reports published by the e-envoy. The societal impact of the development of the Internet's potential is conceived as strongly focused on consumers, and the new medium's possible role in enhancing an informed and democratically active citizenry is downplayed. Moreover, the potential need for a more integrated policy aimed at fomenting home access is smothered by the conclusions drawn from usage patterns of public access points. Here, the fact that *some* usage is made of these access points – however limited – is emphasized and the question of whether there is evidence for *sustained* use is sidelined.

It is true that the 2003 annual report does also refer in places to 'e-citizens', but this concept is defined only by inference, in a manner which is highly revealing of the policy-makers' thinking. The claim is made, for example, that '96% of Britain's population are aware of a place where they can readily access the internet' (2003: 5) and that 'with 61% of the population now reporting that they have used the Internet at some time, "e-citizens" now make up a majority of the adult population' (2003: 6). In other words, the mere fact of possessing Internet access (or even just the knowledge of where access might be gained) is apparently conflated with the exercising of the full set of rights and obligations of an active citizenry. Similarly, much is made of the existence of 'UK online centres', cyber cafés, and so on, to the extent that 'the race for physical access is over' (2003: 6) and that 'opportunities to physically access the internet are now available to all' (2003: 4, 5). Such claims, however, seem to ignore the crucial importance of home access, despite the fact that the report itself cites Sweden as a 'benchmarked country' precisely because it has the highest home Internet access levels in Europe, and goes on to recognize that home users tend to spend more time on-line and are more likely to become consistent and sophisticated users (2003: 12).[6]

Against this constraining backdrop, therefore, the Assembly has sought to develop its own policies relating to ICT technologies generally and to the Internet in particular. In doing so, the NAfW consistently links them to its ten-year economic strategy development. For example, in developing an overall aim for fully Wales-wide broadband access by 2010, the NAfW government's policy is based on the idea of aggregating public sector demand for broadband as leverage to encourage private sector investment, and for local authorities to set their own interim broadband connection targets. Doubts have been raised, however, about the viability of the success of such an approach. Downing (2002: 24–5), for example, cites the relatively small size of the market in Wales as a reason for concluding that 'universal access to broadband is unlikely to be achieved by market forces alone and is likely to require some form of substantial public investment or subsidy, an issue that will need to be addressed at both national and UK government level'.

As discussed in chapter 7, the flagship of the Assembly's ICT strategy, launched in November 2001, is Cymru Ar-lein/Online for a Better Wales. This programme prioritizes its policy objectives as follows: 'to ensure First Class Infrastructure, to promote Wales in the world, to improve understanding and awareness, to improve services and facilities and to develop and maintain skills and expertise' (National Assembly for Wales, 2003). In Selwyn and Gorard's words, the NAfW see their own policy-making position as 'mirroring the role of the Westminster government in avoiding the extremes of *dirigiste* state

control and laissez-faire marketism and, instead, act
and "steward" in stimulating the use of ICT in Wale.
NAfW's policy initiatives have met with a significant ar.
However, further policy debate in Wales is likely to foct
of key issues. The Welsh Consumer Council has marked ᴄ
policy priorities for the NAfW to take up, based on its own rᴇ
reveals that 'a staggering 55% of Welsh consumers currently make no
use of the Internet at all' (Tuck, 2003: 17). The council calls for a more
fully developed prioritizing of rural areas and for the commissioning of
further research to gain a better understanding of reasons for non-use.
It also makes a pointed call for the allocation of public funding
designed to 'make broadband access available in areas where it may not
be justifiable on commercial grounds alone' (Downing, 2002: 33).

These recommendations fall short, however, of any explicit exhort-
ation to tackle the problem of the absence of home access, merely saying
that 'targeted measures should be introduced to ensure that people of
school age do not suffer disadvantage as a result of lack of home
internet access' (Downing, 2002: 33). It is here, therefore, that the ideas
of the Institute for Public Policy Research (IPPR) may be relevant (as
outlined in Tambini, 2000). The IPPR argues in favour of the creation
of a Universal Service Fund (USF), to which all network owners would
contribute and whose overarching objective would be to facilitate
universal domestic access to the Internet, based on the idea that this USF
would also expect contributions from general taxation; from an access
fee (analogous to the existing television licence fee); from a national
e-lottery; and from the sale of advertising space on public service Internet
portals. This argument also extends to the proposed creation of a discrete
department within OfCom with specific responsibility for promoting
universal access. Such a move would clearly involve a radical re-
evaluation, on the UK government's part, of the relationship between the
new regulatory system and Internet technology, and would also involve
a questioning of the ethos and policy thinking which precedes and
underlies the Communications Act 2003.

Wales and its media

Scotland, Wales and England had been locked for four centuries in an
uneasy relationship. From 1940 to 2000 they not only rediscovered their
core national identities, they also re-imagined themselves shedding many

of the assumptions about class, race, gender and religion which once denied millions of people the right to belong to their nation. (Weight, 2002: 2)

Richard Weight has summarized the ways in which the United Kingdom of 1939 became less united by 2000. The core national identities of Scotland, Wales and England gained wider cultural acceptance internally and across the UK, finding legislative expression in devolution. It is not necessary to accept that there is such a thing as a core national identity to subscribe to the view that what happened was a profound shake-up in how the peoples of the UK understood their relations with each other.

These changes were embedded in wider shifts in the ethnic, sexual, cultural, economic and political fabric of the British islands in which Wales was as involved as any other part of the UK. The period after 1945 was also the time when radio, TV and subsequently satellite, digital and Internet services spread across the UK and became key windows through which Welsh society viewed itself, viewed the world and was observed.

These changes in communications were rooted in longer-term changes in mass communications going back at least to the nineteenth century. From the era of industrialization, after 1780, there emerged forms of communications which, like the railway, the telegraph, mechanized printing, photography and cinema, both shaped and were shaped by the new, modern, urban Wales of the last two hundred years.

So, thinking about the media in Wales demands that we see communications as embedded in wider social, cultural and political change in industrialized societies in general and in the UK in particular. This helps us avoid too heavy a stress on the short term and the particular, and helps us make important connections between the media and wider transformations.

It also helps us think about the media historically. The communication networks of Wales in 1800 were radically different to those of 1900. In the intervening years rapid industrialization and demographic change were accompanied by changes in popular literacy, the explosion of a bilingual newspaper and periodical press and the beginnings of the modern audio-visual industry in the form of the early cinema. Anxieties about these changes were voiced in the press in Wales, but they also found expression in concerns about the print media (A. Jones, 1996). The period 1900 to 2000 saw equally dramatic demographic, cultural and economic change. A worker in rural Wales in 1900 had less access to information about Wales and the world than did her counterpart in 2000, if only because of the spread of radio and TV.

During the period from 1800 to 2000 the mental landscape of Wales changed profoundly. The media were part of these changes and as such were a constant source of comment, both praise and condemnation. A historical perspective can help us recognize the sheer differences between periods and challenge the creation of too simplistic a set of generalizations. Yet, just as it allows us to respect the different worlds of 1800, 1850 or 1970, so it allows us to see continuities in the issues connected with the media in Wales. There are key, recurring themes, many of which we have touched on in this book, including economics, technology, geography, politics, language, class and the national question, which illuminate our understanding of the media in Wales.

Economics

The media in Wales have been shaped by economics. The relation of Wales to the English economy has always been very important. The press in Wales has, since the late nineteenth century, been subordinated increasingly to the economic power of the London press. With few exceptions, the press in 2004 in Wales was dominated by a few large UK-wide companies. Most people in Wales have been reading English-language, often London-produced papers, for over a century.

The film industry in Wales has never had the economic strength seriously to challenge the dominance of the English or American industries. It has survived as a result of the dedication and ingenuity of individuals and of various forms, direct or otherwise, of state support. Broadcasting in Wales has relied on the central economic support of the British state, in the form of either the licence fee, the regulated allocation of advertising revenue to programme making in Wales or the subsidies for S4C. Even the Internet's take-up and use is shaped by the economic capacities of the people of Wales.

On balance, the powerful impetus of profit-making has driven the cinema and the press in the UK and Wales, while broadcasting and some film-making have relied on state subsidy or indirect support. It has been this economic weakness of the Welsh media industries that has underpinned anxieties about media concentration, concerns about Anglicization and the information deficit. The cultural fears that have driven so much public debate about the media in Wales have always had the ghost of economic weakness hovering in the background.

The economic theory which by 2004 informed UK government media policy assumed that in future the diverse communicative needs of the peoples of Wales would be met by a mix, in which the market played the major role, and public service the minor one. Yet, the economic history of the media in Wales points in another direction. The economic weakness of the Welsh economy relative to the English has meant that the British state has had constantly to intervene to address communicative deficiencies, if only in the form of active support for a Welsh radio, TV and, to some extent, film industry. The debates over these issues will doubtless continue to rage in Wales as in the UK as a whole.

Technology

A similar case can be made in relation to technology. In the case of the early phases of the newspaper, cinema and radio industries the technologies involved were relatively inexpensive. As these industries matured, so too did the sophistication of the technology and the cost of sustaining viable networks of production and distribution. The benefits of broadcasting technology, in the form of universal access to TV and radio signals came about because of government-sponsored investment in infrastructure such as masts, studios and programming. The geographical obstacles to road transport posed by the Welsh mountains have also meant that the technological cost of the roll-out of radio, TV and broadband technologies in Wales is higher than in the UK as a whole. The data we have on the Internet, a privately driven system, points to significant inequalities of access across Wales, often driven by differentials in income. The cost of digital TV to subscribers is also a key factor in take-up.

This all points away from seeing technological change as an independent force in the development of the media industries in Wales. The deployment and diffusion of media technologies have always been, and will remain, embedded in the health of the economy, in the economics of the media industries and in the willingness of governments or industry to invest so as to achieve universal access. This, in turn, is based upon political decisions, decisions which cannot be avoided, no matter how hard some politicians wish to believe that technologies fused with markets will deliver universal access and fair distribution of the benefits associated with media technologies.

Geography

Geography has also been more than just an issue to do with technological roll-out. The industrial geography of Wales has shifted over time.

The concentration of communications networks and centres (roads, rail, airports) in south Wales has exacerbated perceptions of the divisions that exist within Wales between the north, the south and the west. Wales, as the nature of its newspaper press illustrates, can be viewed more as a set of linked local cultures that have stayed more salient there than in England because of the physical problems associated with transport. This local dimension has also been reflected in the different dialects within Welsh, and the older perceptions, erroneous as the 2001 census pointed out, that Welsh was not spoken to any great extent in the south. It has also fed into criticism of the Assembly, which has been viewed by some as a southern institution rather than a truly national one.

Yet, set against this has been the way the press, cinema and especially broadcasting have provided communicative bridges across the geographical boundaries. The conception of Wales as a unified geographical and cultural space in the period after 1800 has been rooted in the ways various media have sought to articulate that unity. This was particularly true of broadcasting, which for the first time in Welsh history allowed people in Wales to witness representations of their country in real time, simultaneously. A further, complicating factor has been the porous boundary between England and Wales. Wales and England are co-occupants of a small geographical space, and so it is not surprising that the media has been, in important senses, a mixed media, especially since the transport revolutions of railways and cars; a situation that for much of the twentieth century provoked grave concerns amongst cultural nationalists in Wales, fearing the eventual absorption of Welsh culture by its powerful neighbour.

Language

The differences between the ways in which Welsh is spoken in different parts of the country point to the importance of the language in thinking about the media in Wales. Bilingualism within Wales reflects the normal experience of peoples the world over. It has been the idea that monolingualism based on English should be the norm that the language debates and activism in Wales challenged in the last century.

In 2001 most Welsh people were monolingual English speakers and around 20 per cent were bilingual, that is speaking both Welsh and English. The secular decline in Welsh speakers in the twentieth century was, as we have outlined, frequently blamed, in part or whole, on the popularity and availability of English-language media, be it in print, film or broadcast form. Yet the issues have always been more complex than that. Linguistic change is rooted in economic, demographic, political, social, cultural and technological change. For example, both the influx of workers into the south Wales industrial belt at the start of the twentieth century and the impact of changes in education and transport combined with the spread of cinema and broadcasting to facilitate change. The geographical proximity of Wales and England, always a factor in the fortunes of the Welsh language, was made more important by the rapid changes of the twentieth century. There is no doubt that the media in Wales have been part of these changes, but the jury is out, and perhaps always will be, on the extent to which they have been the prime cause of linguistic change.

Yet language is the bearer of memory, richness, specificity and tradition. It is not at all surprising that it became, as it did in other countries around the world facing industrialization and the demographic and political changes brought in its wake, a central issue in the cultural and political life of Wales. What was won out of these battles was the placing of the Welsh language at the heart of broadcasting in Wales, in the form of BBC and commercial provision and then of S4C. What was overlooked in the policy-making process was the need, advocated by nationalists for many years, of a broadcasting structure for Wales that met the needs of both language groups.

The undoubted success of the language movement in relation to TV and radio has not, to date, been replicated in other areas of the media, such as film or the press. While public support for ventures like the planned all-Welsh, national daily, *Y Byd* (N. Thomas, 2003/4), may help it flourish and for the first time provide Wales with a national, Welsh-language daily, there can be no doubt that the survival of the Welsh language on TV in the digital age will need further effort and imagination on the part of all those in Wales keen to ensure its growth as a living language. For the successes in broadcasting were based on the assumption that the state should ensure that public service broadcasting really did provide a service to the people of Wales, significant numbers of whom used Welsh as their primary form of communication. It was the policy framework that allowed a space for people to argue for this change. The new, market-driven framework embedded primarily in the Communications Act 2003 makes such argument redundant. For, if the market cannot sustain a Welsh-language channel, why should the government subsidize one? This is likely to be one of the most controversial issues to face Welsh communications in the next decade.

On this issue, as on others, the media in Wales have figured as places where wider anxieties about cultural and social change are focused. In this sense the Welsh experience, its fear of being swamped by a separate language and culture, has prefigured the English experience. While grave concerns have always existed in the UK about the Americanization of culture through the influence of cinema, TV and music, the arrival of a multi-channel universe has posed for England, more intensely than before, the same problems of how to protect and sustain a particular set of cultural values as the arrival of English-language broadcasting posed for Wales in the 1920s and 1930s. It remains to be seen how these global influences are absorbed in cultural debate and policy in the UK in the coming period.

The national question

Arguably the problems faced by Welsh-language broadcasting in the more commercially driven, less state-sponsored, digital age could best be dealt with by reconstructing the UK system of broadcasting and media regulation to give more power and autonomy to Wales. This might allow the coordination of resources to promote media culture, in both languages, in structures which were linked through mechanisms of democratic accountability to the Welsh people. This, in turn, leads into thinking about the issue of the Welsh nation; for if there is meaning in the idea of Welsh nationhood then perhaps this should find expression in the extent to which people in Wales control their own media.

We have argued throughout this book that the issues of nationalism and national identity are complex. On the one hand, the Welsh nation has been subordinated in terms of the media to the UK power bases in the industries we have surveyed. On the other, there has never been unanimity in Wales about how to combat this, or whether or not this subordination is desirable. The question of whether the media helped invent or disseminate a particular version of Welshness in the nineteenth and twentieth centuries; or, rather, which particular versions they disseminated and whether or not they had an effect on people's ideas, is a subject of continuing debate. Yet this debate matters to an understanding of the media in Wales.

If Wales stands for anything it is a geographical area containing diverse traditions, at least two languages and a distinctive political and cultural history. The rapid changes of the nineteenth and twentieth centuries both promoted a sense of the political distinctiveness of Wales and led to anxieties about its continuance as a separate entity. Socialists in Wales for many years were opposed to the establishment of separate institutions for Wales which took it away from the power base of Westminster, often because of their internationalism and their view that real power to benefit Wales was in London and not Cardiff or Swansea. For many of these people, then and now, nationalism, be it English nationalism or Welsh nationalism, is a mix of the acceptable and the dangerous: the acceptable in that it rightly stresses the importance of sustaining real, lived traditions; the dangerous in that it is nationalist sentiment that is frequently mobilized to justify crimes against other peoples. Yet, by the end of the twentieth century, a measure of consensus had been achieved, one which considered that Wales, for all its complexities, merited its own democratically elected Assembly.

Given the way in which the political structures in Wales had, by the end of the twentieth century, adapted to the idea of a distinctive Welsh dimension to UK political structures, the issue of its relation to the media was always going to arise. The question of whether Wales should have its own national broadcasting structures has been around for many years. The Assembly has provided a platform for furthering this debate. While the market has delivered a vast amount of differing kinds of media in Wales, it has not been able to deliver diversity in broadcasting, film or the press. If the media in Wales is to become a vehicle for further promoting cultural diversity then the question is: what mechanisms exist to ensure this? We have outlined some of these issues above. It is unlikely that this issue will be resolved easily, or outside of wider changes in UK media policy, but the national question will remain a key dimension in thinking about the media in Wales in the twenty-first century.

Approaches, diversity and voices

Our approach throughout this book has been to stress the political, economic and historical factors shaping the media in Wales. We have tried to address the political economy of the industry in order to grasp many of its key features, to understand change and to see what the related issues of public concern and policy have been. It is clear that the factors we have surveyed in this book are extremely important in understanding the media in Wales, as elsewhere, and, while we have argued the case for particular interpretations of the evidence we have surveyed, we consider that there are many gaps in knowledge about all the areas we have covered. Further research on the history and political economy of the media in Wales is essential if we are to gain a full grasp of its evolving relationship to society.

We have tried also to stress the importance of considering the extent to which the media have contributed to public life and debate in Wales. Drawing on Habermas, we have stressed the normative dimensions of these debates. While we consider that only detailed empirical research, disciplined by the requirements of objectivity and accuracy, will yield useful knowledge about the media in Wales, we also consider that the issue of the aims and purpose of communications needs to be assessed constantly. In this context we have viewed the media in Wales as a vital part of the public life of the country and have, in our survey, seen some areas of real quality and success and others where we have cause for concern.

While we do not hold with the idea that the media in Wales, and the media workers who staff these institutions, have produced increasingly low-quality material in recent years, and we do not think that there is a profound lack of diversity in the media available to the people of Wales, we remain concerned. Our concern has focused on the ways in which the market operates to promote concentration and centralized control over communicative resources, as in the film and press industries, and, in addition, on the ways in which the achievements of public control over broadcasting, so evident in the creation of BBC Wales and S4C, are now under threat from governments that want market forces to shape communications in the UK. The evidence points towards the conclusion that public intervention in the media is a necessary basis for ensuring diversity and plurality of media outlets. That does not mean state control over the media, but it does mean the state intervening to promote substantial amounts of diversity.

Wales, as we argued at the beginning, has a range of voices. There is no one single 'Wales'. It is made up of people who occupy different ethnic, social, economic, linguistic and cultural positions. Its peoples have a variety of levels of political involvement. It is marked by its particular history but not frozen in it. The real challenge for those interested in promoting a Wales in which as many voices as possible can hear and listen to each other with respect will be how to find the instruments with which to achieve this normative goal.

It may be that readers of this book do not consider this an appropriate or desirable outcome for any media policy. It may be, as the current seemingly unbending orthodoxy asserts, that the only way properly to govern the media is to let the market decide. In this we beg to differ. Like health, education, transport and food, communications are 'goods' from which individuals and societies draw sustenance. Because they bring common benefits to all, these goods should be governed accordingly and not left to the vagaries of the market. The media in Wales must therefore be structured to help achieve diversity and plurality and, through this, to allow the voices of the peoples of Wales to be heard on their own terms in the nation, the UK and around the world.

Notes

[1] Morris (1998: 29) notes how commercial operators have been subsidized as a means of ensuring that (at least some) Welsh films, including shorts, are shown in Wales, one example being Ceri Sherlock's *Cameleon/Chameleon* (1997).

[2] This festival began life as the Aberystwyth Film Festival in 1989. It was relocated to Cardiff and became the Welsh International Film Festival, then the International Film Festival of Wales, before being transformed into the Cardiff Screen Festival in 2003.

[3] See chapter 4.

[4] Only one cinema in Wales, Chapter in Cardiff, received funding under this programme in 2002–3. This might be contrasted with the situation in 1993–4 when eight cinemas around Wales received support through the RFT network (British Film Institute, 1993, 1994).

[5] See chapter 7 for a discussion of the influence of the Bangemann Report to the EU (1994) and of parallel developments in the United States with the 1996 Telecommunications Reform Act.

[6] Selwyn and Gorard (2002: 196) see the type of policy thinking discernible in this report as 'indicative of New Labour's underlying philosophy of new paternalism, using the state to enforce rather than merely encourage conformity to generally non-controversial but important values for national success in the global economy'.

[7] See, for example, the views of Downing (2002: 32), Mackay and Powell (1998: 213) and Selwyn and Gorard (2002: 46). These are discussed in more detail in chapter 7.

References

Aaron, W. (1979). 'Film', in M. Stephens (ed.), *The Arts in Wales 1950–75*, Cardiff, Welsh Arts Council, pp. 297–308.

Airflash (1993). No. 45, summer.

Aitchison, J. and Carter, H. (2003/4). 'Turning the tide?', *Agenda*, Winter, Cardiff, Institute of Welsh Affairs, 55–8.

Aitken, I. (1997). 'The British documentary film movement', in R. Murphy (ed.), *The British Cinema Book*, London, British Film Institute, pp. 60–8.

Allan, S. and O'Malley, T. (1999). 'The media in Wales', in D. Dunkerley and A. Thompson (eds), *Wales Today*, Cardiff, University of Wales Press, pp. 126–47.

Anderson, B. (1983). *Imagined Communities: Reflections on the Origins and Spread of Nationalism*, London, Verso.

Andrews, L. (2004). Paper presented to the conference, Communication in Wales after the Communications Act, University of Wales, Aberystwyth, 29 March.

Annan Committee (1977). *Report of the Committee on the Future of Broadcasting*, London, HMSO.

Anon (1967). 'Swansea, "ideal for radio station"', *Western Mail*, 7 February.

—— (1983). 'Council protest over radio station', *South Wales Argus*, 8 June.

Ashcroft, B. (2001). *Post-Colonial Transformation*, London, Routledge.

Bangemann, M. (1994). *Europe and the Global Information Society:*

Recommendations to the European Council, Brussels, European Union.

BARB (2003). 'Cable and satellite development 1992–2001', *www.-barb.co.uk*, accessed 9 October.

Barber, B. R. (1984). *Strong Democracy: Participatory Politics for a New Age*, Berkeley, University of California Press.

Barlow, D. M. (2001). 'Cymru reservation: health devolved but not *Casualty!*', *Free Press*, 117.

—— (2002). 'Conceptions of access and participation in Australian Community Radio stations', in N. W. Jankowski (ed.) *Community Media in the Information Age: Perspectives and Practice*, New Jersey, Hampton Press.

—— (2005). 'What's in the "post"? Mass media as a "site of struggle"', in C. Williams and J. Aaron (eds), *Postcolonial Wales*, Cardiff, University of Wales Press, pp. 193–214.

Barlow, D. M., Mitchell, P. and O'Malley, T. (2003). 'Commercial radio in Wales, 1972–2003: radio and the public sphere', paper presented to Annual Conference of the Media, Cultural and Communication Studies Association, University of Sussex, 20 December.

—— (2005). 'The communicative dimension of civil society: media and the public sphere', in G. Day, D. Dunkerley and A. Thompson (eds), *Civil Society in Wales*, Cardiff, University of Wales Press (forthcoming).

Barnard, S. (1989). *On the Radio: Music Radio in Britain*, Milton Keynes, Open University Press.

—— (2000). *Studying Radio*, London, Edward Arnold.

Barnett, S. (2000a). 'A surprising win for quality over quantity', *The Observer*, Media Section, 17 December, 7.

—— (2000b). 'Caught between Alastair and the deep Tory blue sea', *The Observer*, Media Section, 13 July, 7.

—— (2000c). 'Will pressure derail the Government's rush to market?', *The Observer*, Media Section, 22 June, 8.

—— and Seaton, J. (2002). *Evidence to the Joint Scrutiny Committee on the Draft Communications Bill*, London, University of Westminster.

—— and Seymour, E. (1999). *A Shrinking Iceberg Travelling South: Changing Trends in British Television*, London, Campaign for Quality Television.

BBC (2003). 'Profits priority kills *Welsh Mirror*', *www.news.bbc.co.uk*, 6 August.

BBC Cymru Wales (2002). *Annual Review 2001/2002*, BBC, Cardiff.
BBC Wales (2003a). *Annual Report*, BBC, Cardiff.
BBC Wales (2003b). *Welsh Language Scheme*, BBC, Cardiff.
—— (2004). *www.bbc.co.uk/wales*, last accessed 21 February.
Beddoe, D. (1986). 'Images of Welsh women', in T. Curtis (ed.), *Wales: The Imagined Nation: Studies in Cultural and National Identity*, Bridgend, Poetry Wales Press, pp. 225–38.
Berland, J. (1993). 'Radio space and industrial time: the case of music formats', in T. Bennett, S. Frith, J. Grossberg, J. Shepherd and G. Turner (eds), *Rock and Popular Music: Politics, Policies, Institutions*, New York, Routledge, pp. 104–18.
Berry, D. (1994). *Wales and Cinema: The First Hundred Years*, Cardiff, University of Wales Press.
—— (1996). 'Film and television in Wales', in J. Hill and M. McLoone (eds), *Big Picture Small Screen: The Relations Between Film and Television*, Luton, John Libbey, pp. 196–204.
—— (2000). 'Unearthing the present: television drama in Wales', in S. Blandford (ed.), *Wales on Screen*, Bridgend, Seren, pp. 128–51.
Bevan, D. (1984). 'The mobilisation of cultural minorities: the case of Sianel Pedwar Cymru', in *Media, Culture and Society*, 6, 103–17.
Blair, T. (1999). 'Why the internet years are vital', *Guardian*, 25 October.
Blanchard, S. and Harvey, S. (1983). 'The post-war independent cinema – structure and organisation', in J. Curran and V. Porter (eds), *British Cinema History*, London, Weidenfeld and Nicholson, pp. 226–44.
Blandford, S. (1999). 'Aspects of the live and recorded arts in contemporary Wales', in D. Dunkerley and A. Thompson (eds), *Wales Today*, Cardiff, University of Wales Press, pp. 111–26.
—— (ed.), (2000a). *Wales on Screen*, Bridgend, Seren.
—— (2000b). 'Introduction', *Wales on Screen*, in S. Blandford (ed.), Bridgend, Seren, pp. 11–37.
—— (2000c). 'Making *House of America*: an interview with Ed Thomas and Marc Evans', in S. Blandford (ed.), *Wales on Screen*. Bridgend, Seren, pp. 66–89.
Bonner, P. and Ashton, L. (1998). *Independent Television in Britain. Volume V: ITV and IBA, 1981–92: The Old Relationship Changes*, London, Macmillan.
Boyd-Barrett, O. (1995). 'The political economy approach', in O. Boyd-Barrett and C. Newbold (eds), *Approaches to Media*, London, Arnold, pp. 186–92.

—— and Newbold, C. (eds) (1995). *Approaches to Media*, London, Arnold.

Briggs, A. (1965). *The History of Broadcasting in the United Kingdom*. Volume II. *The Golden Age of Wireless*, Oxford, Oxford University Press.

—— (1979). *The History of Broadcasting in the United Kingdom*. Volume IV. *Sound and Vision*, Oxford, Oxford University Press.

—— (1995). *The History of Broadcasting in the United Kingdom*. Volume V. *Competition*, Oxford, Oxford University Press.

British Film Institute (1985). *Film and TV Handbook*, London, British Film Institute (BFI).

—— (1986). *Film and TV Handbook*, London, BFI.

—— (1987). *Film and TV Handbook*, London, BFI.

—— (1988). *Film and TV Handbook*, London, BFI.

—— (1989). *Film and TV Handbook*, London, BFI.

—— (1990). *Film and TV Handbook*, London, BFI.

—— (1991). *Film and TV Handbook*, London, BFI.

—— (1992). *Film and TV Handbook*, London, BFI.

—— (1993). *Film and TV Handbook*, London, BFI.

—— (1994). *Film and TV Handbook*, London, BFI.

—— (1995). *Film and TV Handbook*, London, BFI.

—— (1996). *Film and TV Handbook*, London, BFI.

—— (1997). *Film and TV Handbook*, London, BFI.

—— (1998). *Film and TV Handbook*, London, BFI.

—— (1999). *Film and TV Handbook*, London, BFI.

—— (2000). *Film and TV Handbook*, London, BFI.

—— (2001). *Film and TV Handbook*, London, BFI.

—— (2002). *Film and TV Handbook*, London, BFI.

—— (2003). *Film and TV Handbook*, London, BFI.

—— (2004). *Film and TV Handbook*, London, BFI.

Bromley, M. (2000). 'Our market driven media', *Planet*, 139, 124–6.

Brooks, X. (1999). 'Human Traffic', *Sight and Sound*, 9, 6, 46–7.

Brown, L. (1985). *Victorian News and Newspapers*, Oxford, Oxford University Press.

Bryan, J., Clarke, D., Hill, S., Munday, M. and Roberts, A. (1998). *The Economic Impact of the Arts and Cultural Industries in Wales*, Cardiff, Cardiff Business School.

Butt Phillip, A. (1975). *The Welsh Question: Nationalism in Welsh Politics 1945–1970*, Cardiff, University of Wales Press.

Calhoun, C. (1992). 'Introduction: Habermas and the public sphere', in C. Calhoun (ed.), *Habermas and the Public Sphere*, Cambridge, MA, MIT Press, pp. 1–48.

Campaign for Press and Broadcasting Freedom (2001). *Response to the White Paper 'A New Future for Communications'*, London, Campaign for Press and Broadcasting Freedom (CPBF).

—— (2002a). *The Puttnam Report: 'Making a Good Bill Better'*, London, CPBF.

—— (2002b). *Submission to the Joint Committee on the Draft Communications Bill*, London, CPBF.

Carter, M. (1998). *Independent Radio: The First 25 Years*, London, Radio Authority.

Carter, S. (2003). *The Communications Act: Myths and Realities*, London, OfCom.

Cayford, J. (1992). 'The *Western Mail* 1869–1914: the politics and management of a provincial newspaper', Cardiff, University of Wales, Ph.D. thesis.

Chanan, M. (1983). 'The emergence of an industry', in J. Curran and V. Porter (eds), *British Cinema History*, London, Weidenfeld and Nicholson, pp. 39–58.

Chaney, P., Hall, T. and Dicks, B. (2000). 'Inclusive governance? The case of minority and voluntary sector groups and the National Assembly for Wales', *Contemporary Wales*, 13, 98–112.

Collins, R. (1996). *New Media, New Policies*, Cambridge, Polity Press.

—— (2003). 'Internet governance in the UK', paper presented to the Annual Conference of the Media, Communications and Cultural Studies Association, University of Sussex, 19 December.

Commercial Radio Companies Association (1998). *Memorandum Submitted to Select Committee on Welsh Affairs – Second Report*, www.parliament.the-stationery-office.co.uk.

—— (2003). *The 2003 Communications Act – An Aide Memoire for CRCA members*, London, Commercial Radio Companies Association.

Communications Update (1994). 'Consumers and the 1997 Review', *Communications Update*, 102, 15–16.

Competition Commission (2003). 'Carlton/Granada get go-ahead for merger', press release, London, Competition Commission, 7 October.

Cormack, M. (1998). 'Minority language media in western Europe', *European Journal of Communication*, 13 (1), 33–52.

Corrigan, P. (1983). 'Film entertainment as ideology and pleasure: towards a history of audiences', in J. Curran and V. Porter (eds), *British Cinema History*, London, Weidenfeld and Nicholson, pp. 24–38.

Courtney, I. and Gibson, S. (1999). *Cymru. Com: Here's How*, Cardiff, Wales Media Forum.

Crisell, A. (1997). *An Introductory History of British Broadcasting*, London, Routledge.

Crisell, A. (1998). 'Local radio: attuned to the times or filling time with tunes?', in B. Franklin and D. Murphy (eds), *Making the Local News: Local Journalism in Context*, London, Routledge, pp. 24–35.

—— (2002). 'Radio', in A. Briggs and P. Cobley (eds), *The Media: An Introduction*, 2nd edn, Harlow, Longmans, pp. 121–34.

Crookes, P. and Vittet-Philippe, P. (1986). *Local Radio and Regional Development in Europe*, Manchester, European Institute for the Media/European Centre for Political Studies.

Crooks, C. and Light, P. (2002). 'Virtual society and the cultural practice of study', in S. Woolgar (ed.), *Virtual Society: Technology, Cyberbole, Reality*, Oxford, Oxford University Press, pp. 153–75.

Culture Committee (2000a). *Broadcasting in Wales – CC–2–00*, Cardiff, NAfW.

—— (2000b). *Broadcasting in Wales – CC–3–00*, Cardiff, NAfW.

—— (2003). *Report on the First Four Years: 1999–2003*, Cardiff, NAfW.

Curran, J. (1996). 'Mass media and democracy revisited', in J. Curran and M. Gurevitch (eds), *Mass Media and Society*, 2nd edn, London, Arnold, pp. 81–119.

—— and Gurevitch, M. (eds), (2000). *Mass Media and Society*, 3rd edn, London, Arnold.

—— and Seaton, J. (1997). *Power without Responsibility: The Press, Broadcasting and New Media in Britain*, 5th edn, London, Routledge.

—— (2003). *Power without Responsibility: The Press, Broadcasting and New Media in Britain*, 6th edn, London, Routledge.

Dahlgren, P. (1991). 'Introduction', P. Dahlgren (ed.), *Communication and Citizenship: Journalism and the Public Sphere in the New Media Age*, London, Routledge, pp. 1–24.

—— (1996). 'Media logic in cyberspace: repositioning journalism and its publics', *Javnost/The Public*, 3, 3, 59–72.

Davies, G. (1991). 'Local radio comes to rural Wales', *Planet*, 85, 109–11.

Davies, J. (1994a). *Broadcasting and the BBC in Wales*, Cardiff, University of Wales Press.
—— (1994b). *A History of Wales*, London, Penguin.
—— (1999). *The Welsh Language*, Cardiff, University of Wales Press/*Western Mail*.
Day, G. and Suggett, R. (1985). 'Conceptions of Wales and Welshness: aspects of nationalism in nineteenth-century Wales', in G. Rees, J. Bojra, P. Littlewood, H. Newby and T. Rees (eds), *Political Action and Social Identity: Class, Locality and Ideology*, London, Macmillan, pp. 91–115.
Day, G., Fitton, M. and Minhinnick, M. (1998). 'Finding our voices', in J. Osmond (ed.), *The National Assembly Agenda*, Cardiff, Institute of Welsh Affairs, pp. 290–300.
Delamont, S. (1987). 'S4C and the grassroots? A review of past and future research on the mass media and the Welsh language', *Contemporary Wales*, 1, 91–105.
Department of Communication and the Arts (1994). *Creative Nation*, Canberra, Commonwealth Government of Australia.
Department of Culture, Media and Sport (2000). *Concordat between the Department for Culture, Media and Sport and the Cabinet of the National Assembly for Wales*, London, Department for Culture, Media and Sport (DCMS).
—— (2003a). *Government Response to the Select Committee Report on the British Film Industry*, London, DCMS.
—— (2003b). 'Communications act gets royal assent', press release, London, DCMS, 17 July.
—— (2004). *S4C: An Independent Review*, London, DCMS.
Department of Trade and Industry (1999). *Regulating Communications: The Way Ahead*, London, Department of Trade and Industry (DTI).
Department of Trade and Industry/Department of Culture, Media and Sport (1998). *Regulating Communications: Approaching Convergence in the Information Age*, executive summary, London, DTI/DCMS.
—— (2000). *A New Future for Communications*, London, DTI/DCMS.
—— (2002). *Draft Communications Bill*, London, DTI/DCMS.
Desjardins, M. (1995). 'Cinema and communication', in J. Downing, A. Mohammadi and A. Sreberny-Mohammadi (eds), *Questioning the Media: A Critical Introduction*, 2nd edn, London, Sage, pp. 394–412.
Dickinson, M. (1983). 'The state and the consolidation of monopoly',

in J. Curran and V. Porter (eds), *British Cinema History*, London, Weidenfeld and Nicholson, pp. 74–98.

Digital Europe (2003). *Cymru Ar-lein and Sustainable Development: Case Study Summary*, Brussels, European Union.

Docherty, D. (1987). 'Who goes to the RFTs?', *Sight and Sound*, Summer, 161–4.

Downing, J. (2002). *Net Gain? Access to and Use of the Internet in Wales*, Cardiff, Wales Consumer Council.

Downing, J., Mohammadi, A. and Sreberny-Mohammadi, A. (1995). 'Preface', in J. Downing, A. Mohammadi and A. Sreberny-Mohammadi (eds), *Questioning the Media: A Critical Introduction*, 2nd edn, London, Sage, pp. xv–xxiv.

Doyle, G. (2002). *Media Ownership*, London, Sage.

DTI Policy Action Team (PAT) 15 (2000). 'Closing the digital divide: information and communication technologies in deprived areas', 15 June, *www.cabinet-office.gov.uk/seulindex.htm*.

Dutton, W. H. (1999). *Society on the Line: Information Politics in the Digital Age*, Oxford, Oxford University Press.

Ellis, G. (2000). 'Stereophonic nation: the bilingual sounds of Cool Cymru FM', *International Journal of Cultural Studies*, 3, 2, 188–98.

Equity (2002). *Submission to the National Assembly Culture Committee on the Communications Bill*, Cardiff, NAfW.

European Union (2000). *Directive 2000/31/EC of the European Parliament and the Council on Certain Legal Aspects of Information Society Services*, Brussels, European Union.

Evans, D. (1989). *A History of Wales 1815–1906*, Cardiff, University of Wales Press.

Evans, G. (1944). *The Radio in Wales*, Aberystwyth, The New Wales Union.

—— (1997). *Fighting For Wales*, Talybont, Y Lolfa.

—— (2001). *For the Sake of Wales*, Cardiff, Welsh Academic Press.

Evans, I. (1997). '"Drunk on hopes and ideals": the failure of Wales television, 1959–1963', *Llafur*, 7, 2, 81–93.

Evans, M. (2003). 'Director Marc Evans supports the Cardiff Screen Festival', press release, Cardiff, Cardiff Screen Festival, 16 November.

Fairchild, C. (1999). 'Deterritorializing radio: deregulation and the continuing triumph of the corporatist perspective in the USA', *Media, Culture and Society*, 21, 549–61.

Ferguson, M. (ed.) (1986). *New Communication Technologies and the Public Interest*, London, Sage.

Film Council (2002). *Working Together, Making a Difference: The Work of the Public Film Agencies in the UK*, London, Film Council.

—— (2003). *Response to the Culture, Media and Sport Committee Enquiry "Is there a British Film Industry?"*, London, Film Council.

Film Education Working Group (1999). *Making Movies Matter: Report of the Film Education Working Group*, London, British Film Institute.

Film Policy Review Group (1998). *A Bigger Picture: The Report of the Film Policy Review Group*, London, Department of Culture, Media and Sport.

Fishlock, T. (1972). 'The struggle to be heard in Welsh', *The Times*, 12 July.

—— (1973). 'BBC Wales now stronghold of spoken Welsh', *The Times*, 12 February.

Foot, K. A. (2002). 'Online structure for political action', *Javnost/The Public*, 9, 2, 43–60.

Forgan, I. and Tambini, D. (2001). *Content*, London, Institute for Public Policy Research.

Fornatale, P. and Mills, J. E. (1980). *Radio in the Television Age*, Overlook Press, Woodstock, NY.

Freshfields Bruckhaus Deringer (2003). *Communications Act*, www.freshfields.com, accessed 17 February.

Future Foundation (2000). *The Renaissance of Regional Nations*, London, Newspaper Society/Harrison Cowley.

Garnham, N. (1986). 'The media and the public sphere', *Intermedia*, 14, 1, 28–33.

—— (1992). 'The media and the public sphere', in C. Calhoun (ed.), *Habermas and the Public Sphere*, Cambridge, MA, MIT Press, pp. 359–76.

—— (1998). 'Policy', in A. Briggs and P. Cobley (eds), *The Media: An Introduction*, London, Longman, pp. 210–23.

Gates, B. (1995). *The Road Ahead*, New York, Viking.

German, M. (2001). 'Film industry is valuable asset to North Wales economy says Michael German', press release, Cardiff, NAfW, 20 February.

Goldberg, D., Prosser, T. and Verhulst, S. (1998). *Regulating the Changing Media: A Comparative Study*, Oxford, Clarendon Press.

Golding, P. (1994). 'Telling stories: sociology, journalism and the informed citizen', *European Journal of Communication*, 9, 4, 461–84.

Golding, P. and Murdock, G. (2000). 'Culture, communications and political economy', in J. Curran and M. Gurevitch (eds), *Mass Media and Society*, 3rd edn, London, Arnold, pp. 70–92.

Goodwin, P. (1998). *Television under the Tories: Broadcasting Policy 1979–1997*, London, British Film Institute.

Gorst, J. (1971). *Commercial Radio . . . the Beast of Burden*, London, Aims of Industry Publications.

Gower, J. (2002). 'Internet in Wales', *www.bbc.co.uk*.

Greenough, M. (2002). 'Spinning the web', *Planet*, 154, 71–5.

Griffiths, A. (1993). 'The construction of national and cultural identity in a Welsh language soap opera', in P. Drummond, R. Paterson and J. Willis (eds), *National Identity and Europe*, London, British Film Institute, pp. 9–24.

—— (1994). 'Ethnography and popular memory: postmodern configurations of Welsh identities', *Continuum*, 7, 2.

Guest, K. (2002). 'All hail the Cool Caledonians', *Independent*, Friday Review, 25 January, 7.

Habermas, J. (1964). 'The public sphere: an encyclopedia article', *New German Critique*, 3, 49–55.

—— (1989). *The Structural Transformation of the Public Sphere*, Cambridge, Polity.

—— (1992). 'Further reflections on the public sphere', in C. Calhoun (ed.), *Habermas and the Public Sphere*, Cambridge, MA, MIT Press, 421–61.

Hagemann, C. (2002). 'Participation in and contents of two Dutch political party discussion lists on the internet', *Javnost/The Public*, 9, 2, 61–76.

Hall, J. (2001). *Online Journalism: a Critical Primer*, London, Pluto Press.

Hamelink, C. J. (1994). *Trends in World Communication: On Disempowerment and Self-Empowerment*, Penang, Southbound.

Hannan, P. (1998). 'Who's asking the questions?', *Planet*, 126, 7–12.

Hanson, S. (2000). 'Spoilt for choice? multiplexes in the 90s', in R. Murphy (ed.), *British Cinema of the 90s*, London, British Film Institute, pp. 48–59.

Hargreaves, I. (1999) 'Foreword', in G. Talfan Davies, *Not by Bread Alone: Information Media and the National Assembly*, Cardiff, Wales Media Forum, pp. 1–2.

—— and Thomas, J. (2002). *New News, Old News*, London, Independent Television Commission.

Harper, C. (1998). *And That's the Way it Will Be: News and*

Information in a Digital World, New York, New York University Press.

Haywood, T. (1998). 'Global networks and the myth of equality: trickle down or trickle away?', in D. B. Loader (ed.), *Cyberspace Divide: Equality, Agency and Policy in the Information Society*, London, Routledge, pp. 19–34.

Hechter, M. (1986). 'Towards a theory of ethnic change', in I. Hume and W. T. R. Pryce (eds), *The Welsh and their Country*, Llandysul, Gomer Press, pp. 217–33.

Hendy, D. (2000). *Radio in the Global Age*, Cambridge, Polity Press.

Herman, E. (2002). 'The propaganda model: a retrospective', in D. McQuail (ed.), *McQuail's Reader in Mass Communication Theory*, London, Sage, pp. 60–8.

—— and Chomsky, N. (1988). *Manufacturing Consent: The Political Economy of the Mass Media*, New York, Pantheon.

Hesmondhalgh, D. (2002). *The Cultural Industries*, London, Sage.

Higson, A. (2000). 'The limiting imagination of national cinema', in M. Hjort and S. MacKenzie (eds), *Cinema and Nation*, London, Routledge, pp. 63–74.

Hill, J. (1996). 'British film policy', in A. Moran (ed.), *Film Policy: International, National and Regional Perspectives*, London, Routledge, pp. 101–13.

—— (1999). *British Cinema in the 1980s*, Oxford, Clarendon Press.

Hill, J., McLoone, M. and Hainsworth, P. (eds). (1994). *Border Crossing: Film in Ireland, Britain and Europe*, Belfast, Institute of Irish Studies in association with University of Ulster.

HM Government (2002), *In the Service of Democracy*, London, HMSO.

HMSO (1975). *Report of the Working Party on a Fourth Television Service in Wales*, Cmnd. 6290, Cardiff, HMSO.

—— (1977). *Report of the Committee on the Future of Broadcasting*, Cmnd. 6753, London, HMSO.

—— (2003). *Explanatory Notes to Communications Act 2003*, London, HMSO.

Hobsbawm, E. (1990). *Nations and Nationalism Since 1780: Programme, Myth, Reality*, Cambridge, Canto.

Hogenkamp, B. (1985). 'Miners' cinemas in south Wales in the 1920s and 1930s', *Llafur*, 4, 2, 64–75.

—— (1987). 'To-day we live: the making of a documentary in a Welsh mining valley', *Llafur*, 5, 1, 45–52.

Hollander, E., Van der Linden, C. and Vergeer, M. (1995). 'Access in the age of commercialisation of information: the case of local radio in the Netherlands', *Javnost/The Public*, 2, 4, 75–85.

Home Office (1986). *Report of the Committee on Financing the BBC*, Cmnd. 9824, London, HMSO.

Hood, S. (1983). 'John Grierson and the documentary film movement', in J. Curran and V. Porter (eds), *British Cinema History*, London, Weidenfeld and Nicholson, pp. 99–112.

Hooper, R. (2001). 'Keynote speech', Manchester Symposium, 1 May, London, Radio Authority.

House of Commons (1946). *House of Commons Debates 5th Series* Volume 428, 29 October, col. 466.

—— (1966). *Parliamentary Debates 5th Series*, Volume 725, cols 1559, 1561–2, 3 March 1966.

—— (1969). *Parliamentary Debates 5th Series*, Volume 792, cols 1595–8, 3 December.

—— (1971). *Parliamentary Debates 5th Series*, Volume 818, col. 422, 26 May.

—— (1973). *Parliamentary Debates 5th Series*, Volume 854, oral answers, cols 1–3, 2 April.

—— (1974). *Parliamentary Debates 5th Series*, Volume 872, written answers, col. 212, 10 April.

—— (1975a). *Parliamentary Debates 5th Series*, Volume 884, written answers, col. 176, 16 January.

—— (1975b). *Parliamentary Debates 5th Series*, Volume 901, written answers, col. 105, 25 November.

—— (1977a). *Parliamentary Debates 5th Series*, Volume 928, cols 608–9, 24 March.

—— (1977b). *Parliamentary Debates 5th Series*, Volume 932, col. 1109, 23 May.

—— (1978). *Parliamentary Debates 5th Series*, Volume 954, cols 1559–88, 26 July.

—— (2002). *Parliamentary Debates*, col. 825, 3 December.

HTV (2002). *HTV Wales Evidence on the Draft Communications Bill*, Cardiff, NAfW.

Hume, I. (1986). 'Mass media and society in the 1980s', in I. Hume and W. T. R. Pryce (eds), *The Welsh and their Country*, Llandysul, Gomer Press, pp. 324–47.

—— and Pryce, W. T. (eds) (1986). *The Welsh and their Country*, Llandysul, Gomer Press.

Husband, C. (1994). 'General introduction: ethnicity and media democratization within the nation-state', in C. Husband (ed.), *A Richer Vision: The Development of Ethnic Minority Media in Western Democracies*, London, John Libbey, pp. 1–19.

Huston, G. (2002). 'Telecommunications policy and the internet', *www.isoc.org/oti/articles/1201/huston.html*.

Hutchison, D. (1999). *Media Policy: An Introduction*, London, Blackwell.

Hutchison, R. (1977). *Three Arts Centres: A Study of South Hill Park, the Gardner Centre and Chapter*, London, Arts Council of Great Britain.

Huws, G. (1996). 'The success of the local: Wales', *Mercator Media Forum*, 2, 84–93.

Independent Broadcasting Authority (1977a). *The Annan Report: The Authority's Comments*, London, Independent Broadcasting Authority (IBA).

—— (1977b). *Independent Broadcasting in Wales*, Cardiff, IBA.

—— (1978). *Annual Report and Accounts 1977–8*, London, IBA.

—— (1981). *Annual Report and Accounts, 1980–1*, London, IBA.

—— (1986). *Annual Report and Accounts, 1985–6*, London, IBA.

Independent Television Commission (1998). *Annual Report and Accounts 1997*, London, Independent Television Commission (ITC).

—— (1999). *Annual Report and Accounts 1998*, London, ITC.

—— (2002a). *Memorandum to the Culture Committee of the National Assembly of Wales on the Communications Bill*, Cardiff, NAfW.

—— (2002b). *The Public's View*, London, ITC.

Jakubowicz, A. (1995). 'Media in multicultural nations', in J. Downing, A. Mohammadi, and A. Sreberny-Mohammadi (eds), *Questioning the Media: A Critical Introduction*, London, Sage, pp. 165–83.

Jankowski, N., Prehn, O. and Stappers, J. (eds), (1992). *The People's Voice: Local Radio and Television in Europe*, London, Libbey.

Jays, D. (2000). 'Very Annie-Mary', *Sight and Sound*, 11, 6, 56–7.

Jones, A. (1993). *Press, Politics and Society: A History of Journalism in Wales*, Cardiff, University of Wales Press.

—— (1996). *Powers of the Press: Newspapers, Power and the Public in Nineteenth-Century England*, Aldershot, Scolar Press.

—— (1998). 'The newspaper press in Wales 1804–1945', in P. H. Jones and E. A. Rees (eds), *A Nation and its Books: A History of the Book in Wales*, Aberystwyth, National Library of Wales, pp. 209–19.

—— (2000a). 'The nineteenth-century media and Welsh identity', in

L. Brake, B. Bell and D. Finkelstein (eds), *Nineteenth-Century Media and the Construction of Identities*, Basingstoke, Palgrave, pp. 310–25.

—— (2000b). 'The Welsh newspaper press', in H. T. Edwards (ed.), *A Guide to Welsh Literature c. 1800–1900*, Vol. V, Cardiff, University of Wales Press, pp. 1–23.

Jones, G. S. (2001–2). *Chairman's Report, Annual Review*, Cardiff, Sgrîn.

Jones, H. P. (1983). 'The referendum and the Welsh-language press', in D. Foulkes, J. B. Jones and R. A. Wilford (eds), *The Welsh Veto: The Wales Act and the Referendum*, Cardiff, University of Wales Press, pp. 169–83.

Jones, J. and Wilford, R. (1983). 'Implications: two salient issues', in D. Foulkes, J. B. Jones and R. A. Wilford (eds), *The Welsh Veto: The Wales Act and the Referendum*, Cardiff, University of Wales Press, pp. 216–30.

Jones, J. B. and Balsom, D. (2000). 'Conclusion', in J. B. Jones and D. Balsom (eds), *The Road to the National Assembly for Wales*, Cardiff, University of Wales Press, pp. 275–83.

Jones, S. G. (1987). *The British Labour Movement and Film*, London, Routledge and Kegan Paul.

Jury, L. (2002). 'Welsh rival to Catherine Cookson's crown sells BBC the rights to screen eight novels', *Independent*, 6 June, 5.

Kinsey, C. (2001). 'Chapter Arts Centre – the early years' (Christine Kinsey interviewed by Gilly Adams), *www.chapter.org*, accessed 9 August.

Kleinsteuber, H. J. (1990). 'Beyond public service and private profit: international experience and non-commercial local radio', *European Journal of Communication*, 5, 1, 87–106.

Knapp, J. A. (1997). 'Essayistic messages: Internet newsgroups as an electronic public sphere', in D. Porter (ed.), *Internet Culture*, London, Routledge, pp. 181–97.

Koss, S. (1990). *The Rise and Fall of the Political Press in Britain*, London, Fontana.

Kruger, D. (1999). *Access Denied*, London, Demos.

Labour Research (n.d., but 1922). *The Press*, London, Labour Research.

Lee, A. (1976). *The Origins of the Popular Press*, London, Croom Helm.

Lee, B. (1992). 'Textuality, mediation, and public discourse', in C. Calhoun (ed.), *Habermas and the Public Sphere*, Cambridge, MA, MIT Press, pp. 402–18.

Leigh, D. (2000). 'Rancid Aluminium', *Sight and Sound*, 10, 3, 50–1.

Lewis, P. M. and Booth, J. (1989). *The Invisible Medium: Public, Commercial and Community Radio*, London, Macmillan.

Liff, S., Steward, F. and Watts, P. (2002). 'New public places for internet access: networks for practice-based learning and social inclusion', in S. Woolgar (ed.), *Virtual Society: Technology, Cyberbole, Reality*, Oxford, Oxford University Press, pp. 78–98.

Llewellyn, M. (1998). 'Welsh – the language of rock!', *Planet*, 129, 56–64.

Local Radio Workshop (1978). *Submission to the Parliamentary Select Committee on Nationalised Industries, on the Administration of Independent Local Radio by the Independent Broadcasting Authority*, London, Local Radio Workshop.

—— (1983). *Capital: Local Radio and Private Profit*, London, Comedia.

Lockard, J. (1997). 'Progressive politics, electronic individualism and the myth of virtual community', in D. Porter (ed.), *Internet Culture*, London, Routledge, pp. 219–32.

Louvish, S. (1999). 'Solomon and Gaenor', *Sight and Sound*, 9, 5, 56.

Lovering, J. (2001). 'Why the dragon has no teeth', *Planet*, 146, 7–10.

Lucas, R. (1981). *The Voice of a Nation? A Concise Account of the BBC in Wales*, Llandysul, Gomer.

Luckett, M. (2000). 'Image and nation in 1990s British cinema', in R. Murphy (ed.), *British Cinema of the 90s*, London, British Film Institute, pp. 88–99.

Mackay, H. (1999). 'New media technologies, Welsh identities', paper presented to the conference Languages and Discourses, Communities and Selves, Values and Representations, University of Wales, Gregynog, December.

Mackay, H. and Powell, A. (1997). 'Wales and its media: production, consumption and regulation', *Contemporary Wales*, 9, 8–39.

Mackay, H. and Powell, T. (1998). 'Connecting Wales: the internet and national identity', in B. D. Loader (ed.), *Cyberspace Divide: Equality, Agency and Policy in the Information Society*, London, Routledge, pp. 203–16.

Macpherson, D. (1980). *Traditions of Independence: British Cinema in the Thirties*, London, British Film Institute.

Mansfield, H. (1978). 'Letter', *The Times*, 3 May.

Martin, W. J. (1995). *The Global Information Society*, Aldershot, Aslib Gower.

McArthur, C. (1985). 'Scotland's story', *Framework*, 26/7, 64–74.
—— (1993). 'In praise of a poor cinema', *Sight and Sound*, 3, 8, 30–2.
—— (1994). 'The cultural necessity of a poor celtic cinema', in J. Hill, M. McLoone and P. Hainsworth (eds), *Border Crossing: Film in Ireland, Britain and Europe*, Belfast, Institute of Irish Studies, University of Ulster.
McChesney, R. (2002). *Theses on Media Deregulation*, London, Campaign for Press and Broadcasting Freedom.
McGuigan, J. (1996). *Culture and the Public Sphere*, London, Routledge.
McIntyre, S. (1996). 'Art and industry: regional film and video policy in the UK', in A. Moran (ed.), *Film Policy: International, National and Regional Perspectives*, London, Routledge, pp. 215–33.
McLaughlin, L. (1993). 'Feminism, the public sphere, media and democracy', *Media, Culture and Society*, 15, 599–620.
McQuail, D. (2003). *Media Accountability and Freedom of Publication*, Oxford, Oxford University Press.
Medhurst, J. (1998). 'Mass media in 20th century Wales', in P. H. Jones (ed.), *A Nation and its Books*, Aberystwyth, National Library of Wales, pp. 329–40.
Meech, P. and Kilborn, R. (1992). 'Media and identity in a stateless nation: the case of Scotland', *Media, Culture and Society*, 14, 245–59.
Miller, D. (1994). *Don't Mention The War*, London, Pluto.
Miskell, P. (1997). 'Film exhibition in Wales: a study of circuits and cinemas c. 1918–1951', *Llafur*, 7, 2, 53–67.
Monger, C. (2000). 'Foreword', in S. Blandford (ed.), *Wales on Screen*, Bridgend, Seren, pp. 7–10.
Monk, C. (1997). 'Darklands', *Sight and Sound*, 7, 9, 37.
Montagu, I. (1980). 'Film censorship', in D. Macpherson (ed.), *Traditions of Independence: British Cinema in the Thirties*, London, British Film Institute, pp. 113–15.
Moran, A. (ed.) (1996). *Film Policy: International, National and Regional Perspectives*, London, Routledge.
Morris, N. (1995). 'Film and broadcasting in Wales', *Books in Wales*, 1, 5–8.
—— (1998). 'Projecting Wales', *Planet*, 126, 24–30.
Mosco, V. (1996). *The Political Economy of Communication*, London, Sage.
Mottram, R. (1990). 'Cinema and communication', in J. Downing, A. Mohammadi and A. Sreberny-Mohammadi (eds), *Questioning the Media: A Critical Introduction*, London, Sage, pp. 318–29.
Mungham, G. and Williams, K. (1998). 'The press and media', in

J. Osmond (ed.), *The National Assembly Agenda*, Cardiff, Institute of Welsh Affairs, pp. 116–29.

Murphy, R. (2000). *British Cinema of the 90s*, London, British Film Institute.

National Assembly for Wales (1999). *The Official Record: Broadcasting in Wales*, Cardiff, NAfW.

—— (2000). *www.betterwales.com*, Cardiff, NAfW.

—— (2001a). *Response to the Government's Consultation, by the Cabinet of the National Assembly for Wales*, Cardiff, NAfW.

—— (2001b). *The Official Record: Broadcasting and Communication*, Cardiff, NAfW.

—— (2001c). *Strategic Statement on the Preparation of 'Plan for Wales'*, Cardiff, NAfW.

—— (2002a). 'Richard Commission starts work', press release, Cardiff, NAfW, September.

—— (2002b). *Welsh Assembly Government Response to the Draft Communications Bill*, Cardiff, NAfW.

—— (2002c). *The Official Record: Broadcasting*, Cardiff, NAfW.

—— (2002d). *Minority Party Debate*, Cardiff, NAfW.

—— (2003). *Cymru Ar-lein, www.cymruarlein.wales.gov.uk*, last accessed 11 December.

National Library of Wales (2001). *Rhestr o Bapurau Bro Gorffennaf 2001*, Aberystwyth, National Library of Wales, on-line catalogue.

National Union of Journalists (2002). *Submission to Welsh Assembly on Broadcasting Bill*, Cardiff, NAfW.

Naughton, J. (1999). *A Brief History of the Future: the Origins of the Internet*, London, Weidenfeld and Nicolson.

Negroponte, N. (1995). *Being Digital*, New York, Vintage Books.

Negus, K. (1996). 'Globalization and the music of the public spheres', in S. Braman and A. Sreberny-Mohammadi (eds), *Globalization, Communication and Transnational Civil Society*, Cresskill, NJ, Hampton Press, pp. 179–96.

Nettleton, S., Pleace, N., Burrows, R., Muncer, S. and Loader, B. (2002). 'The reality of virtual social support', in S. Woolgar (ed.), *Virtual Society: Technology, Cyberbole, Reality*, Oxford, Oxford University Press, pp. 176–88.

Newspaper Society (2003a). *www.newspapersoc.org.uk*, accessed 11 August 2003.

—— (2003b). 'Regional newspaper coverage', *www.newspapersoc.org.uk*, accessed 17 April 2003.

Nurse, K. (2001). 'Taffy was a Welshman . . . ', *New Welsh Review*, 54, 36–8.

Oblak, T. (2002). 'Dialogue and representation: communication in the electronic sphere', *Javnost/The Public*, 9, 2, 7–22.

OfCom (2003). 'Advisory Committees for the nations', press release, London, OfCom, 12 September.

—— (2004a). *OfCom's Annual Plan, April 2004–March 2005*, London, OfCom.

—— (2004b). *Consultation on OfCom Guidance on the Public Interest Test for Media Mergers*, London, OfCom.

OfCom Advisory Group (2003). *Wales and OfCom: A Report by an Advisory Group to the Minister for Culture, Sport and the Welsh Language, Welsh Assembly Government*, Cardiff, NAfW.

Office for National Statistics (1999). *Family Expenditure Survey*, London, HMSO.

—— (2000). *Family Expenditure Survey*, London, HMSO.

—— (2001). *Family Expenditure Survey*, London, HMSO.

—— (2002). *Family Expenditure Survey*, London, HMSO.

—— (2003). *Family Expenditure Survey*, London, HMSO.

O'Malley, T. (1994). *Closedown? The BBC and Government Broadcasting Policy, 1979–92*, London, Pluto Press.

—— (1997). 'Labour and the 1947–9 Royal Commission on the press', in M. Bromley and T. O'Malley (eds), *A Journalism Reader*, London, Routledge, pp. 126–58.

—— (1998). 'Demanding accountability: the press, the Royal Commissions and the pressure for reform, 1945–77', in M. Bromley and H. Stephenson (eds), *Sex, Lies and Democracy*, Longman, pp. 84–96.

—— (2001). 'The decline of public service broadcasting in the UK, 1979–2000', in M. Bromley (ed.), *No News is Bad News: Radio, Television and the Press*, London, Longman, pp. 28–45.

—— (2002a). *The State of the Media – Media Policy and the Need for Reform*, London, Campaign for Press and Broadcasting Freedom.

—— (2002b). *A Submission to the National Assembly's Culture Committee on the Communications Bill and its Implications for the Media in Wales*, London, Campaign for Press and Broadcasting Freedom.

—— (2003). 'The BBC adapts to competition', in M. Hilmes (ed.), *The Television History Book*, London, British Film Institute, pp. 86–9.

—— and Soley, C. (2000). *Regulating the Press*, London, Pluto.

O'Malley, T., Allan, S. and Thompson, A. (1997). 'Tokens of antiquity: the newspaper press and the shaping of national identity in Wales, 1870–1900', in M. Harris and T. O'Malley (eds), *Studies in Newspaper and Periodical History 1995 Annual*, Westport, Connecticut and London, Greenwood Press, pp. 127–52.

Oppe, F. (2000). 'Diary of two mad housewives', in S. Blandford (ed.), *Wales on Screen*, Bridgend, Seren, pp. 168–79.

Osmond, J. (1983). 'The referendum and the English language press', in D. Foulkes, J. B. Jones and R. A. Wilford (eds), *The Welsh Veto: The Wales Act and the Referendum*, Cardiff, University of Wales Press, pp. 153–68.

—— (1992). *The Democratic Challenge*, Llandysul, Gomer.

—— (1993). 'The last outpost of imperialism', *Planet*, 99, 40–3.

—— (1994). 'Re-making Wales', in J. Osmond (ed.), *A Parliament for Wales*, Llandysul, Gomer pp. 5–35.

—— (1995). *Welsh Europeans*, Bridgend, Seren.

—— (1998). *Memorandum Submitted to Welsh Affairs Select Committee by the Institute of Welsh Affairs*, London, HMSO.

O'Sullivan, C. (1999). 'Mad Cows', *Sight and Sound*, 9, 12, 51.

Parker, A. (2002). *Building a Sustainable UK Film Industry: A Presentation to the UK Film Industry*, London, Film Council.

Patelis, K. (2000). 'The political economy of the Internet', in J. Curran (ed.), *Media Organisations in Society*, London, Arnold, pp. 84–106.

Paterson, L. and Wyn Jones, R. (1999). 'Does civil society drive constitutional change?', in B. Taylor and K. Thompson (eds), *Scotland and Wales: National Again?*, Cardiff, University of Wales Press, pp. 169–97.

Pavlik, J. V. (2001). *Journalism and New Media*, New York, Columbia University Press.

Perrins, D. (2000). 'This town ain't big enough for the both of us', in S. Blandford (ed.), *Wales on Screen*, Bridgend, Seren, pp. 152–67.

Peters, J. D. (1993). 'Distrust of representation: Habermas on the public sphere', *Media, Culture and Society*, 15, 541–71.

Petley, J. (1989). 'Future film policy', *Sight and Sound*, Spring, 86–90.

Petrie, D. (1996). 'Peripheral visions: film-making in Scotland', in W. Everett (ed.), *European Identity in Cinema*, Exeter, Intellect Books, pp. 93–102.

—— (2000). 'The new Scottish cinema', in M. Hjort and S. MacKenzie (eds), *Cinema and Nation*, London, Routledge, pp. 153–69.

Phillips, W. (1982). 'The frozen waves: radio in 1982', *Admap*, July, 380–8.

—— (1983). 'Radio '83: out of steam', *Admap*, July/August, 348–52.

Pilkington Committee (1962), *Report of the Committee on Broadcasting*, London, HMSO.

Plaid Cymru (2003). *Election Manifesto*, Cardiff, Plaid Cymru.

Poole, R. (1989). 'Public spheres', in H. Wilson (ed.), *Australian Communications and the Public Sphere*, Melbourne, Macmillan, pp. 16–26.

Porter, V. (1983). 'The context of creativity: Ealing Studios and Hammer Films', in J. Curran and V. Porter (eds), *British Cinema History*, London, Weidenfeld and Nicholson, pp. 179–207.

Post-16 Education and Training Committee (2000a). *A Culture in Common*, Cardiff, NAfW.

—— (2000b). *Policy Review: Arts and Culture in Wales – ETR 10–00*, Cardiff, NAfW.

—— (2000c). *Meeting with Broadcasters – ETR 14–00*, Cardiff, NAfW.

Poster, M. (1997). 'CyberDemocracy: Internet and the public sphere', in D. Porter (ed.), *Internet Culture*, London, Routledge, pp. 201–18.

Postman, N. (1993). *Technopoly: The Surrender of Culture to Technology*, New York, Vintage Books.

Potter, J. (1989). *Independent Television in Britain*. Vol. 3: *Politics and Control 1968–80*, London, Macmillan.

Press Council (various dates), *The Press and the People*, London, Press Council (being the Press Council's annual reports covering the years 1966–1990).

Radio Authority (1998). *Response to 'Regulating Communications: Approaching Convergence in the Information Age'*, London, Radio Authority.

—— (1999). *Radio Authority Licensing Award Procedures and Strategy for Independent Radio*, London, Radio Authority, www.ofcom.org.uk.

—— (2002). *Local News on ILR – A Consultation*, London, Radio Authority.

Rajar (2004). *Quarterly Summary of Radio Listening*, www.rajar.co.uk, London, Rajar Ltd.

Randerson, J. (2002a). 'Written evidence to Richard Commission', Cardiff, NAfW.

—— (2002b). 'Call for strong Welsh voice in communications', press release, Cardiff, NAfW, 9 July.

—— (2002c). '10 year plan for culture unveiled', press release, Cardiff, NAfW, 7 February.

—— (2003). 'Big screen beckons Wales to celebrate cinema', press release, Cardiff, NAfW, 27 January.

Rees, R. D. (1961–3). 'South Wales and Monmouthshire newspapers under the Stamp Act', *Welsh History Review*, 1, 301–24.

Rheingold, H. (1995). *The Virtual Community*, London, Minerva.

Richards, J. (1997). *Films and British National Identity: From Dickens to Dad's Army*, Manchester, Manchester University Press.

Ridgwell, S. (1997). 'Pictures and proletarians: South Wales miners' cinemas in the 1930s', *Llafur*, 7, 2, 69–80.

Robertson, G. (1991). *Freedom, the Individual and the Law*, London, Penguin.

Robins, T. and Webster, C. (2000). 'Between nation and animation: the fear of a Mickey Mouse planet', in S. Blandford (ed.), *Wales on Screen*, Bridgend, Seren, pp. 110–27.

Rowlands, J. B. (2001–2). *Chief Executive's Report*, Cardiff, Sgrîn.

—— (2002–3). *Chief Executive's Report*, Cardiff, Sgrîn.

Ryan, M. (1986). 'Blocking the channels: T.V. and Film in Wales', in T. Curtis (ed.), *Wales: The Imagined Nation*, Bridgend, Poetry Wales Press, pp. 181–96.

—— (2000). 'A woman's place: women and film in Wales', in S. Blandford (ed.), *Wales on Screen*, Bridgend, Seren, pp. 38–49.

Ryan, T. (1983). ' "The new road to progress": the use and production of films by the Labour movement', in J. Curran and V. Porter (eds), *British Cinema History*, London, Weidenfeld and Nicholson, pp. 113–28.

S4C (2002). *S4C's Response to the Draft Communications Bill*, Cardiff, NAfW.

—— (2003). 'Top Welsh programmes – week ending 14.9.2003', *www.s4c.co.uk*, accessed 9 October.

—— (2004). *S4C Review: A Welsh Language Television Service Fit for the 21st Century*, Cardiff, S4C.

Sabin, M. (2002). *Consultation Paper for the National GI Strategy for Wales 2003–2008*, Aberystwyth, Cymru Ar-lein.

Sassi, S. (2001). 'The transformation of the public sphere?' in B. Axford and R. Huggins (eds), *New Media and Politics*, London, Sage, pp. 89–108.

Scannell, P. (1989). 'Public service broadcasting and modern public life', *Media, Culture and Society*, 11, 135–66.

—— and Cardiff, D. (1991). *A Social History of British Broadcasting.* Volume I. *1922–1939*, Oxford, Blackwell.

Schiller, H. (1991). 'Not yet the post-imperialist era', *Critical Studies in Mass Communication*, 8, 13–28.

—— (1996). *Information Inequality*, New York/London, Routledge.

Schlesinger, P. (1987). *Putting 'Reality' Together*, London, Methuen.

—— (1991). 'Media, the political order and national identity', *Media, Culture and Society*, 13, 297–308.

Schudson, M. (1997). 'Why conversation is not the soul of democracy', *Critical Studies in Mass Communication*, 14, 4, 297–309.

Schuler, D. (1996). *New Community Networks: Wired for Change*, New York, ACM Press.

Selwyn, N. and Gorard, S. (2002). *The Information Age: Technology, Learning and Exclusion in Wales*, Cardiff, University of Wales Press.

Sendall, B. (1982). *Independent Television in Britain. Volume 1: Origin and Foundation 1946–1962*, London, Macmillan.

—— (1983). *Independent Television in Britain. Volume 2: Expansion and Change 1958–1968*, London, Macmillan.

Sgrîn (2001–2). *Annual Review*, Cardiff, Sgrîn Cymru.

—— (2002–3). *Annual Review*, Cardiff, Sgrîn Cymru.

—— (2003). *Sgrîn Cinema Exhibitors News* (September), Cardiff, Sgrîn Cymru.

Shaw, M. (1996). *Civil Society and Media in Global Crises*, London, Pinter.

Slevin, J. (2000). *The Internet and Society*, Cambridge, Polity Press.

Smith, A. (1991). 'The nation: invented, imagined, reconstructed?', *Journal of International Studies*, 20, 3, 353–68.

Smith, C. (1998). *Creative Britain*, London, Faber and Faber.

Smith, D. (1999). *Wales: A Question For History*, Bridgend, Seren.

Sparks, C. (1999). 'The press', in J. Stokes and A. Reading (eds), *The Media in Britain: Current Debates and Developments*, London, Macmillan, pp. 41–60.

Speers, T. (2001). *Welcome or Over Reaction? Refugees and Asylum Seekers in the Welsh Media*, Cardiff, Wales Media Forum.

Spencer, L. (1997). 'House of America', *Sight and Sound*, 7, 9, 45–6.

Starling, P. (2001). 'British Broadcasting Censor', *Mirror*, 5 November.

Stead, P. (1986). 'Wales in the movies', in T. Curtis (ed.), *Wales: The Imagined Nation: Studies in Cultural and National Identity*, Bridgend, Poetry Wales Press, pp. 159–80.

—— (1987). '"Kameradschaft" and after: the miners and film', *Llafur*, 5, 1, 37–44.

Stein, L. (2002). 'Democratic talk, access television and participatory political communication', *Javnost/The Public*, 5, 2, 21–34.

Stevenson, N. (2002). *Understanding Media Cultures*, 2nd edn, London, Sage.

Stoller, T. (2001). Speech to Cardiff Communications Summit, London, Radio Authority, 12 June.

Stromer-Galley, J. (2002). 'New voices in the public sphere: a comparative analysis of interpersonal and online political talk', *Javnost/The Public*, 9, 2, 23–42.

Tacchi, J. (2001). 'Who listens to the radio? The role of industrial audience research', in M. Bromley (ed.), *No News is Bad News*, London, Longman, pp. 136–56.

Talfan Davies, G. (1992). 'Broadcasting and the nation', *Planet*, 92, 16–25.

—— (1999). *Not By Bread Alone: Information, Media and the National Assembly*, Cardiff, Wales Media Forum.

—— (2003). 'Oral evidence', Cardiff, Richard Commission.

Tambini, D. (1999). 'New media and democracy: the civic networking movement', *New Media and Society*, 1, 3, 305–29.

—— (2000). *Universal Internet Access: A Realistic View*, London, Institute for Public Policy Research.

—— (2002). 'The end of public service TV?', *Media Guardian*, 22 December, 8.

Tang, P. (1998). 'Managing the cyberspace divide: government investment in electronic information services', in B. D. Loader (ed.), *Cyberspace Divide: Equality, Agency and Policy in the Information Society*, London, Routledge, pp. 183–202.

Tepper, M. (1997). 'Usenet communities and the cultural politics of information', in D. Porter (ed.), *Internet Culture*, London, Routledge, pp. 39–54.

Thomas, D. (1996). 'Welsh language publications: is public support effective?', *Contemporary Wales*, 9, 40–55.

Thomas, J. (1997). '"Taffy was a Welshman, Taffy was a thief", anti-Welshness, the press and Neil Kinnock', *Llafur*, 7, 2, 95–108.

—— (2003/4). 'Buried without tears: the death of the *Welsh Mirror*', *Planet*, 162, 23–7.

—— Jewell, J. and Cushion, S. (2003). *Media Coverage of the 2003 Welsh Assembly Elections*, Cardiff, Wales Media Forum.

Thomas, N. (2003/4). 'Y Byd. Papur dyddiol cenedlaethol', *Agenda*, Cardiff, Institute of Welsh Affairs, 62–4.

Thompson, B. (1997). 'Twin Town', *Sight and Sound*, 7, 4, 53–4.

Thompson, J. B. (1994). 'Social theory and the media', in D. Crowley and D. Mitchell, (eds), *Communication Theory Today*, Cambridge, Polity, pp. 27–49.

Tomos, A. (1982). 'Realising a dream', in S. Blanchard and D. Morley (eds), *What's this Channel Fo[u]r? An Alternative Report*, London, Comedian, pp. 37–53.

Tracey, M. (1998). *The Decline and Fall of Public Service Broadcasting*, Oxford, Oxford University Press.

Tsaliki, L. (2002). 'Online forums and the enlargement of public space: research findings from a European perspective', *Javnost/The Public*, 9, 2, 95–112.

Tuck, R. (2003). *Internet Inequality in Wales*, Cardiff, Wales Consumer Council.

Tunstall, J. (1983). *The Media in Britain*, London, Constable.

—— (1986). *Communications Deregulation*, Oxford, Basil Blackwell.

UK Online (2003). *Annual Report*, London, HMSO.

Underwood, M. (2002) 'Internet', at *www.cultsock.ndirect.co.uk/MUHome/cshtml*, accessed 10 November.

Verstraeten, H. (1996). 'The media and the transformation of the public sphere', *European Journal of Communication*, 11, 3, 347–70.

Wainwright, M. (2004). 'Films fade out for country folk', *Guardian*, 4 March, 5.

Wales, World, Nation (2003). 'Broadcast media', *www.walesworldnation.com*, accessed 27 November.

Walker, D. (2001). 'MPs off-message on internet revolution', *Guardian*, 11 January.

Warner, M. (1992). 'The mass public and the mass subject', in C. Calhoun (ed.), *Habermas and the Public Sphere*, Cambridge, MA, MIT Press, pp. 377–401.

Waterman, P. (1996). 'A new world view: globalization, civil society, and solidarity', in S. Braman and A. Sreberny-Mohammadi (eds), *Globalization, Communication and Transnational Civil Society*, Cresskill, NJ, Hampton Press, pp. 37–62.

Waters, D. (2000). 'And the winner is . . . the Welsh Film Industry', *Western Mail*, 22 March, 12.

Webster, F. (2002). *Theories of the Information Society*, 2nd edn, London, Routledge.

Weight, R. (2002). *Patriots: National Identity in Britain 1940–2000*, London, Pan.

Welsh Affairs Select Committee (1999). *Broadcasting in Wales and the National Assembly*, London, HMSO.

Welsh Assembly Government (2002). *Creative Future/Cymru Greadigol: A Culture Strategy for Wales*, Cardiff, Welsh Assembly Government.

Welsh Development Agency (1998). 'Wales Information Society – Leading the way into the information age', *www.wis.org.uk*.

Welsh Economy Research Unit (2001). *Economy and Culture: S4C in Wales. Present and Potential Economic Impacts*, Cardiff, S4C/ University of Glamorgan/Cardiff University.

Welsh Conservative Party (2003). *Election Manifesto*, Cardiff, Welsh Conservative Party.

Welsh Labour Party (2003). *Election Manifesto*, Cardiff, Welsh Labour Party.

Welsh Office (1997). *A Voice for Wales/Llais dros Gymru: The Government Proposals for a Welsh Assembly*, Cardiff, HMSO.

White, B. (2003). 'It's still bad news', *Free Press*, 135, 7.

Williams, C. and Aaron, J. (eds) (2005). *Postcolonial Wales*, Cardiff, University of Wales Press.

Williams, Glanmor (1979). 'Language, literacy and nationality in Wales', in G. Williams (ed.), *Religion, Language and Nationality in Wales*, Cardiff, University of Wales Press, pp. 121–47.

Williams, Granville (1996). *Britain's Media: How They Are Related: Media Ownership and Democracy*, London, Campaign for Press and Broadcasting Freedom.

Williams, G. A. (1991). *When Was Wales?*, London, Penguin.

Williams, K. (1994). 'Are we being served? The press, broadcasting and a Welsh parliament', in J. Osmond (ed.), *A Parliament For Wales*, Llandysul, Gomer, pp. 245–59.

—— (1997a). *Shadows and Substance: The Development of a Media Policy for Wales*, Llandysul, Gomer.

—— (1997b). 'Dear Ron', *Planet*, 123, 61–4.

—— (1998). *Get Me A Murder A Day! A History of Mass Communication in Britain*, London, Arnold.

—— (2000). 'No dreads, only some doubts: the press and the referendum campaign', in J. Jones and D. Balsom (eds), *The Road to the National Assembly for Wales*, Cardiff, University of Wales Press, pp. 96–122.

—— (2002). 'ITV – past and present', *Planet*, 154, 66–70.

Williams, R. (1974). *Television: Technology and Cultural Form*, London, Fontana.

—— (1979). 'Introduction', in M. Stephens (ed.), *The Arts in Wales 1950–75*, Cardiff, Wales Arts Council, pp. 1–4.

—— (1983). 'British film history: new perspectives', in J. Curran and V. Porter (eds), *British Cinema History*, London, Weidenfeld and Nicholson, pp. 9–83.

—— (1989). 'Are we becoming more divided?', *Radical Wales*, 23, 8–9.

Wright, A. (1980). *Local Radio and Local Democracy: A Study in Political Education*, London, Independent Broadcasting Authority.

Wyn Jones, R. (1998). *Memorandum Submitted to Welsh Affairs Select Committee, 'Broadcasting and Political Culture in Wales'*, London, HMSO.

—— (2004). 'The continuing failure to take Wales seriously', *Independent*, 4 August, 29.

—— Trystan, D. and Taylor, B. (2000). 'Voting patterns in the referendum', in J. Barry Jones and D. Balsom (eds), *The Road to the National Assembly for Wales*, Cardiff, University of Wales Press, pp. 161–75.

Y Byd (2004). 'Website', *www.ybyd.com/english.shtml*, accessed on 30 November 2004.

Index

HTV 10 n., 14, 72, 86, 133, 137–41,
    143–4, 191, 196, 199, 204,
    206–7, 213 n.
    see also ITV1 Wales
Human Traffic 88
Hume, I. 6, 22–3, 28
Hylton, J. 130

In the Service of Democracy 158
Independent Broadcasting Authority
    (IBA) 106–8, 112, 133, 137–41,
    222
    General Advisory Council for
    Wales 140
Independent Local Radio (ILR)
    14–15, 17, 22, 30 n., 96, 98,
    107–24, 125 n.
Independent Television 127, 129–30,
    138, 140–1, 145
Independent Television Authority
    (ITA) 28, 106, 129–32, 134,
    139, 147
Independent Television Commission
    (ITC) 133, 145–6, 202, 204–5,
    207, 223
information deficit 61, 205, 213 n.,
    229
Institute for Public Policy Research
    (IPPR) 174, 180–1, 227
Internet 6, 8, 18, 26, 35, 114, 132–3,
    153–83, 214, 224–7
    access difficulties 160–70
    age 166–7
    broadband 18, 159–60, 171, 183,
    226–7, 230
    class 164
    Communications Decency Act 157
    Connectivity Indicator 160
    e-mail 153, 164–5, 173, 176, 182 n.
    free market versus public service
    157–8
    freedom 156–7
    gender 167
    'Internetphilia' 156, 181

newsgroups and bulletin boards
    153, 177–8, 183 n.
    online journalism 175
    policy 224–7, 228, 229, 230
    Universal Service Fund (USF)
    181, 227
Ireland 89, 99, 209
Irish Times 176
ITV1 142, 144
ITV1 Wales 3, 10, 14, 17, 29, 72, 91,
    142, 144, 191, 194, 222

Jacob, I. 134
Jenkins, R. 136
Joint Committee (House of Lords and
    House of Commons) 195, 196
Jones, A. 6, 9, 27, 29, 35–8, 41–2,
    44–5, 47, 50–7, 59–61, 97, 103,
    107, 120, 228
Jones, H. M. 139
Jones, M. 139
Jones, Thomas 36
Jones, Tom 13

Kameradschaft 94 n.
Kemsley, Viscount *see* Berry, Gomer
Kinnock, N. 57–8

Labour Party 57, 61, 136
    see also New Labour; Welsh
    Labour Party
Labour Research 54
land reform 52
Last Days of Dolwyn, The 81, 94 n.
'leakage' 25, 205
    see also 'transmission overlap'
Lewis, Saunders 100, 106, 134
libel 36, 215
Liberal Democrat Party 57
Liberal Party 37, 42, 44,
Licensing Act 36
Liverpool Daily Post 37–8, 46, 62 n.,
    130
Llais Llafur 54